ESSENTIAL GERMAN

PHRASEBOOK & DICTIONARY

Nicole Irving, Leslie Colvin and Kate Needham

Illustrated by Ann Johns

Designed by Lucy Parris
Edited by Nathalie Abi-Ezzi and Ben Denne
Series editor: Susan Meredith

Language consultants: Anke Kornmüller, Sandy Walker
and Gene O. Stimpson.

Cover designed by Stephen Wright.
With thanks to Lucy Owen and Helen Wood.
Cover photograph: Brandenburg Gate © AP.

The material in this book was originally published in
two separate volumes: *Essential German* and
Essential German Dictionary.

Original designs by Adrienne Kern and Kathy Ward.

First published in 2000 by Usborne Publishing Ltd, Usborne
House, 83-85 Saffron Hill, London EC1N 8RT, England.
www.usborne.com
Copyright © 2000, 1994, 1990 Usborne Publishing Ltd.

Printed in Italy.

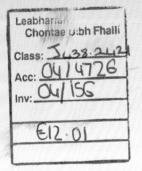

Contents

About the phrasebook

This book gives simple, up-to-date German to help you to get by, travel and socialize in Germany. It also gives basic information about Germany and tips for low-budget travellers.

Finding the right words

Use the Contents list on page 3 to find the section of the book you need. If you don't find a phrase where you expect it to be, try a related section. There are food words, for example, on several pages. If you still can't find the word, try looking it up in the dictionary.

Go for it

Remember that you can make yourself clear with very few words, or words that are not entirely right. Saying "Frankfurt?" while pointing at a train will provoke *ja* or *nein* (yes or no). The German listed on the opposite page is absolutely essential.

You will feel more confident if you have some idea of how to pronounce German correctly and of how the language works. If German is new to you, try looking through the sections on pages 55-60. A good pronunciation tip is to try to make your voice go up at the end of a question.

Being polite

Words like *Entschuldigung* (excuse me), *bitte* (please) or *danke* (thank you) make anything sound more polite and will generally guarantee a friendly response.

There are other ways of being polite in German. German has three different words for "you": *du, ihr* and *Sie*. You can use the casual *du* for a friend, or someone of your own age or younger. It is important, though, always to use the polite *Sie* when you talk to an older person, whether you know them or not. Saying *du* to someone who doesn't expect it can be very rude. For more than one person, the informal *du* becomes *ihr*, but *Sie* remains the same in the plural. In this book *du* or *Sie* is given depending on the situation. Sometimes you will have to judge which is best, so both are given. If you are ever in doubt, use *Sie*.

The language in this book is everyday, spoken German, ranging from the formal to the colloquial. An asterisk after a German word shows that it is slang or fairly familiar, e.g. telly: *die Glotze**. Common slang words and phrases are listed on pages 50-51.

Masculine, feminine or neuter

German nouns all have a gender: they are either masculine, feminine or neuter. The German word for "the" or "a" changes to agree with the gender of the noun. In the phrasebook, "the" and "a" are given in the form likely to be most useful when they are put together with the noun in a sentence. You can find out more about this on page 56.

German nouns always start with a capital letter.

Entschuldigung, wir haben uns verlaufen.
Excuse me, we're lost.

Wohin gehen Sie?
Where are you going?

yes	ja
no	nein
maybe	vielleicht
I don't know.	Ich weiß nicht.
I don't mind.	Das ist mir egal.
please	bitte
thank you	danke
excuse me	Entschuldigung
sorry	tut mir leid
I'm very sorry.	Es tut mir sehr leid.
It doesn't matter.	Es macht nichts.
It's nothing/ Don't mention it.	Keine Ursache.
hello	guten Tag
goodbye	auf Wiedersehen
hi	hallo
bye	tschüs
good morning	guten Morgen
good evening	guten Abend
good night	gute Nacht
see you soon	bis bald
Mr, Sir	Herr
Mrs, Madam	Frau
Miss	Fräulein
and	und
or	oder
when?	wann?
where is?	wo ist?
why?	warum?
because	weil
how?	wie?
how much/ many?	wie viel?
How much is it?	Wieviel kostet es?
What is it/this?	Was ist es/das?
it/this is	es/das ist
is there?	gibt es?
there is	es gibt
I'd like	Ich möchte

Getting help with German

I don't understand.
Ich verstehe nicht.

Can you write it down?
Können Sie das aufschreiben?
Kannst du das aufschreiben?

Can you say that again?
Können Sie das wiederholen?
Kannst du das wiederholen?

A bit slower, please.
Ein bisschen langsamer, bitte.

What does this word mean?
Was heißt dieses Wort?

What's the German for this?
Wie sagt man das auf Deutsch?

Have you got a dictionary?
Haben Sie ein Wörterbuch?
Hast du ein Wörterbuch?

Do you speak English?
Sprechen Sie Englisch?
Sprichst du Englisch?

Langsamer, bitte.
Slower, please.

Signs you may see

Notausgang	**Emergency exit**
Vorsicht	**Beware/Danger**
Bissiger Hund	**Beware of the dog**
Kein Eintritt	**Keep out/No entry**
Rauchen verboten	**No smoking**
Nichtraucher	**Non-smoking**
Privatbesitz	**Private property**
Trinkwasser	**Drinking water**
Kein Trinkwasser	**Not drinking water**
Camping verboten	**No camping**
Schwimmen verboten	**No swimming**

Ist Stefan da, bitte?
Is Stefan there, please?

Asking the way

Ich habe mich verlaufen.
I'm lost.

Können Sie mir bitte helfen?
Can you help me, please?

Wo ist die Touristeninformation?
Where is the tourist office?

Können Sie mir das aufzeichnen?
Can you draw me a map?

Gibt es hier in der Nähe eine öffentliche Toilette?
Is there a public toilet around here?

Fact file

You will find a *Touristeninformation* in most big towns and cities, often near the station or town hall. In tourist areas even small towns have one. Most tourist offices provide town plans and leaflets about local sights. They also give advice on places to stay and travel arrangements, and often employ someone who speaks English. Some tourist offices sell maps and specialist booklets about local footpaths, wildlife etc.

Directions

It's on the left/right.	Es ist auf der linken/ rechten Seite.
Turn left/right.	Biegen Sie nach links/rechts ab.
Go straight ahead.	Gehen Sie geradeaus.
Take ...	Nehmen Sie ...
the first on the left	die erste Straße links
It's ...	Es ist ...
Go ...	Gehen Sie ...
Turn ...	Biegen Sie ab nach ...
left	links
right	rechts
straight ahead	geradeaus
on the left/right	auf der linken/rechten Seite

the second on the right	die zweite Straße rechts
the third	die dritte
the fourth	die vierte
Follow the signs ...	Folgen Sie dem Schild ...
for Bonn	nach Bonn
for the station	zum Bahnhof

crossroads, junction	Kreuzung
roundabout	Kreisverkehr
traffic lights	Ampel
pedestrian crossing	Fußgängerüberweg
zebra crossing	Zebrastreifen
subway	Unterführung
Cross ...	Überqueren Sie ...
Follow ...	Folgen Sie ...
street, road	die Straße
alley	der Weg, die Gasse
path, footpath	der Fußweg
cycle path	der Fahrradweg
main/high street	die Hauptstraße

square	der Platz
dual carriageway	die Schnellstraße
motorway	die Autobahn
ringroad	Umgehungsstraße
one way	Einbahnstraße
no entry	keine Einfahrt
dead end	Sackgasse
no parking	Parken verboten
car park	der Parkplatz
parking meters	Parkuhren
ticket machine	der Parkscheinautomat
pedestrian area	die Fußgängerzone
pedestrians	Fußgänger
pavement	der Bürgersteig
town centre	die Stadtmitte, das Zentrum, die City
area, part of town	das Stadtviertel
suburb	der Vorort
outskirts, suburbs	der Stadtrand
town hall	das Rathaus
bridge	die Brücke
river	der Fluss
railway line	die Eisenbahnlinie
post office	die Post, das Postamt
shops	die Geschäfte
church	die Kirche
school	die Schule
cinema	das Kino
museum	das Museum
park	der Park
just before/after	kurz vor/nach
at the end	am Ende
on the corner	an der Ecke
next to	neben
opposite	gegenüber
in front of/behind	vor/hinter
over/under	über/unter
in/on	in/auf
here/there	hier/dort
over there	da drüben
far	weit
near, nearby	in der Nähe
near here, around here	hier in der Nähe
in this area	in der Gegend
somewhere	irgendwo
10 minutes walk/drive/by bike	zehn Minuten zu Fuß/ im Auto/mit dem Rad

Wie kommt man am besten zum Campingplatz?
What's the best way to the campsite?

Können Sie mir das auf dem Plan zeigen?
Can you show me on the map?

Wo ist der nächste Strand?
Where's the nearest beach?

Wie weit ist das?
How far is it?

Wie komme ich zur Jugendherberge?
How do I get to the youth hostel?

Travel: trains, underground, buses

Getting information

Wann geht der nächste Zug nach Berlin?
What time is the next train to Berlin?

Wie lange dauert die Fahrt?
How long is the journey?

Muss ich umsteigen?
Do I have to change?

Fact file

DB (German national railways) runs a good rail network. *IC* (*InterCity*), *EC* (*EuroCity*) and *ICE* (*InterCityExpress*) are high speed trains for which you pay a supplement. You can get cheap deals (*Sparpreise*) for weekends (e.g. *Schönes-Wochenende-Ticket*), evenings (*Guten-Abend-Ticket*), groups, and young people. *Surf & Rail* is for direct connections between towns - you book online at http://www.bahn.de/ Special offers alter frequently, so check on the web site, at the station, or with a travel agent.

Local city transport is usually a mixture of bus, tram, underground and *S-Bahn* (suburban rail network). The same tickets are often valid for all of these. There are ticket machines at stations, and at bus and tram stops, but you can often buy tickets from bus or tram drivers. Tickets are sold singly or in blocks. Most cities also have cheap local travel deals such as a *Tageskarte* (day pass). You usually have to stamp your ticket in a special machine before travelling, or as you get on the bus or tram.

Wo steige ich um, um in die Friedrichstraße zu kommen?
Where do I change for Friedrichstraße?

Was wurde gerade über Lautsprecher gesagt?
What did they just say over the loudspeaker?

Von welchem Bahnsteig fährt der Zug zum Marienplatz?
Which platform for Marienplatz?

Tickets

Wo kann ich eine Fahrkarte kaufen?
Where can I buy a ticket?

Einmal Mainz einfach, bitte.
Can I have a single to Mainz?

Bekomme ich Ermäßigung?
Can I get a reduction?

Wie funktioniert dieser Automat?
How does this machine work?

I'd like to reserve a seat.	Ich möchte einen Sitzplatz reservieren.
railway station	der Bahnhof
underground station	die U-Bahn-Station
bus station	der Busbahnhof
bus stop	die Bushaltestelle
train	der Zug
underground train	die U-Bahn
tram	die Straßenbahn
bus	der Bus
coach	der (Reise)bus
leaves at 2 o'clock	fährt um zwei Uhr ab
arrives at 4 o'clock	kommt um vier Uhr an
first	erste
last	letzte
next	nächste
cheapest	billigste
ticket	eine Fahrkarte
ticket office	der Fahrkartenschalter
ticket machine	der Fahrkartenautomat
fare	der Fahrpreis

student fare	Studentenermäßigung
youth fare	Fahrpreis für Jugendliche
a single	einfach
a return	hin und zurück
book of tickets	eine Mehrfahrtenkarte
supplement	ein Zuschlag
left luggage lockers	Schließfächer
connection	der Anschluss
timetable	ein Fahrplan
arrivals/departures	Ankunft/Abfahrt, Abflug
long distance	Fernzug
local, suburban	Nahverkehr
every day	täglich
weekdays	wochentags
Sundays and holidays	an Sonn- und Feiertagen
except	außer

Buses

Ist das der richtige Bus nach Hamburg?
Is this the right bus for Hamburg?

Wohin fährt dieser Bus?
Where does this bus go?

Können Sie mir sagen, wo ich aussteigen muß?
Can you tell me where to get off?

Travel: air, sea, taxis

> *Kann ich meinen Flug bestätigen?*
> **Can I confirm my flight?**

> *Wann muss ich einchecken?*
> **What time should I check in?**

> *Wo ist die Abfertigung?*
> **Where do I check in?**

Fact file

Airports and ports usually have signs and announcements in English. There is often a bus or train from the airport into town.

Taxis have a standard pick-up charge plus a metered fare; each large bag is charged extra. Taxis often take only three passengers, but they can be good value.

> *Mein Gepäck ist nicht angekommen.*
> **My luggage hasn't arrived.**

> *Frau Schulz sollte mich abholen.*
> **Mrs Schulz is supposed to be meeting me.**

Where is the taxi stand?
Wo ist der Taxistand?

Take me to ...
Ich möchte nach ...

What's the fare to ...?
Was kostet es zur/zum/nach ...?

Please drop me here.
Setzen Sie mich bitte hier ab.

airport	der Flughafen
port	der Hafen
aeroplane	das Flugzeug
ferry	die Fähre
hovercraft	das Hovercraft
flight	der Flug
North Sea	Nordsee
Baltic Sea	Ostsee
rough	stürmisch
calm	ruhig
I feel sick.	Mir ist schlecht.
on board	an Bord
suitcase	der Koffer
backpack, rucksack	der Rucksack
bag	die Tasche
hand luggage	Handgepäck
trolley	Gepäckwagen
information	die Auskunft
customs	der Zoll
passport	ein Pass
departure gate	Ausgang
boarding pass	die Bordkarte
foot passenger	ein Passagier
No smoking	Nichtraucher
travel agent	ein Reisebüro
cut price	herabgesetzt
standby	Standby
charter flight	Charterflug
flight number	die Flugnummer
a booking	eine Reservierung
to change	ändern
to cancel	stornieren
a delay	Verspätung

Fact file

Cyclists will find a good network of cycle paths, and cycle lanes in cities and towns are common. You can hire bikes from bike shops and some train stations. On most trains, you can travel with a bike but check for extra charges.

You can ride mopeds from the age of fifteen, but must be insured and wear a helmet. Remember that in Germany people drive on the right.

Give way to traffic coming from the right.
Dem Rechtsverkehr die Vorfahrt lassen.

Fill it up, please.
Volltanken, bitte.

I have a puncture.
Ich habe einen Platten.

The engine won't start.
Der Motor springt nicht an.

The battery's flat.
Die Batterie ist leer.

How much will it cost?
Was wird das kosten?

for hire
zu vermieten

Can I hire ...?
Kann ich ... mieten?

Where are you going?
Wohin fahren Sie?

I'm going to Bonn.
Ich fahre nach Bonn.

driving licence	ein Führerschein
car documents	die Wagenpapiere
petrol station	eine Tankstelle
petrol	Benzin
lead-free petrol	bleifreies Benzin
oil	Öl
litre	ein Liter
car	ein Auto
motorbike	ein Motorrad
moped	ein Moped
bicycle	ein Fahrrad
bike	ein Rad
crash helmet	ein Sturzhelm
battery	eine Batterie
jump leads	ein Starthilfekabel
spark plugs	Zündkerzen
fan belt	ein Keilriemen
radiator	der Kühler
to hitch	trampen
lights	das Licht
chain	die Kette
wheel	das Rad
gears	die Gänge
brakes	die Bremsen
pump	eine Pumpe
tyre	der Reifen
inner tube	der Schlauch

Ich habe eine Panne.
I've broken down.

Wo ist die nächste Werkstatt?
Where's the nearest garage?

Die Bremsen funktionieren nicht.
The brakes don't work.

Ich weiß nicht, was kaputt ist.
I don't know what's wrong.

Können Sie das reparieren?
Can you fix it?

Accommodation: places to stay

At the tourist office

Haben Sie ein Campingplatzverzeichnis?
Do you have a list of campsites?

Fact file

The *Touristeninformation* will supply lists of places to stay, and can make bookings for you, but there might be a fee for this service. There are lots of *Jugendherbergen* (youth hostels) in Germany. These are generally very good and cheap, but you will need to be a member of the IYHA.† Alternatively, you will get cheap bed and breakfast accommodation in a private house with rooms to let; these are quite common in Germany.

Camping

Fact file

Campingplätze (campsites) can be found all over Germany. They are generally good and can be cheap.

Is there a campsite around here?
Gibt es einen Campingplatz in der Nähe?

Where are the showers?
Wo sind die Duschen?

tent	ein Zelt
caravan	ein Wohnwagen
hot water	warmes Wasser
cold water	kaltes Wasser
drinking water	Trinkwasser
camping gas	Campinggas
tent peg	ein Hering
mallet	ein Holzhammer
sleeping bag	ein Schlafsack
torch	eine Taschenlampe
matches	Streichhölzer
loo paper	Klopapier
can opener	ein Dosenöffner

Haben Sie noch Platz?
Do you have a space?

Wir sind zu dritt mit einem Zelt.
There are three of us with a tent.

Gibt's hier einen Laden?
Do you have a shop?

Kann man das Wasser trinken?
Is it OK to drink the tap water?

†International Youth Hostel Association.

Hotels

Haben Sie ein Zimmer?
Do you have a room?

Wir sind belegt.
We're full.

Gibt es hier in der Nähe noch ein Hotel?
Is there another hotel nearby?

Was kostet ein Zimmer?
How much for a room?

Fact file

Hotels in Germany can be pricey, but a *Pension* (guest house) or *Gasthof* (country inn) will provide cheaper *Fremdenzimmer* (guest rooms). These are usually clean and comfortable.

Ist das mit Frühstück?
Does that include breakfast?

Kann ich das Zimmer sehen?
Can I see the room?

Rooms to let
Zimmer frei.

There are three of us.
Wir sind drei Personen.

How many nights?
Wie lange bleiben Sie?

How much do you want to pay?
Wieviel möchten Sie bezahlen?

Can I leave a message for someone?
Kann ich eine Nachricht für jemanden hinterlassen?

Can I have my passport back?
Kann ich meinen Pass zurückhaben?

one/two night(s)	eine Nacht/zwei Nächte
single room	ein Einzelzimmer
double room	ein Doppelzimmer
room with three beds	ein Dreibettzimmer
full/half board	Voll/Halbpension
clean	sauber
cheap	billig
expensive	teuer
lunch	das Mittagessen
dinner (evening)	das Abendessen
key	der Schlüssel
room number	die Zimmernummer
registration form	das Anmeldeformular

Ich möchte ein Zimmer für zwei Personen.
I'd like a room for two people.

Können Sie für mich ein Zimmer reservieren?
Can you book a room for me?

Accommodation: staying with people

Greetings

> *Hallo.*
> **Hello.**

> *Wie geht's?*
> **How are you?**

> *Wo soll ich mein Zeug hin tun?*
> **Where can I put my things?**

> *Wo schlafe ich?*
> **Where am I sleeping?**

For more polite or formal greetings it is best to say *Guten Tag* (good day) or *Guten Abend* (good evening). Also use the polite form: *Wie geht es Ihnen?* (How are you?)

> *Wann frühstücken Sie?*
> **What time do you have breakfast?**

> *Können Sie mich um sieben wecken?*
> **Could you wake me up at seven?**

Washing

> *Wie funktioniert die Dusche?*
> **How does the shower work?**

Is it OK if I have a bath?
Ist es okay, wenn ich bade?
Do you mind if I wash a few things?
Darf ich ein paar Sachen waschen?
Where can I dry these?
Wo kann ich das trocknen?

bathroom	das Badezimmer
bath	das Bad
shower	die Dusche
toilet	die Toilette
loo	das Klo
bidet	das Bidet
towel	das Handtuch
soap	die Seife
shampoo	das Shampoo
toothpaste	die Zahnpasta
toothbrush	die Zahnbürste
deodorant	der Deo(dorant)
hairdryer	der Föhn
hairbrush	die Haarbürste
washing powder	das Waschpulver

Being polite

Kann ich etwas dazu beisteuern?
Can I pay my share?

Nein, es ist in Ordnung.
No, it's OK.

Nett von euch, dass ich hier wohnen kann.
It's nice of you to let me stay.

Wenn ich was brauche, frag' ich.
I'll ask if I need anything.

alarm clock	ein Wecker
on the floor	auf dem Boden
an extra ...	noch ein/eine ...
blanket	eine Decke
quilt, duvet	eine Bettdecke
sheet	ein Laken
pillow	ein Kopfkissen
electric socket	eine Steckdose
T.V.	das Fernsehen
needle	Nadel
thread	Faden
scissors	eine Schere
iron	ein Bügeleisen
upstairs	oben
downstairs	unten
cupboard	ein Schrank
bedroom	das Schlafzimmer
living room	das Wohnzimmer
kitchen	die Küche
garden	der Garten
balcony	der Balkon

Can I have a key?
Kann ich einen Schlüssel haben?

What is there to do in the evenings?
Was kann man abends machen?

Where's the nearest phone box?
Wo ist die nächste Telefonzelle?

I'm tired.
Ich bin müde.

I'm knackered.
Ich bin völlig kaputt.

I'm cold.
Mir ist kalt.

I'm hot.
Mir ist heiß.

Saying goodbye

Vielen Dank.
Thank you for everything.

Auf Wiedersehen.
Goodbye.

Was kostet es, in England anzurufen?
How much is it to call Britain?

Kann ich das Telefon benutzen?
Can I use your phone?

Ich bezahle das Gespräch.
I'll pay for the call.

For more about making phone calls, see page 17.

Banks

Nehmen Sie Kreditkarten?
Do you accept credit cards?

Kann ich Ihren Pass sehen?
Can I see your passport?

Ich möchte das wechseln.
I want to change this.

Post office

Wo ist der nächste Briefkasten?
Where's the nearest postbox?

Kann ich hierfür eine Briefmarke haben?
Can I have a stamp for this?

Fact file

The unit of currency is the *Deutsche Mark* (DM), or the *Euro* from January 2002. 1 DM = 100 *Pfennige*. Most banks in town centres are open Monday to Friday 9-4, (until 6 on Thursday).

Wechselstuben (foreign exchange offices) are often open outside banking hours but you may get a poorer rate of exchange.

Money problems

Ich habe meine Reiseschecks verloren.
I've lost my traveller's cheques.

Die Nummern waren ...
The serial numbers were ...

Wie bekomme ich sie ersetzt?
How do I get replacements?

Ich erwarte Geld, ist es da?
I'm expecting some money; has it arrived?

bank	eine Bank
cashier's desk, till	die Kasse
foreign exchange	Devisen
enquiries	Information
money	Geld
small change	Kleingeld
notes	Noten, Scheine
traveller's cheques	Reiseschecks
credit card	eine Kreditkarte
exchange rate	der Wechselkurs
commission	die Provision
money transfer	eine Überweisung
post office	ein Postamt
postcard	eine Postkarte
letter	ein Brief
parcel	ein Paket
envelope	ein Umschlag
writing paper	Schreibpapier
by airmail	per Luftpost
by registered post	per Einschreiben
stamp	eine Briefmarke
telephone	ein Telefon
mobile phone	ein Handy
telephone box	eine Telefonzelle
directory	das Telefonbuch

phone number	die Telefonnummer
wrong number	falsch verbunden
reverse charge call†	ein R-Gespräch
Hang on.	Bleib' am Apparat.

The cashpoint machine (ATM) has swallowed my credit card.
Der Geldautomat hat meine Kreditkarte verschluckt.

Where can I send an e-mail from?
Von wo kann ich eine E-Mail schicken?

Fact file

There are payphones on the street, in post offices, cafés and department stores. All take *Telefonkarten* (phone cards), which you can buy at a post office or a newsagent; few take coins. You can make international calls from most payphones. For useful phone numbers see page 49. You can get stamps from machines outside post offices and on some post boxes.

Phones

†Reverse charge calls are not possible within Germany, but to make a reverse charge call to another country, dial 01308 00044.

Das Telefon ist kaputt.
This phone doesn't work.

Ist das die Vorwahl für Berlin?
Is this the code for Berlin?

Hallo. Ist Steffie da, bitte?
Hello. Is Steffie there, please?

Sagen Sie ihr/ihm bitte, dass ich angerufen habe.
Please tell her/him I called.

Wann ist sie zurück?
When will she be back?

Meine Nummer ist ...
My number is ...

Kann ich eine Nachricht für ... hinterlassen?
Can I leave a message for ...?

Kann sie/er mich zurückrufen?
Can she/he call me back?

Cafés

café	ein Café
pub/bar	eine Kneipe
at the bar	an der Bar
Cheers!	Prost!
something to drink	etwas zu trinken
something to eat	etwas zu essen
snack	der Snack
black/white coffee	Kaffee ohne/mit Milch
a (large) coffee	ein (großer) Kaffee
decaffeinated	koffeinfrei
tea (with milk)	ein Tee mit Milch
hot chocolate	eine heiße Schokolade
fruit juice	ein Fruchtsaft
orange juice	Orangensaft
coke	eine Cola
still/fizzy mineral water	ein Mineralwasser ohne/mit Kohlensäure
soda water	das Soda(wasser)
beer (bottled)	eine Flasche Bier
beer (draught)	ein Bier vom Fass
a bottle of ...	eine Flasche ...
half a bottle of white wine	eine halbe Flasche Weißwein
glass of red wine	ein Glas Rotwein
milk	Milch
sugar	Zucker
ice	Eis
slice of lemon	eine Scheibe Zitrone
cheese sandwich	ein Käsebrot
ham sandwich	ein Schinkenbrot
omelette (plain)	ein Omelett
ice cream	ein Eis

Fact file

Cafés are open during the day. Other options: Italian ice cream places, *Café-Konditorei* (for coffee and cakes), *Gaststätte* (food at mealtimes, soft drinks or beer all day) or *Weinstube* (wine etc. in the evening).
Drinks: try *Apfelschorle* (apple juice with soda). Snacks: these include *Käsetoast* (toasted cheese sandwich), *belegtes Brot* (open sandwich), *Kaffee und Kuchen* (coffee and cakes), and *Torten* (gâteaux).

Eating out

Choosing a place

- *Wo gehen wir hin?* **Where shall we go?**
- *Ich mag keine Pizza.* **I don't like pizza.**
- *Lasst uns einen Kebab essen gehen.* **Let's go for a kebab.**

German food	deutsches Essen	**sausages**	Würstchen
Italian ...	italienisches ...	**mashed potato**	Kartoffelbrei
Greek ...	griechisches ...	**mixed salad**	ein gemischter Salat
cheap restaurant	ein billiges Restaurant	**green salad**	ein Salat
fast-food restaurant	ein Schnellrestaurant	**spaghetti**	Spaghetti
to take away	zum Mitnehmen	**rare**	englisch gebraten
menu	die Karte	**medium**	halb durchgebraten
starter	eine Vorspeise	**well done**	durchgebraten
main course	ein Hauptgericht	**mustard**	Senf
dessert	eine Nachspeise, ein Nachtisch	**salt**	Salz
price	der Preis	**pepper**	Pfeffer
soup	Suppe	**dressing**	die Salatsoße
fish	Fisch	**mayonnaise**	die Mayonnaise
meat	Fleisch		
vegetables	Gemüse	**Is everything all right?**	
cheese	Käse	Ist alles in Ordnung?	
fruit	Obst	**Yes, it's very good.**	
chips	Fritten/Pommes frites	Ja, es ist sehr gut.	

Deciding what to have

- *Kann ich einen ohne Käse haben?* **Can I have one without cheese?**
- *Was ist das?* **What's that?**
- *Ich nehme so einen.* **I'll have one of those.**

Problems

Ich habe Schnitzel bestellt.
I ordered Schnitzel.

Haben Sie kein Tomatenketchup?
Don't you have any ketchup?

Das ist nicht durch.
This isn't cooked enough.

Hallo!
Excuse me!

Zahlen, bitte!
Can we have the bill please?

Das habe ich nicht bestellt.
I didn't order this.

Fact file

German food varies from region to region. Specialities you will find everywhere include *Schnitzel* (pork or veal, often in breadcrumbs), many kinds of *Würstchen* (sausages), *Frikadelle* (meatballs), *Knödel* (dumplings), *Rotkohl* (red cabbage), *eingelegte Heringe* or *Rollmöpse* (pickled herrings), and various breads and cakes (see pages 18 and 27). Restaurants are often quite pricey. *Gaststätten* specialize in local food. Look out for the *Tagesmenü* (set menu), which is displayed outside with its price. It is usually three courses and often good value.

Cheap places to eat are department store cafeterias, hamburger places and *Imbissbuden* (snackbars, many of them Turkish). *Frittenbuden* (food stalls) serve sausages, chips, pizza, etc. Some foreign restaurants are also good value. Try Italian, Greek or Balkan.

The bill always includes service and VAT but tipping is normal practice, so it's best to leave a small tip.

The best times for eating out are lunch at 12 or 1, and dinner at about 7.30. However, it's often cheaper to buy your own food (see page 27).

Eating in

Fact file

The standard breakfast is coffee or tea with rolls or toast, and butter and jam. Muesli, yoghurt, eggs, cheese or ham are sometimes also served.

The main meal is lunch and is often hot. The evening meal is usually cold, and people may eat *Wurst* (various types of sausage, such as salami or liver sausage), or different kinds of *Schinken* (ham) and *Käse* (cheese) with bread and salads.

Enjoy your meal.
Guten Appetit!

I'm hungry/thirsty.
Ich habe Hunger/Durst.

I'm not hungry/thirsty.
Ich habe keinen
  Hunger/Durst.

Das Essen ist fertig!
It's ready.

Greift zu!
Help yourselves.

Was ist da drin?
What's in this?

Kann ich die Butter haben?
Can you pass the butter?

Ich bin satt, danke.
I've had enough, thanks.

Möchtest du Salat?
Would you like some salad?

Es war köstlich.
That was delicious.

Ein wenig.
Just a little.

Noch etwas Brot?
Some more bread?

Helping

Kann ich helfen?
Can I help?

Kann ich den Tisch decken?
Can I lay the table?

Kann ich abwaschen?
Can I do the washing-up?

meal	das Essen	**pasta**	Nudeln
breakfast	das Frühstück	**dumplings**	Knödel
lunch	das Mittagessen	**rice**	Reis
dinner (evening)	das Abendessen	**potatoes**	Kartoffeln
bowl	eine Schüssel	**onions**	Zwiebeln
glass	ein Glas	**garlic**	Knoblauch
plate	ein Teller	**tomatoes**	Tomaten
knife	ein Messer	**cucumber**	(Salat)gurke
fork	eine Gabel	**beans**	Bohnen
spoon	ein Löffel	**peas**	Erbsen
muesli	Müsli	**carrots**	Karotten
bread/roll	Brot/Brötchen	**spinach**	Spinat
boiled egg	gekochtes Ei	**pickled gherkin**	Gewürzgurke
jam	Konfitüre	**cabbage**	Kohl/Kraut
margarine	Margarine	**cauliflower**	Blumenkohl
chicken	Hähnchen	**celery**	Stangensellerie
pork	Schweinefleisch	**raw**	roh
beef	Rindfleisch	**(too) hot, spicy**	(zu) scharf
veal	Kalbfleisch	**salty**	salzig
liver	Leber	**sweet**	süß

Special cases

Ich mag keinen Fisch.
I don't like fish.

Ich bin Vegetarier.†
I'm a vegetarian.

Ich bin allergisch gegen Eier.
I'm allergic to eggs.

†If you're a girl, say *Vegetarierin*.

Shopping

Fact file

Shops are open Monday to Friday until 8. Food shops often open early but close at 6. On Saturdays, shops close at 4, but on the first Saturday of the month, large shops in main shopping areas may stay open until 6. Shops usually close on Sundays, except for bakers, which open 11-3. Shops in and near train stations may be open late and at weekends.

Some news kiosks sell blocks of bus/tram tickets, as well as papers and postcards. An *Apotheke* sells mainly medicines. For everyday things like soap, make-up, etc., the cheapest place is a *Drogeriemarkt*, a supermarket or a department store. Department stores are often cheapest for most things. They are usually found in a *Fußgängerzone* (pedestrian area). Some names to look out for are *Karstadt* and *Kaufhof*.

The *Abteilung für Haushaltsartikel* (household goods section of a department store) sells handy things for camping, but for proper camping equipment you will need a camping department or sports shop.

For food shopping, most department stores have a self-service *Lebensmittel* (food) hall. Along with supermarkets, these are the easiest and cheapest options. Specialist shops may offer better quality and choice, though. Bakers offer a fantastic range of breads and rolls and are well worth a visit. Markets are held regularly. They are colourful and lively as well as being good for food and local produce. There are few greengrocers; people tend to buy fruit and vegetables from markets or supermarkets.

shopping centre	Einkaufszentrum
shop	ein Laden, ein Geschäft
department store	ein Kaufhaus
market	der Markt
supermarket	ein Supermarkt
grocer	ein Lebensmittelgeschäft
baker	eine Bäckerei
butcher	eine Metzgerei, eine Schlachterei
cake shop	eine Konditorei
delicatessen	ein Delikatessgeschäft
fruit/veg stall, greengrocer	ein Obst- und Gemüsehändler
fishmonger	eine Fischhandlung
healthfood shop	ein Bioladen
hardware shop	ein Haushaltswarengeschäft
dispensing chemist	eine Apotheke
non-dispensing chemist	eine Drogerie, ein Drogeriemarkt
jeweller	ein Juwelier
gift shop	ein Geschenkartikelgeschäft
news kiosk	ein Zeitungskiosk
newsagent	ein Zeitungshändler
bookshop	ein Buchladen
stationer	ein Schreibwarenladen
record shop	ein Plattenladen
computer store	ein Computergeschäft
video shop	eine Videothek
flea market	ein Flohmarkt
junk shop	ein Trödelladen
sports shop	ein Sportartikelgeschäft
camping department	die Campingabteilung
shoe shop	ein Schuhgeschäft
cobblers	ein Schuster
hairdresser, barber	ein Friseur/eine Friseuse (m/f)
launderette	ein Waschsalon
dry-cleaner	eine Reinigung
travel agent	ein Reisebüro
open	geöffnet
closed	geschlossen
entrance	der Eingang
exit	der Ausgang
checkout	die Kasse
stairs	die Treppe
escalator	die Rolltreppe
price	der Preis

Wo ist das Haupteinkaufsviertel?
Where's the main shopping area?

Haben Sie Batterien?
Do you sell batteries?

Wo bekomme ich welche?
Where can I get some?

Wo kann ich das reparieren lassen?
Where can I get this repaired?

Wo kauft man am besten eine Sonnenbrille?
Where's a good place to buy sunglasses?

Kann ich Ihnen helfen?
Can I help you?

Kann ich mal sehen?
Can I see that?

Was kostet das?
How much is it?

Ich sehe mich nur um.
I'm just looking.

Ich überleg's mir.
I'll think about it.

sunscreen	Sonnenschutzmittel
make-up	Make-up
(hair) gel	Gel, Haargel
hair spray	Haarspray
tampons	Tampons
tissues	Papiertaschentücher
razor	eine Rasierklinge
shaving foam	Rasierschaum
painkiller	Schmerzmittel
contact lens solution	Kontaktlinsenflüssigkeit
plasters	Pflaster
film	ein Film
English newspapers	englische Zeitungen
postcard	eine Postkarte
writing paper	Schreibpapier
envelope	ein Umschlag
notebook	ein Notizblock
pen	ein Stift
pencil	ein Bleistift
poster	ein Poster
stickers	Aufkleber
badges	Buttons
sunglasses	Sonnenbrille
jewellery	Schmuck
watch	eine Uhr
earrings	Ohrringe
ring	ein Ring
purse	ein Portemonnaie
wallet	eine Brieftasche
bag	eine Tüte
smaller	kleiner
cheaper	billiger
another colour	eine andere Farbe

Ich brauche eine Sonnencreme.
I need some suntan lotion.

Haben Sie das in größer?
Is there a bigger one?

Ich möchte zwei Brötchen.
I'd like two bread rolls.

Kann ich für drei Mark Weintrauben haben?
Can I have 3 marks worth of grapes?

Kann ich ein Stück Leberwurst haben?
Can I have a piece of liver sausage?

carrier bag	eine Tragetasche	**chocolate**	Schokolade
small	klein	**crisps**	Chips
big	groß	**peanuts**	Erdnüsse
a slice of	eine Scheibe	**yoghurt**	ein Joghurt
a bit more/less	etwas mehr/weniger	**fruit**	Obst
a portion of	eine Portion	**apples**	Äpfel
a piece of	ein Stück	**pears**	Birnen
a kilogram	ein Kilo	**peaches**	Pfirsiche
half a kilo	ein Pfund	**bananas**	Bananen
250 grammes	zweihundertfünfzig Gramm	**plums**	Pflaumen
		strawberries	Erdbeeren
health food	Naturkost/Gesundheitskost	**raspberries**	Himbeeren
organic	Bio-		
roast chicken	ein Brathähnchen		
white/brown/rye bread	Weiß-/Grau-/Roggenbrot		
cake	Kuchen		
pastry	Gebäckstück		
jam doughnut	Berliner		
sweets	Süßigkeiten		

Fact file

Bakers and supermarkets sell many types of bread and rolls, often with seeds on or in them. If you want wholemeal, ask for *Vollkorn*, or try *Schwarzbrot* (black bread).

Etwas mehr, bitte.
A bit more please.

Soviel?
Like that?

Das ist genug, danke.
That's enough, thanks.

clothes	Kleider
shirt	ein Hemd
T-shirt	ein T-Shirt
vest top	ein T-Shirt, ein Top
sweatshirt	ein Sweatshirt
jumper	ein Pulli
fleece	ein Fleece
dress	ein Kleid
skirt	ein Rock
trousers	Hosen
shorts	Shorts
jogging	eine Trainings-
bottoms	hose
top	oberteil
trainers	Sportschuhe
shoes	Schuhe
sandals	Sandalen
boots	Stiefel
belt	ein Gürtel
jacket	ein Mantel
raincoat	ein Regenmantel
underpants	Unterwäsche
knickers	eine Unterhose
bra	ein BH†
tights	eine Strumpfhose
socks	Socken
swimsuit, trunks	ein Badeanzug, eine Badehose
a small size	klein
a medium size	mittelgroß

Fact file

Goods can often be exchanged within 8-14 days, but this may vary. All high-streets and shopping precincts have shops that sell clothes for young people, or try the department stores *H & M* or *C & A* for reasonable prices. You may find a *Secondhand-Laden* (second-hand shop) in a side street.

a large size	groß
too big	zu groß
smaller	kleiner
long	lang
short	kurz
tight	eng
baggy	(zu) weit
fashion	die Mode
style	der Stil
look	der Look
fashionable	modisch
trendy	flott
untrendy	unmodern
out-of-date	altmodisch
smart	schick
dressy	elegant
scruffy	ungepflegt
second-hand	gebraucht
sale	Ausverkauf
changing room	die Umkleidekabine

Kann man in Jeans kommen?
Are jeans all right?

Leihst du mir deine Jacke?
Can I borrow your jacket?

Soll ich meine Badesachen mitbringen?
Shall I bring my swimming stuff?

†Pronounced *beh-ha*.

Music

Wo kann man gute CDs kaufen?†
Where's a good place to buy CDs?

Can I put some music on?
Kann ich Musik hören?
I listen to (lots of) ...
Ich höre (viel) ...
I've never heard any ...
Ich habe nie ... gehört.
Can you tape this for me?
Kannst du das für mich aufnehmen?

Turn it up.
Lauter.
It's too loud.
Das ist zu laut.
Turn it down.
Dreh' das leiser.

Kennst du das Video?
Have you seen the video?

Haben Sie das auf Kassette?
Do you have this on cassette?

Gibt's eine Jazz-Abteilung?
Do you have a jazz section?

Von wem ist das?
Who's this by?

Playing an instrument

Do you play an instrument?
Spielst du ein Instrument?

I play the guitar.
Ich spiele Gitarre.

I'm learning the drums.
Ich lerne Schlagzeug.

Which instrument do you like best?
Welches Instrument magst du am liebsten?

I play in a band.
Ich spiele in einer Band.

I sing in a band.
Ich singe in einer Gruppe.

Was für Musik magst du?
What kind of music do you like?

Leihst du mir mal die neuste CD?
Can I borrow the latest CD?

Die kannst du vergessen.*
They're useless.

Hast du diese CD gehört?
Have you heard this CD?

Das ist geil.*
It's brilliant.

music	Musik
music shop	ein Plattenladen
radio	das Radio
radio cassette player	ein Kassettenradio
(radio) station	ein Sender
CD player	ein CD-Spieler
personal CD player	ein tragbarer CD-Spieler
personal stereo	ein Walkman†
hi-fi	eine Hi-fi-Anlage
headphones	die Kopfhörer
single	eine Single
album	eine LP, ein Album
mini disc	eine Mini-Disk
a blank tape	eine leere Kassette
music/pop video	ein Videoclip
track	ein Stück
song	ein Song
lyrics	der Text
tune, melody	eine Melodie
rhythm, beat	der Rhythmus
live	live
group, band	eine Gruppe, eine Band
orchestra	das Orchester
solo	ein Solo
singer	ein Sänger (m), eine Sängerin (f)
accompaniment	die Begleitmusik
fan	ein Fan
tour	eine Tour
concert, gig	ein Konzert, ein Gig, ein Auftritt
charts	Charts, die Hitparade
the Top 50	die Top fünfzig
number one	die Nummer eins
hit	ein Hit
latest	neuste
new	neu
piano	Klavier
keyboards	Tastatur, Keyboard
synthesizer	Rhythmusmaschine
electric guitar	elektrische Gitarre
bass guitar	Bass
acoustic guitar	Konzertgitarre
saxophone	Saxophon
trumpet	Trompete
violin	Geige
flute	Flöte
choir	ein Chor

Types of music

This list includes music you're likely to hear in Germany. For other types of music, just try using the English word - as you can see, the names are often the same.

house music	House Music
heavy metal	Heavy Metal
rock	Rock
rap	Rap
hip-hop	Hip-Hop
techno	Techno
reggae	Reggae
funk	Funk
soul	Soul
African music	afrikanische Musik
rock & roll	Rock 'n' Roll
jazz	Jazz
blues	Blues
folk	Folk
pop	Pop
dance, disco	Tanz-/Discomusik
70's music	der Siebziger-Jahre-Sound
retro	Retro
classical	klassische Musik

Na, was steht an?*
What's happening?

Hast du 'ne Idee?
Have you got any ideas?

Machen wir heut' Abend was?
Shall we do something tonight?

Ich kann nicht, hab' keine Zeit.
I can't, I'm busy.

Wann?
What time?

Wo treffen wir uns?
Where shall we meet?

Ich treff' dich am Brunnen.
See you at the fountain.

What is there to see here?	Was gibt es hier zu sehen?
Is there an admission charge?	Gibt es einen Eintrittspreis?
Is there a reduction for students?	Gibt es eine Studentenermäßigung?
Can I get a ticket in advance?	Gibt es Karten im Vorverkauf?
Do you know a good place to ...	Wo kann man gut ...
go dancing?	tanzen gehen?
listen to music?	Musik hören?
eat?	essen?
go for a drink?	etwas trinken gehen?
I'm busy tonight.	Heute Abend bin ich nicht frei.
What time does it ...	Wann ...
start?	fängt es an?
finish?	hört es auf?
open?	öffnet es?
close?	macht es zu?
today	heute
tomorrow	morgen
day after tomorrow	übermorgen
(in the) morning	morgens
(in the) afternoon	nachmittags
(in the) evening	abends
this week	diese Woche
next week	nächste Woche
entertainment guide, listing	ein Programm, Veranstaltungskalender
club, nightclub	ein (Nacht)klub
disco	eine Disco
rave	ein Rave
party	eine Party
show, entertainment	eine Show
(go to the) cinema	(ins) Kino (gehen)
(go to the) theatre	(ins) Theater (gehen)
ballet	das Ballett
opera	die Oper
ticket office	Kartenschalter
box office	Theaterkasse
student ticket	Studentenkarte
performance, film showing	eine Vorstellung
guide book	der (Reise)führer
tour	eine Tour, Rundfahrt

Fact file

If you want to find out what to visit, go to the tourist office (see page 6). The service there is generally extremely efficient and helpful.

Local papers have a *Tageskalender* (list of events and entertainments), often best on Saturdays. In the street, *Litfaßsäulen* (pillars) carry posters of events and cinema programmes. Cities have *Veranstaltungsanzeiger* or *Stadtmagazine* (listings magazines). Films are usually dubbed. Student discounts are common.

region	die Umgebung, die Gegend	**cathedral**	der Dom
countryside	die Landschaft	**church**	eine Kirche
mountains	die Berge	**castle**	ein Schloss
lake	der See	**tower**	ein Turm
river	der Fluss	**city walls**	eine Stadtmauer
forest	der Wald	**ruins**	eine Ruine
coast	die Küste	**amusement arcade**	eine Spielhalle
on the beach	am Strand	**theme park**	ein Vergnügungspark
in town	in der Stadt	**festival**	ein Festival
at X's place	bei X	**picnic**	ein Picknick
museum	ein Museum	**fireworks**	Feuerwerk
art gallery	eine Galerie	**beer garden**	ein Biergarten
exhibition	eine Ausstellung	**wine tasting**	eine Weinprobe
art exhibition	eine Kunstausstellung	**interesting**	interessant
the old town	die Altstadt	**dull, boring**	langweilig
		beautiful	schön

Films, TV, books

cinema	ein Kino	director (film)	der Regisseur
film society/club	ein Filmklub	cast	die Besetzung
theatre	ein Theater	actor/actress	der Schauspieler/
library	eine Bibliothek		die Schauspielerin
film, movie	ein Film	film buff	ein Kinofan
play	ein Stück,	production	eine Produktion
	ein Schauspiel	plot	die Handlung
book	ein Buch	story	die Geschichte
magazine	eine Zeitschrift	set	das Bühnenbild
comic	ein Comic	special effects	die Special Effects
novel	ein Roman	photography	die Aufnahmen
poetry	Gedichte	TV, telly	das Fernsehen, die Glotze*
author	der Autor	cable TV	Kabelfernsehen

satellite TV	Satellitenfernsehen	**detective film**	ein Detektiv-Film
digital TV	Digitalfernsehen	**sci-fi**	ein Sciencefiction-Film
programme	die Sendung	**suspense**	Spannung
channel	das Programm	**sex**	Sex
news	die Nachrichten	**violence**	Gewalt
weather	Wetter	**political**	politisch
documentary	ein Dokumentarfilm	**satirical**	satirisch
cartoons	Zeichentrickfilm	**serious**	ernst
game show	eine Game-Show	**offbeat**	ungewöhnlich
serial	eine Sendereihe	**commercial**	kommerziell
soap	Soap, eine Serie	**exciting, gripping**	aufregend, spannend
ads	die Werbung	**over the top**	übertrieben
dubbed	synchronisiert	**good**	gut
in English	auf Englisch	**OK, not bad**	nicht schlecht
with subtitles	mit Untertiteln	**bad, lousy**	schlecht, schrecklich
well known	bekannt	**silly**	blöde
award-winning	preisgekrönt	**funny, fun**	lustig
fringe	avantgardistisch	**soppy**	schmalzig
block buster	ein Kinohit	**sad**	traurig
a classic	ein Filmklassiker	**It's scary.**	Es ist gruslig.
comedy	eine Komödie		
thriller	ein Krimi, ein Thriller	**Where can I hire a video?**	Wo kann ich ein Video ausleihen?
musical	ein Musical	**Do I have to be a member?**	Muss ich Mitglied sein?
horror film	ein Horrorfilm		
adventure story	ein Abenteuerfilm	**What age certificate is the film?**	Für welches Alter ist der Film zugelassen?
war film	ein Kriegsfilm		
western	ein Western		

Kannst du mir was zu lesen leihen?
Can I borrow something to read?

Das haben wir in der Schule gelesen.
I did that book at school.

Um was geht's da?
What's it about?

Das ist spitze.*
It's brilliant.

Hast du das gelesen?
Have you read this?

Das ist total öde.*
It's so boring.

Von wem ist es?
Who's it by?

I'm English.
Ich bin aus England.

My family is from ...
Meine Familie kommt aus ...

I've been here for two weeks.
Ich bin seit zwei Wochen hier.

I'm on an exchange.
Ich bin als Austauschstudent hier.

I'm on holiday.
Ich bin auf Urlaub.

I'm staying with friends.
Ich wohne bei Freunden.

I am a friend of ...
Ich bin Freund/Freundin von ...

I'm studying German.
Ich studiere Deutsch.

I'm travelling around.
Ich reise rum.

My parents are divorced.
Meine Eltern sind geschieden.

My birthday is on the ...
Mein Geburtstag ist am ...

I'm an only child.
Ich habe keine Geschwister.

My name is ...	Ich heiße ...
I live ...	Ich wohne ...
in the country	auf dem Land
in a town	in einer Stadt
in the suburbs	am Stadtrand
by the sea	am Meer
in a house	in einem Haus
in a flat	in einer Wohnung
I live with ...	Ich wohne zusammen mit ...
I don't live with ...	Ich wohne nicht mit ... zusammen
my	mein(e)†
your	dein(e)†
family	die Familie
parents	die Eltern
father/mother	der Vater/die Mutter
stepfather	der Stiefvater
stepmother	die Stiefmutter
husband/wife	der Mann/die Frau
boyfriend	der Freund
girlfriend	die Freundin
brother/sister	der Bruder/die Schwester
step/half brother	der Stief-/Halbbruder
step/half sister	die Stief-/Halbschwester
alone	allein
single	single
married	verheiratet
surname	der Nachname
nickname	ein Spitzname
my address	meine Adresse
my e-mail address	meine E-Mail-Adresse

†This word changes according to the gender of the word it refers to. See page 58.

Other people

Kennst du Klaus?
Do you know Klaus?

Er ist groß.
He's tall.

Sie geht mir auf den Wecker.*
I can't stand her.

Wer ist das?
Who's that?

Mit ihm hat man seinen Spaß.
He's a good laugh.

Ich mag ihn.
I like him.

Was ist aus Petra geworden?
What's happened to Petra?

Wie ist sie?
What's she like?

Sie sieht recht gut aus.
She's quite pretty.

Wir kommen ganz gut miteinander aus.
We get on well.

friend	ein Freund (m), eine Freundin (f)	**he/she is ...**	er/sie ist ...
boy	ein Junge	**tall**	groß
girl	ein Mädchen	**short**	klein
bloke, guy	ein Kerl, ein Typ	**fat**	dick
someone	jemand	**thin**	dünn
has ...	hat ...	**fair**	blond
long hair	lange Haare	**dark**	dunkel
short hair	kurze Haare	**pretty**	hübsch
curly hair	lockige Haare	**good-looking**	gutaussehend
straight hair	glatte Haare	**OK (looks)**	okay
brown eyes	braune Augen	**not good-looking**	nicht gutaussehend
		ugly	hässlich

Kennst du jemanden hier?
Do you know anyone here?

Wie ist deine Telefonnummer?
What's your phone number?

Willst du was trinken?
Do you want a drink?

Hast du Lust zu tanzen?
Do you want to dance?

a bit, a little	etwas, ein wenig	a creep	ein fieser Typ
very	sehr	an idiot, a prat	ein Trottel
so	so	in a bad mood	schlecht gelaunt
really	wirklich	in a good mood	gut gelaunt
completely	völlig, total	angry, annoyed	sauer
nice, OK	nett	depressed	down*, deprimiert
not nice, horrible	unangenehm	happy	glücklich
horrible, nasty	gemein	temperamental	launenhaft
cool, trendy, hip	in*, cool*, stark*		
old-fashioned, square	altmodisch, out		
clever	clever	**Have you heard that ... ?**	
thick	blöd	Hast du gehört ... ?	
boring	langweilig		
shy	schüchtern	**Petra is going out with Klaus.**	
mad, crazy	verrückt	Petra geht mit Klaus.	
weird	seltsam		
lazy	faul	**Stefan got off with Christa.**	
laid back	gelassen	Stefan hat Christa aufgerissen.*	
up-tight	verklemmt		
mixed up, untogether	konfus, durcheinander	**He/she kissed me.**	
selfish	egoistisch	Er/Sie hat mich geküsst.	
jealous	neidisch		
rude	unhöflich	**They split up.**	
annoying	lästig	Sie haben sich getrennt.	
macho	macho		
stuck up	eingebildet	**We had a row.**	
sloaney, yuppie	schickimicki*, ein Yuppie	Wir haben uns gestritten.	
loaded, rich	(schwer) Kohle haben*	**Leave me alone.** Lass mich allein.	

Können wir uns mal treffen?
Can I see you again?

Kann ich auch kommen?
Can I come too?

Tut mir leid, ich kann nicht.
Sorry, I can't.

Möchtest du mitkommen?
Want to come?

Vielleicht ein andermal.
Maybe some other time.

Sports

Catch!
Fang!

Throw it to me.
Wirf ihn mir zu.

In!/Out!
In!/Aus!

You're cheating!
Du mogelst!

Who won?
Wer hat gewonnen?

How do you play this?
Wie spielt man das?

What are the rules?
Wie sind die Regeln?

What team do you support?
Für welche Mannschaft bist du?

Is there a match we could go to?
Gibt es ein Spiel, zu dem wir gehen können?

Fact file

Football is probably the most popular sporting game in Germany. It has the biggest TV audiences, particularly for *Bundesliga* (top league) games.

Tennis, cycling, windsurfing, inline-skating and swimming are also popular. More people go swimming in summer, when they can use a *Freibad* (open air pool). In winter, many people in the south go to the German Alps at weekends for downhill skiing. Cross-country skiing and ice-hockey are also popular.

sport	Sport	once a week	einmal pro Woche
match	ein Spiel	twice a week	zweimal pro Woche
doubles	Doppel	I play ...	ich spiele ...
singles	Einzel	I don't play ...	ich spiele nicht ...
race	ein Rennen	tennis	Tennis
marathon	ein Marathon	squash	Squash
championships	die Meisterschaften	badminton	Federball
Olympics	die Olympischen Spiele	football	Fußball
World Cup	die Fußballweltmeisterschaft	American football	amerikanisches
club	ein Klub, ein Verein		Football
team	die Mannschaft	basketball	Basketball
referee	der Schiedsrichter	volleyball	Volleyball
supporter	ein Fan	table tennis	Tischtennis
training, practice	das Training	cricket	Kricket
a goal	ein Tor	baseball	Baseball
to lose	verlieren	I do, I go ...	ich mache, gehe
a draw	unentschieden		(zum) ...†
sports centre	ein Sportzentrum	I don't do, go ...	ich mache, gehe
stadium	das Stadion		nicht (zum) ...†
gym	die Turnhalle	judo	Judo
court	ein Platz	karate	Karate
indoor ...	Hallen-...	keep-fit	Fitnesstraining
outdoor	im Freien	running	laufen
ball	ein Ball	aerobics	Aerobic
bat	ein Schlagholz	weight-training	Hanteltraining
net	ein Netz	body-building	Bodybuilding
trainers	Sportschuhe	bowling	Bowling
Tennis shoes	Tennisschuhe	dancing	tanzen
sports clothes	ein Trainingsanzug	yoga	Joga

Wie steht's?
What's the score?

Kick!
Kick it!

Hier!
Here!

Schnell!
Quick!

Kann ich mal spielen?
Can I play?

Spiel den Ball zu.
Pass the ball.

Renn!
Run!

†Use *zum* in front of the nouns, i.e. *Ich gehe zum Fitnesstraining/Hanteltraining/Bowling.*

Ich finde Tauchen nicht so toll.
I'm not keen on scuba diving.

Ich gehe gern Drachen fliegen.
I love hang gliding.

Ich fahre lieber Wasserski.
I prefer water-skiing.

Ich hab's nie versucht.
I've never tried.

Ich kann nicht schwimmen.
I can't swim.

Ist die Strömung stark?
Are the currents strong?

Ist das nicht gefährlich?
It's not dangerous, is it?

I like ...	Ich gehe gern ...
I don't like ...	Ich gehe nicht gern ...
I love ...	Ich gehe besonders gern ...
I prefer ...	Ich ziehe ... vor
swimming	schwimmen
(scuba) diving	tauchen
sailing	segeln
surfing	surfen
canoeing	Kanu fahren
rowing	rudern
sunbathing	sonnenbaden
boat	ein Boot
sail	das Segel
surfboard	ein Surfbrett
windsurfer	ein Windsurfer
sea	das Meer
beach	der Strand
swimming pool	ein Schwimmbad
in the sun	in der Sonne
in the shade	im Schatten
mask	eine Tauchermaske
snorkel	ein Schnorchel
flippers	Schwimmflossen
wetsuit	ein Taucheranzug
life jacket	eine Schwimmweste
fishing	fischen

fishing rod	eine Angel
cycling	Rad fahren
racing bike	ein Rennrad
mountain bike	ein Mountainbike
touring bike	ein Tourenrad
horse riding	reiten
horse	ein Pferd
walking, hiking	wandern
footpath	ein Fußweg
skateboarding	Skateboard fahren
roller skating	Rollschuh laufen
ice rink	eine Schlittschuhbahn
skates	Schlittschuhe
skiing	Ski laufen
cross-country skiing	Langlauf
snowboarding	Snowboard fahren
ski run	die Skipiste
ski pass	eine Liftkarte
ski lifts	Skilifte
chair lift	ein Sessellift
drag lift	ein Schlepplift
skis	Skier
ski boots	Skistiefel
ski goggles	eine Skibrille
snow	der Schnee

Studying

Was machst du?
What do you do?

Wo studierst du?
Where are you studying?

Was für eine Hochschule ist das?
What sort of college is it?

Um wieviel Uhr bist du fertig?
What time do you finish?

Musst du viel arbeiten?
Do you have a lot of work?

Ja, massenhaft.
Yes, loads.

I do ...	Ich studiere ...
computer studies	Informatik
maths	Mathematik
physics	Physik
chemistry	Chemie
biology	Biologie
natural sciences	Naturwissenschaften
geography	Geographie
history	Geschichte
economics	Volkswirtschaftslehre (VWL)
business studies	Betriebswirtschaftslehre (BWL)
languages	Sprachen
French	Französisch
English	Englisch
Spanish	Spanisch
German	Deutsch
Italian	Italienisch
literature	Literatur
philosophy	Philosophie
sociology	Soziologie
psychology	Psychologie
religious studies	Theologie
general studies	Allgemeinwissenschaften
art	Kunst
drama	Theaterwissenschaften
music	Musik
PE	Sport
school	eine Schule
mixed	gemischt
boarding school	ein Internat
private school	eine Privatschule
(school) term	ein Halbjahr
(university) term	ein Semester
graduation (uni)	die Graduierung
holidays	die Ferien

uniform	eine Uniform
school club	ein Schulklub
lesson, lecture	eine Stunde/Vorlesung
tuition, coaching, private lessons	Nachhilfeunterricht
homework	Hausaufgaben
essay	ein Aufsatz
translation	eine Übersetzung
project	ein Referat
revision	eine Wiederholung, Prüfungsvorbereitung
test	eine Klassenarbeit
oral	mündlich
written	schriftlich
continuous assessment	studienbegleitende Leistungskontrolle
mark, grade	die Note
teacher, lecturer	der Lehrer (m), die Lehrerin (f)
(language) assistant	der Assistent (m), die Assistentin (f)
good	gut
bad	schlecht
strict	streng
easy going	lasch
to repeat (a year)	sitzen bleiben
to be suspended	vom Unterricht ausgeschlossen werden
to be expelled	von der Schule verwiesen werden
to skip a lesson	eine Stunde schwänzen
a grant	ein Stipendium

Fact file

Types of schools and colleges:
- For 10 to 15 year olds, *Realschule* or *Hauptschule* (these are similar to comprehensive schools) or *Gymnasium* (grammar school).
- 16 to 19 year olds doing the *Abitur* (university entrance exam) stay on in a *Gymnasium* for the three *Oberstufe* years (similar to sixth form).
- *Berufsschule* (for 16 to 18 year olds doing apprenticeships or job training, or for people with the *Abitur* who are on training schemes).
- *Universität*, or *Uni* (university).
The school year is split into two *Halbjahre* (half years) and begins at different times in the different *Bundesländer* (states). The day begins at 7.30 or 8 and often ends at lunchtime. Schools are mixed and there is no uniform. School starts with *Erste Klasse* (first class) at age six and carries on up to *Dreizehnte* (thirteenth class). *Wehrdienst* (national service) is compulsory for men at 18, but it can be deferred while studying. *Zivildienst* (community service) can be served instead.

I'm a student.
Ich bin Student.

I'm still at school.
Ich bin noch in der Schule.

I want to do ...
Ich will ... machen.

He is skiving, bunking off.
Er schwänzt.

Was willst du nach dem Studium machen?
What do you want to do when you finish college?

Welche Fächer studierst du?
What subjects are you doing?

Wann ist dein Examen?
When are your exams?

In welcher Klasse bist du?
What year are you in?

Was machst du am liebsten?
What do you like best?

Ich arbeite in einem Laden.
I work in a shop.

Was machst du so?
What sort of things do you do?

Hast du viel Freizeit?
Do you get a lot of spare time?

Ich interessiere mich für Photographie.
I'm interested in photography.

Ich habe einen PC.
I've got a PC.

Hast du einen Internetanschluss?
Are you on the Internet?

Welche Tasten muss ich drücken?
What keys do I have to press?

Was mache ich jetzt?
What do I do now?

Wer ist dran?
Whose go is it?

I do a lot of sport.	**I write poetry.**
Ich gehe oft zum Sport.	Ich schreibe Gedichte.
I listen to a lot of music.	**I work in a café.**
Ich höre mir oft Musik an.	Ich arbeite in einem Café.
I write songs.	**I do babysitting.**
Ich schreibe Lieder.	Ich gehe babysitten.

I collect ...	Ich sammle ...
postcards	Postkarten
all sorts of things	alles Mögliche
I like drawing.	Ich zeichne gern.
I like painting.	Ich male gern.
I like acting.	Ich spiele gern Theater.
I like making jewellery.	Ich mache gern Schmuck.
a part-time job	eine Teilzeitbeschäftigung
pocket money	Taschengeld
computer	ein Computer
laptop	ein Laptop
software	Software
computer games	Computerspiele
word processing	Textverarbeitung
Web site	eine Website
disk	eine Diskette
joystick	ein Joystick
mouse	eine Maus
game	ein Spiel
chess	Schach
board games	Brettspiele
cards	Karten
table football	Tischfußball
What are the rules?	Wie sind die Regeln?
My go.	Ich bin dran.
Your go.	Du bist dran.

What do you want to do later?	**I want ...**		Ich will ...
Was möchtest du später machen?	**to live/work abroad**		im Ausland leben/arbeiten
When I finish ...	**to travel**		reisen
Wann ich fertig bin ...	**to have a career**		eine Laufbahn einschlagen
One day ...	**to get a good job**		eine gute Stelle finden
Irgendwann ...	**to get my**		meine Ausbildung
I want to be a ...	**qualifications**		abschließen
Ich möchte ... werden.	**to carry on studying**		weiterstudieren

What do you think about ...?	**I think ...**	**You're right.**
Was hältst du von ...?	Ich glaube ...	Du hast Recht.
I don't know much about ...	**I belong to ...**	**I don't agree.**
Ich verstehe nicht viel von ...	Ich gehöre zu ...	Ich stimme nicht zu.
Can you explain ...?	**I believe in ...**	**I'm for/I support ...**
Kannst du ... erklären?	Ich glaube an ...	Ich bin für ...
I feel angry about (deforestation).	**I don't believe in ...**	**I'm against ...**
Ich bin wütend über (das Abholzen).	Ich glaube nicht an ...	Ich bin gegen ...

the future	die Zukunft	**ozone layer**	die Ozonschicht
(in the) past	(in der) Vergangenheit	**acid rain**	der saure Regen
now, nowadays	heutzutage	**nuclear power**	die Atomkraft, die
religion	die Religion		Kernenergie
God	Gott	**recycling**	das Recycling
human rights	die Menschenrechte	**politics**	die Politik
gay	schwul	**government**	die Regierung
feminist	die Feministin	**democratic**	demokratisch
abortion	Abtreibung	**elections**	die Wahlen
drugs	Drogen	**party**	eine Partei
drug addict	der/die Drogenabhängige	**revolution**	Revolution
HIV	HIV	**the left**	die Linken
Aids	Aids	**the right**	die Rechten
unemployment	die Arbeitslosigkeit	**fascist**	faschistisch
Third World	die Dritte Welt	**communist**	kommunistisch
peace	der Frieden	**socialist**	sozialistisch
war	der Krieg	**green**	grün
terrorism	der Terrorismus	**conservative**	konservativ
environment	die Umwelt	**reactionary**	reaktionär
pollution	die Verschmutzung	**radical**	radikal
conservation	die Erhaltung	**politically active**	politisch engagiert
global warming	globaler	**march, demo**	eine Demo(nstration)
	Temperaturanstieg	**charity**	eine Wohltätigkeits-
greenhouse effect	der Treibhauseffekt		organisation

Illness, problems and emergencies

I am ill.	Ich bin krank.
It hurts.	Es tut weh.
It hurts a little/a lot.	Es tut etwas weh/sehr weh.
I've cut myself.	Ich habe mich geschnitten.
I think I've broken my ...	Ich glaube, ich habe mir den/die/das ... gebrochen.[†]
I've been stung by a wasp.	Mich hat eine Wespe gestochen.
He/she's had too much to drink.	Er/sie hat zuviel getrunken.
I feel dizzy.	Mir ist schwindlig.
I'm constipated.	Ich leide an Verstopfung.
I'm on medication for ...	Ich nehme ein Medikament für ...
I'm allergic to ...	Ich bin allergisch gegen ...
antibiotics	Antibiotika
penicillin	Penizillin
some medicines	einige Medikamente
I have ...	Ich habe ...
food poisoning	eine Lebens- mittelvergiftung
diarrhoea	Durchfall
sunstroke	einen Hitzschlag
a headache	Kopfschmerzen
a stomach ache	Bauchschmerzen
my period	meine Tage
an infection	eine Infektion
a sore throat	Halsschmerzen
a cold	eine Erkältung
flu	eine Grippe
a cough	Husten
hayfever	Heuschnupfen
asthma	Asthma
a toothache	Zahnschmerzen
earache	Ohrenschmerzen
a temperature	Fieber
the shivers	Schüttelfrost
a hangover	einen Kater
doctor	ein Arzt/eine Ärztin (m/f)
dentist	ein Zahnarzt/eine Zahnärztin (m/f)
optician	ein Optiker/eine Optikerin (m/f)
chemist's, pharmacist's	eine Apotheke
pill	eine Tablette, eine Pille
prescription	ein Rezept
injection	eine Spritze

Ich fühle mich nicht wohl.
I don't feel well.

Was fehlt dir?
What's wrong?

Ich muss mich übergeben.
I'm going to be sick.

Das tut mir sehr leid.
I'm really sorry about this.

Ich brauche einen Arzt.
I need to see a doctor.

Hat hier in der Nähe eine Apotheke auf?
Is there a chemist open around here?

Können Sie mir was gegen Heuschnupfen geben?
Can you give me something for hayfever?

[†]*Den* + (m) words, *die* + (f) words and *das* + (n) words.

Fact file

In Germany everyone has to carry their identity card, so keep your passport with you. You may be asked to show your *Papiere* (documents, ID).

For minor health problems, the best place to go is an *Apotheke* (chemist). For something more serious, go to a doctor or the local hospital casualty department. You will probably have to pay, but should be able to claim back expenses on your travel insurance, so make sure you keep all the paperwork.

Emergency phone numbers: police, 110, ambulance and fire brigade, 112. For very serious problems, contact the closest *Britische Konsulat* (British Consulate). The number will be in the telephone directory.

There's been an accident.	Es ist ein Unfall passiert.
Help!	Hilfe!
Fire!	Feuer!
Please call ...	Bitte rufen Sie ...
an ambulance	einen Krankenwagen
the police	die Polizei
the fire brigade	die Feuerwehr
the lifeguard	einen Rettungsschwimmer
the hospital	das Krankenhaus

wallet	ein Portemonnaie
(hand)bag	eine Handtasche
my things	meine Sachen
my papers	meine Papiere
my passport	mein Pass
my key	mein Schlüssel
my mobile	mein Handy
all my money	mein ganzes Geld
lost property	das Fundbüro
I'm lost.	Ich habe mich verlaufen.
I'm scared.	Ich habe Angst.
I'm in trouble.	Ich habe ein Problem.

I need to talk to someone.
Ich muss mit jemandem sprechen.

I don't know what to do.
Ich weiß nicht, was ich machen soll.

I don't want to cause trouble, but ...
Ich möchte keine Umstände machen, aber ...

A man's following me.
Ein Mann verfolgt mich.

Can you keep an eye on my things?
Kannst du auf meine Sachen aufpassen?

Has anyone seen ...?
Hat jemand ... gesehen?

Please don't smoke.
Bitte, rauchen Sie nicht.

It doesn't work.
Es funktioniert nicht.

There's no water/power.
Es gibt kein Wasser/keinen Strom.

Slang and everyday German

50

These two pages list some common words and phrases of informal German and slang. You will also notice that many American and English words have been imported into German, but they are not included here. When using slang it is easy to sound rude without meaning to. Here, as in the rest of the book, an asterisk shows that a word is slang; it is best to avoid using these words in formal situations. You will find more slang in the dictionary.

Slang

very, completely	absolut, irre, wahnsinnig, tierisch, total, echt, unheimlich
great, brilliant, classic	toll, spitzenmäßig, geil, stark, klasse, heiß, voll, ultra, fetzig, scharf, astrein
clever, good idea	witzig
lousy, bad, disgusting	schrecklich, grässlich, saumäßig, ätzend
boring	stinklangweilig*
stupid	beknackt*, bescheuert*
bizarre, weird	abgefahren*
freaked out	ausgeflippt*
stressed, hassled	gestresst*, im Stress
guy, bloke	ein Typ, ein Kerl
girl	eine Tussi*, eine Braut*
wimp	ein Weichei, ein Softie*
gang of friends	die Clique
relationship	die Beziehungskiste*
money, dough	Kies*, Knete*, Kohle*, Schmott, Kröten*
clothes, dress	Klamotten*, Fummel*
shoes	Latschen*
room	Bude*
party	Fete*
pub	Pinte*, Kneipe
quarrel, aggro	Zoff*
rubbish	Mist*
car	Karre*, Kiste*
to turn on	anturnen*
to put off	abturnen*
to flip, go mad	ausflippen*

to talk rubbish	Quatsch reden, schwafeln
to get on your nerves	nerven*
to get the hang of something	etwas checken*, etwas schnallen*
to be really keen on someone/thing	auf jemanden/etwas stehen*
to fancy someone/thing	auf jemanden/etwas abfahren*
to chat someone up	jemanden anmachen*
to sleep	ratzen*, knacken*, abmatten
to tell off	anmotzen*, anmachen*
to rip someone off	jemanden linken
I've got it.	Hab' ich gecheckt.* Logo.* Gebongt.*
I haven't got a clue	Keine Ahnung. Ich hab' keinen Plan*/Dunst.*
Stay cool	Keine Panik.*
Buzz off.	Mach die Fliege.* Putz die Platte.*

Alternative pronunciations

it	's* (es)
they, you	se* (sie)
some, a little	was* (etwas)
just	grad* (gerade)
is	is*(ist)
to have	ham* (haben)
not	nich* (nicht)
no	nee* (nein)
nothing	nix* (nichts)

Abbreviations

chauvinist	ein Chauvi*(-nist)
frustration	Frust*(-ration)
teenager	ein Teenie* (Teenager)
flatsharing	die WG* (Wohngemeinschaft)

Fillers

of course	logo*
("boy"/"man")	Mensch*
(no real meaning)	mal
somehow	irgendwie
so, well	also/na ja
isn't it	oder
isn't that so?	nicht wahr?/gell?

Countries, nationalities, faiths

Countries

country das Land   **continent** der Kontinent
north   Norden   **south**   Süden
east   Osten   **west**   Westen

Africa	Afrika
Asia	Asien
Australia	Australien
Austria	Österreich
Belgium	Belgien
Bosnia	Bosnien
Canada	Kanada
Caribbean Islands	(die) Karibik
Central America	Mittelamerika
Channel Islands	(die) Kanalinseln
China	China
Croatia	Kroatien
Czech Republic	(die) Tschechische Republik
England	England
Europe	Europa
France	Frankreich
Germany	Deutschland
Great Britain	Großbritannien
Greece	Griechenland
Hungary	Ungarn
India	Indien
Ireland	Irland
Italy	Italien
Japan	Japan
Middle East	der Nahe Osten
Netherlands	(die) Niederlande
New Zealand	Neuseeland
Pakistan	Pakistan
Poland	Polen
Russia	Russland
Scotland	Schottland
Serbia	Serbien
Slovakia	(die) Slowakei
Slovenia	Slowenien
South America	Südamerika
Spain	Spanien
Switzerland	(die) Schweiz
Turkey	(die) Türkei
United States	die Vereinigten Staaten
Wales	Wales

Nationalities

You can say "I come from" + country:
   e.g. *Ich komme aus Japan*
With feminine country names, say *Ich komme aus der* + name:
   e.g. *Ich komme aus der Schweiz*
With plural country names, say *Ich komme aus den* + name:
   e.g. *Ich komme aus den Vereinigten Staaten*
Or you can say "I am ..." + adjective for nationality, e.g. *Ich bin:* (m)/(f)

American	Amerikaner/Amerikanerin
Australian	Australier/Australierin
Austrian	Österreicher/Österreicherin
Belgian	Belgier/Belgierin
Canadian	Kanadier/Kanadierin
Czech	Tscheche/Tschechin
Dutch	Niederländer/Niederländerin
English	Engländer/Engländerin
French	Franzose/Französin
German	Deutscher/Deutsche
Indian	Inder/Inderin
Irish	Ire/Irin
Italian	Italiener/Italienerin
Pakistani	Pakistaner/Pakistanerin
Scottish	Schotte/Schottin
Slovakian	Slowake/Slowakin
Spanish	Spanier/Spanierin
Swiss	Schweizer/Schweizerin
Turkish	Türke/Türkin
Welsh	Waliser/Waliserin

Faiths

agnostic	Agnostiker/Agnostikerin
atheist	Atheist/Atheistin
Buddhist	Buddhist/Buddhistin
Catholic	Katholik/Katholikin
Christian	Christ/Christin
Hindu	Hindu
Jewish	Jude/Jüdin
Muslim	Muslim/Muslimin
Protestant	Protestant/Protestantin
Sikh	Sikh

Numbers

0 null	**30** dreißig
1 eins	**31** einunddreißig
2 zwei	**32** zweiunddreißig
3 drei	**40** vierzig
4 vier	**50** fünfzig
5 fünf	**60** sechzig
6 sechs	**70** siebzig
7 sieben	**71** einundsiebzig
8 acht	**80** achtzig
9 neun	**81** einundachtzig
10 zehn	**90** neunzig
11 elf	**91** einundneunzig
12 zwölf	**100** (ein) hundert
13 dreizehn	**101** hunderteins
14 vierzehn	**200** zweihundert
15 fünfzehn	**300** dreihundert
16 sechzehn	**1,000** (ein) tausend
17 siebzehn	**1,100** tausendeinhundert
18 achtzehn	**1,200**
19 neunzehn	tausendzweihundert
20 zwanzig	**2,000** zweitausend
21 einundzwanzig	**2,100**
22 zweiundzwanzig	zweitausendeinhundert
23 dreiundzwanzig	**10,000** zehntausend
24 vierundzwanzig	**100,000** hunderttausend
25 fünfundzwanzig	**1000,000** eine Million

Colours

colour	die Farbe
light	hell
dark	dunkel
blue	blau
navy	marineblau
green	grün
yellow	gelb
orange	orange
purple	lila, violett
pink	rosa
red	rot
white	weiß
grey	grau
brown	braun
black	schwarz

Days and dates

Monday	Montag
Tuesday	Dienstag
Wednesday	Mittwoch
Thursday	Donnerstag
Friday	Freitag
Saturday	Samstag
Sunday	Sonntag
January	Januar
February	Februar
March	März
April	April
May	Mai
June	Juni
July	Juli
August	August
September	September
October	Oktober
November	November
December	Dezember
day	der Tag
week	die Woche
month	der Monat
year	das Jahr
diary	ein Taschenkalender
calendar	ein Kalender
yesterday	gestern
the day before yesterday	vorgestern
today	heute
the next day	am nächsten Tag
tomorrow	morgen
the day after tomorrow	übermorgen
this week	diese Woche
last week	letzte Woche
next week	nächste Woche
What's the date?	Welches Datum haben wir?
on Mondays	montags
in August	im August
(on) 1st April	am ersten April
(on) 2nd January	am zweiten Januar
in the year 2000	im Jahr 2000

Time

hour	die Stunde
What time is it?	Wie spät ist es?/ Wieviel Uhr ist es?
It's 1 o'clock.	Es ist ein Uhr.
2 o'clock	zwei Uhr
minute	die Minute
morning	der Morgen
afternoon	der Nachmittag
evening	der Abend
midday	Mittag
midnight	Mitternacht
quarter past two	Viertel nach zwei
half past two	halb drei
half past three	halb vier
quarter to two	Viertel vor zwei
five past two	fünf nach zwei
ten to two	zehn vor zwei
What time ... ?	Wann ...?/ Um wieviel Uhr ...?
in ten minutes	in zehn Minuten
half an hour ago	vor einer halben Stunde
at 13.17	um dreizehn Uhr siebzehn
at 9am	um neun Uhr morgens
at 3pm	um drei Uhr nachmittags
at 9 in the evening	um neun Uhr abends

Seasons and weather

season	die Jahreszeit	sky	der Himmel
spring	der Frühling	sun	die Sonne
summer	der Sommer	clouds	die Wolken
autumn	der Herbst	rain	der Regen
winter	der Winter	snow	der Schnee

What's the weather like?
Wie ist das Wetter?

It's fine.	Es ist schön.
It's sunny.	Es ist sonnig.
It's hot.	Es ist heiß.
It's windy.	Es ist windig.
It's raining.	Es regnet.
It's foggy.	Es ist neblig.
It's snowing.	Es schneit.
It's icy.	Es hat Glatteis.
It's cold.	Es ist kalt.
It's freezing.	Es ist eiskalt.

The fact files below focus on essential, practical information which is different from that given for Germany.

Fact file: Austria

Languages – German spoken throughout. **Travel** – An efficient train service runs throughout Austria. For under 26s, a big discount is available on the *Puzzle ticket*, allowing four days of travel in one of four regions. There is also a good bus service, and trams in larger cities. Bikes can be hired from most train stations. You must be 16 to ride a moped. **Banks, post offices, phones** – Currency is the *Schilling* (öS). 1 öS = 100 *Groschen*. Banks open Mon-Fri 8-12.30 and 1.30-3 (varies in Vienna). Post offices open Mon-Fri 8-12 and 2-6. Phones take coins or phonecards (*Telefonkarten*). **Shopping** – Opening times are Mon-Sat 9-6. Outside cities, shops may close for two hours over lunch, and some may close on Saturday afternoons. **Emergencies** – Police, 133; ambulance, 144; fire, 122.

Fact file: Switzerland

Languages – The official languages are French, German and Italian. **Travel** – Cheap deals include the *Swiss Pass, Swiss Flexi Pass* and *Half Fare Travel Card,* valid on trains, and most bus and lake steamer services. The *PTT* (post office) runs bus services to remote areas. To hire bikes from train stations you must book the day before. You must be 18 to ride a moped. **Banks and phones** – Currency is the Swiss *franc* (SF). In cities banks open Mon-Fri 8.30-4.30, but elsewhere they close from 12-2. Most phones take *taxcards* (phonecards). **Shopping** – Opening times vary. Some shops are closed on Monday mornings. **Emergencies** – There is no national health service, so make sure you are insured. Police, 117; ambulance, 144; fire, 118.

Pronunciation

German pronunciation can be difficult. To pronounce it well, you need the help of a German speaker or some language tapes, but the general points given below will help you to make yourself understood. Bear in mind, however, that there are exceptions and regional variations.

Vowel sounds

a is sometimes long like "a" in arm. Sometimes it is short and sounds like the "a" in "cat" with a hint of the "u" in "cut".

ä sounds like "a" in "care".

au sounds like "ow" in "cow".

äu and *eu* sound like "oy" in "toy".

e sounds like "e" in "get" and, unlike in English, is pronounced even when it is at the end of a word.

ei sounds like "i" in "mine".

i is sometimes short and said like "i" in "fish". When it is long it is the same as *ie* and *ih* and sounds like "ee" in "see".

ö sounds like "u" in "surf".

u sounds like "oe" in "shoe".

ü is a sharp "u" sound. Round your lips to say "oo", try to say "ee" and you will be close.

y sounds the same as *ü*.

Consonants

b at the end of a word sounds nearly like "p".

ch sounds like "ch" in the Scottish word "loch".

d sounds like an English "d" except on the ends of words when it is said like a "t".

g sounds like "g" in "good". If *ig* is at the end of a word, *g* then sounds like *ch* above.

h after a vowel is silent but makes the vowel long.

j sounds like "y" in "young".

qu sounds like "k" + "v".

r is more rolled than an English "r". On the end of a word it sounds like a short "a" sound.

s sounds like "z" in "zoo" when it comes before a vowel. Before consonants or at the end of a word, it sounds like "s" in "sort". When it is at the beginning of a word before "p" or "t", it sounds like "sh" in "short", e.g. *Stadt* (town).

sch sounds like "sh" in "short".

ß is a German letter. It sounds just like "ss" in "dress".

v usually sounds like "f" in "fine".

w sounds like "v" in "very".

z sounds like "ts" in "hits".

German alphabet

Applying the points above, this is how you say the alphabet:
Ah, Beh, C = tseh, Deh, Eh, eFf, Geh, Ha, Ih, Jott, Kah, eLl, eMm, eNn, Oh, Peh, Q = kuh, eRr, eSs, Teh, Uh, V = fau, Weh, X = iks, Y = üpsilon, Z = tset.

How German works

Nouns

All German nouns are either masculine (m), feminine (f), or neuter (n). This is called the gender of the noun. The definite article (the word for "the") shows you which of the three it is. With masculine nouns "the" is *der*, e.g. *der Zug* (the train). With feminine nouns, "the" is *die*, e.g. *die Fähre* (the ferry). With neuter nouns "the" is *das*, e.g. *das Auto* (the car).

For a few nouns the gender is obvious, e.g. *der Mann* (man) is masculine and *die Frau* (woman) is feminine, but for most animals and things, the gender seems random, e.g. *der Zug* (train) is masculine and *die Fähre* (ferry) is feminine. Even with nouns for people, you can't always guess the gender, e.g. *das Mädchen* (girl) is neuter. Some nouns have two forms, e.g. *der Lehrer/die Lehrerin* (teacher m/f), *der Sänger/die Sängerin* (singer m/f). Always learn a noun with its *der*, *die* or *das*. These are given in the dictionary. Nouns always start with a capital letter

Plurals

In the plural (pl), "the" is *die*, e.g. *die Züge* (the trains). Most noun endings change in the plural and some nouns also add an umlaut (¨) over a vowel. The dictionary gives plural noun endings. When you learn a noun, learn its plural as well, e.g. *der Zug*, *die Züge*.

Cases

German nouns have four cases, or forms, depending on the job they are doing in a sentence. When the case changes, the noun ending sometimes changes and the article often changes too. The four cases are as follows:

Nominative - a noun is in the nominative case when it is the subject of a sentence (the person or thing doing the action). In the sentence *Die Frau repariert das Rad* (the woman is repairing the bike), *die Frau* (the woman) is nominative.

Accusative - a noun is in the accusative case when it is the direct object of the sentence (the person or thing that the action is being done to). In the example above, *das Rad* (the bike) is accusative.

Genitive - a noun is in the genitive case when it shows you to whom something belongs. In the sentence *Die Frau repariert das Rad des Mannes* (The woman is repairing the man's bike), *des Mannes* (the man's) is genitive.

Dative - a noun is in the dative case when it is the indirect object (the person or thing for whom something is being done). In the sentence *Die Frau gibt dem Mann das Rad* (The woman gives the bike to the man), *dem Mann* (the man) is dative.

Since *der*, *die* and *das* change with the four cases, it helps to learn them in their different forms as a chart:

singular

	m the man	f the woman	n the child
nom	*der Mann*	*die Frau*	*das Kind*
acc	*den Mann*	*die Frau*	*das Kind*
gen	*des Mannes*	*der Frau*	*des Kindes*
dat	*dem Mann*	*der Frau*	*dem Kind*

plural

	m the men	f the women	n the children
nom	*die Männer*	*die Frauen*	*die Kinder*
acc	*die Männer*	*die Frauen*	*die Kinder*
gen	*der Männer*	*der Frauen*	*der Kinder*
dat	*den Männern*	*den Frauen*	*den Kindern*

Ein/eine/ein ("a", "an")

The indefinite article (the word for "a") is *ein* with (m) and (n) nouns, and *eine* with (f) nouns. It changes according to case in a similar way to *der*, *die* and *das*:

	a man	a woman	a child
nom	ein Mann	eine Frau	ein Kind
acc	einen Mann	eine Frau	ein Kind
gen	eines Mannes	einer Frau	eines Kindes
dat	einem Mann	einer Frau	einem Kind

Adjectives

In sentences like *Das Rad ist neu* (The bike is new), *Der Mann ist jung* (The man is young), or *Die Tasche ist klein* (The bag is small), adjectives don't change. In front of a noun, e.g. *ein neues Rad* (a new bike), *ein junger Mann* (a young man), *eine kleine Tasche* (a small bag), their ending changes to match the noun's case and gender. Adjectives change in different ways with "the" and "a":

Adjectives after ***der/die/das*** ("the"):

singular

nom		**acc**
m	der neue Film	den neuen Film
f	die neue Kirche	die neue Kirche
n	das neue Buch	das neue Buch

gen		**dat**
m	des neuen Films	dem neuen Film
f	der neuen Kirche	der neuen Kirche
n	des neuen Buchs	dem neuen Buch

plural (m)/(f)/(n):

nom	die neuen Filme/Kirchen/Bücher
acc	die neuen Filme/Kirchen/Bücher
gen	der neuen Filme/Kirchen/Bücher
dat	den neuen Filmen/Kirchen/Büchern

Adjectives after ***ein/eine*** ("a"):

nom		**acc**
m	ein neuer Film	einen neuen Film
f	eine neue Kirche	eine neue Kirche
n	ein neues Buch	ein neues Buch

gen		**dat**
m	eines neuen Films	einem neuen Film
f	einer neuen Kirche	einer neuen Kirche
n	eines neuen Buchs	einem neuen Buch

I, you, he, she, etc.

I	ich	**you**	du or ihr or Sie

Du is the familiar (fam) form, and *Sie* is the polite (pol) form of "you". Say *du* to a friend, or someone your own age or younger. Use *Sie* when talking to an adult. If in doubt, use *Sie*. *Ihr* is the plural of *du*. Use it as *du*, but when talking to more than one person. *Sie* stays the same in its plural form.

he	er	**she**	sie
it	er or sie or es		

"It" is *er* when it refers to a (m) noun, *sie* when it refers to a (f) noun, and *es* when it refers to a (n) noun.

we	wir	**they**	sie

Me, you, him, etc.

	I/me	you	he/him/it	she/her/it	it
nom	ich	du	er	sie	es
acc	mich	dich	ihn	sie	es
dat	mir	dir	ihm	ihr	ihm

	we/us	you (fam pl)	you (pol sing/pl)	they/them
nom	wir	ihr	Sie	sie
acc	uns	euch	Sie	sie
dat	uns	euch	Ihnen	ihnen

How German works

My, your, his, her, etc.

In German these words agree with the noun they relate to, e.g. *mein Bruder* (my brother), *meine Schwester* (my sister), etc.

Before:	(m/n) noun	(f/plural) noun
my	mein	meine
your (fam)	dein	deine
your (fam pl)	euer	euere
your (pol sing/pl)	Ihr	Ihre
his/its	sein	seine
her/its	ihr	ihre
our	unser	unsere
their	ihr	ihre

Mein, dein etc. take the same endings as *ein* in the different cases (see 'Ein/eine/ein').

Verbs

German verbs have lots of tenses, but you can get by with two: use the present tense for talking about both present and future, and the perfect for talking about the past.

Present tense

In dictionaries, verbs are listed in the infinitive, e.g. "to like". Many infinitives end in *en*, e.g. *sehen* (to see), and follow the pattern given below. Drop the "en" ending and replace it with the ending you need:

hören (to hear)

I hear	ich	hör	e
you hear	du	hör	st
he/she/it hears	er/sie/es	hör	t
we hear	wir	hör	en
you hear	ihr	hör	t
they hear	sie	hör	en
you hear	Sie	hör	en

Sometimes "e" precedes "t" endings, e.g. *arbeiten*: *er/ihr arbeitet* (he/you (pl) work).

Verbs like *hören* are called weak verbs. Strong verbs have a vowel change with *du* and *er/sie/es*, e.g. **geben** (to give):

I give	ich	geb	e
you give	du	gib	st
he/she/it gives	er/sie/es	gib	t
we give	wir	geb	en
you give	ihr	geb	t
they give	sie	geb	en
you give	Sie	geb	en

Below are useful strong verbs with their *er* (he) forms in brackets. Some strong verbs have a special past participle - a form needed for making the perfect tense (see 'Talking about the past') - so this is given after the *er* form of the verb:

to be	*sein (ist, gewesen)*
to become	*werden (wird, geworden)*
to begin	*beginnen (beginnt, begonnen)*
to come	*kommen (kommt, gekommen)*
to do	*tun (tut, getan)*
to find	*finden (findet, gefunden)*
to go	*gehen (geht, gegangen)*
to go/drive	*fahren (fährt, gefahren)*
to see	*sehen (sieht, gesehen)*
to stand/be	*stehen (steht, gestanden)*
to stay	*bleiben (bleibt, geblieben)*

German doesn't distinguish between the two English present tenses (e.g. I drive, I am driving) so *ich fahre* can mean either.

Useful irregular verbs

to be	**sein**
I am	*ich bin*
you are	*du bist*
he/she/it is	*er/sie/es ist*
we are	*wir sind*
you are	*ihr seid*
they are	*sie sind*
you are	*Sie sind*

to have to/must	müssen
I must	ich muss
you must	du musst
he/she/it must	er/sie/es muss
we must	wir müssen
you must	ihr müsst
they must	sie müssen
you must	Sie müssen

to want to/ intend to	wollen
I want to	ich will
you want to	du willst
he/she/it wants to	er/sie/es will
we want to	wir wollen
you want to	ihr wollt
they want to	sie wollen
you want to	Sie wollen

The last two verbs are really handy for making sentences like *Ich muss einen Rucksack kaufen* (I must buy a backpack), *Ich will mit dem Zug fahren* (I want to go by train). The second verb in the sentences (*kaufen* - to buy, *fahren* - to go) is in the infinitive and goes at the end.

Mögen (to like) is another useful irregular verb. The present is used with a noun to say what you like, e.g. *Ich mag Horrorfilme* (I like horror films). Another form is very often used with an infinitive like the verbs above to say what you'd like to do, e.g. *Ich möchte ins Kino gehen* (I'd like to go to the cinema). Here are both forms:

I like	ich mag
you like	du magst
he/she/it likes	er/sie/es mag
we like	wir mögen
you like	ihr mögt
they like	sie mögen
you like	Sie mögen

I'd like	ich möchte
you'd like	du möchtest
he/she/it would like	er/sie/es möchte
we'd like	wir möchten
you'd like	ihr möchtet
they'd like	sie möchten
you'd like	Sie möchten

Talking about the future

In everyday German the present tense is used, often with *später* (later), *morgen* (tomorrow), etc. to place the action in the future: *Er kauft sich morgen ein Rad* (He's going to buy himself a bike tomorrow).

Talking about the past

To do this, use the perfect tense, e.g. *Ich habe getanzt*, which can mean "I danced" or "I have danced". You make the perfect with the present of *haben* (to have) + something called the past participle of the verb. The past participle is made with "ge" + the verb's stem (infinitive minus the "en" ending) + "t", e.g. *hören* (to hear) = *gehört* (heard); *tanzen* (to dance) = *getanzt* (danced). Past participles go at the end of the sentence, e.g. *Ich habe Fußball gespielt* (I played football).

Some verbs have irregular past participles, e.g. *gehen, gegangen* (to go, went). The most useful are in the list of strong verbs (see 'Present tense').

Some verbs involving movement or change form the perfect with *sein* (to be), e.g. *Er ist gegangen* (he has gone):

to be	sein (ist, gewesen)
to become	werden (wird, geworden)
to come	kommen (kommt, gekommen)
to go/drive	fahren (fährt, gefahren)
to stay	bleiben (bleibt, geblieben)

How German works

Separable verbs

Many common verbs are made up of two separate parts: prefix + verb, e.g. *auf + machen = aufmachen* (to open), *zu + hören = zuhören* (to listen), *weggehen* (to go away). In the infinitive, the prefix stays in place. In the present tense it goes to the end of the sentence: *Ich mache die Tür auf* (I open the door). In the perfect tense the prefix goes to the start of the past participle: *Ich habe die Tür aufgemacht* (I have opened the door).

Here are common prefixes with their usual meanings. Verbs that begin with one of these are separable:

ab	(off)	*nach*	(after)
an	(at, on)	*vor*	(before)
auf	(up)	*weg*	(away)
aus	(out)	*zu*	(to)
ein	(in, into)	*zurück*	(back)

Negatives

To make a sentence negative, put *nicht* (not) after the verb, e.g. *Ich will nicht* (I don't want to), or after the main part of the verb with a separable verb: *ich höre nicht zu* (I'm not listening). In the perfect tense, *nicht* goes before the past participle: *Ich habe es nicht getan* (I didn't do it).

To say "not a", you use *kein*, e.g. *Sie ist keine gute Sängerin* (She's not a good singer, literally "she is no good singer"). *Kein* is the negative of *ein* ("a") and changes like it, e.g. *kein Mann* (no man), *keine Frau* (no woman) etc. (see 'Ein, eine, ein' on page 57).

Other useful negative words include *nie* (never), *niemand* (nobody) and *nichts* (nothing).

Making questions

To make questions, put the subject after the verb, e.g. *Bist du müde?* (Are you tired?), *Ist er fertig?* (Is he ready?). Questions can also begin with words like:

how?	*wie?*	where?	*wo?*
how much?	*wie viel?*	which?	*welch?*
what?	*was?*	who?	*wer?*
when?	*wann?*	why?	*warum?*

Prepositions

Prepositions ("with", "on", etc.) are followed by an accusative or dative case. Some always require the same case, e.g. *ohne* + accusative: *Er ist ohne mich gegangen* (He went without me); *mit* + dative: *Er ist mit mir gegangen* (He went with me). Many prepositions require either the accusative or the dative depending on whether they indicate movement or not. When indicating movement, they use the accusative, e.g. *Er ist auf den Tisch gesprungen* (He leapt onto the table). When indicating static position (no movement), they use the dative: *Er sitzt auf dem Tisch* (He's sitting on the table).

Here are some useful prepositions with the cases they require:

behind	*hinter* (acc or dat)
beside	*neben* (acc or dat)
between	*zwischen* (acc or dat)
in	*in* (dat)
into	*in (acc)*
in front of	*vor* (acc or dat)
on	*auf* (acc or dat)
opposite	*gegenüber* (dat)
out of	*aus* (dat)
over	*über* (acc or dat)
under	*unter* (acc or dat)
with	*mit* (dat)
without	*ohne* (acc)

This dictionary lists essential words. If the word you want is missing, try to think of a different one you could use instead. In the English to German list (pages 62-103), illustrations with labels provide lots of extra words. Below are some tips about using the dictionary.

A typical entry in the English to German list looks like this:

> This is the word you looked up.
>
> This is the German translation.

pink **rosa** *rawzah*

> This is the German pronunciation hint. Read it as if it were an English word and you will be close to the German.

ß is a German letter that is sometimes used instead of "ss". It sounds just like "ss".

"or" introduces an extra German translation. Words in brackets after "or" hint at the difference in meaning:

fat (on meat) **das Fett** *fet*, or (large) **dick** *dik*

der/die/das All German nouns (see page 56) have a gender: masculine, feminine or neuter. So that you know which gender a noun is, each one is listed with the German for "the" - **der** for masculine, **die** for feminine, and **das** for neuter. Some nouns are listed in both a **der** and a **die** form (see page 56).

Some nouns are often used without **der, die** or **das**, but their gender is still given:

[m] stands for masculine
[f] stands for feminine
[n] stands for neuter
[pl] for words that are given in the plural

(n) (se) (-) To form the plural, German nouns usually add various letters. These are shown in brackets at the end of the word. **(-)** means that a word does not change in the plural.

¨ is called an umlaut. It goes over an "a", "o" or "u" and changes its sound slightly. In the plural, many nouns add ¨ to the last "a", "o" or "u" (or to "a" if the last two vowels are "au"):

bike **das Fahrrad(¨er)** *farraht pl: farraider*

> In the plural, put ¨ over the last "a", and add "er": **Fahrräder** (bikes).

pl: introduces any unusual plural and/or an unusual plural pronunciation:

hand **die Hand(¨e)** *hant pl: henda*

[+ acc] [+ dat] German has a system of cases (see page 56). Some words are always followed by the same case. [+ acc] shows that a word takes the accusative case; [+ dat] shows that it takes the dative case; [+ acc or dat] shows that it can take either (see Prepositions, page 60).

~ follows parts of words that you attach to the beginning of a noun:

double **Doppel~** *doppel* e.g. double bed **das Doppelbett**

* indicates that a word is slang, and is best avoided in formal situations.

Verbs (see page 58) are listed in the infinitive form, e.g. "to eat", but you will find them listed under "e" for eat, etc.

' some German verbs are separable (see page 60). ' indicates where they separate:

to arrive **an'kommen** *an-kommen*

a, an *ein [m, n] ine*, or
eine [f] ine-a (These change
in different cases, see p. 57)
about (approximately)
ungefähr oongefair; what's
it about? (film, book) *worum
geht es? vawroom gate ess*
above (higher than) *über*
[+ acc or dat] *oohber*, or
(overhead) *oben awben*
abroad (to be abroad) *im
Ausland im owss-lant*, or
(to go abroad) *ins Ausland
inz owss-lant*
to accept *akzeptieren
aktsepteeren*, or (an offer)
an'nehmen an-naymen
accident *der Unfall(̈e)
oonfal pl: oonfella*
accommodation (places to
stay) *die Unterkunft
oonter-koonft*
to ache (or to have a head/
back etc. ache)
Schmerzen haben
shmairtsen hahben
(see pictures on right)
to act (theatre) *spielen
shpeelen*
actor *der Schauspieler(-)
shaow-shpeeler*
actress *die
Schauspielerin(nen)
shaow-shpeelerin(en)*
to add *hinzu'fügen
hintsoo-foohgen*
address *die Adresse(n)
adressa(n)*
adopted *adoptiert
adopteert*
adult *der/die
Erwachsene(n)
airvaxana(n)*
advantage *der Vorteil(e)
for-tyle(-a)*; to take
advantage of
aus'nutzen [+ acc]
owssnootsen

adventurous (person)
abenteuerlustig
ahbentoyer-loosstikh, or
(journey) **abenteuerlich**
ahbentoyer-likh
advertisement (in paper)
die Anzeige(n) *an-tsye-
ga(n)*, or (at cinema, on TV)
die Werbung(en) *vair-
boong(en)*; classified ads
die Annoncen *annonssen*
advice **der Rat** *raht*

to ache **Schmerzen haben**

Ich
habe Kopfschmerzen.
*ikh hahba
kopf-shmairtsen*

Ich
habe Zahnschmerzen.
*ikh hahba
tsahn-shmairtsen*

Ich habe
Ohrenschmerzen.
*ich hahba
awren-shmairtsen*

Ich habe
Bauchschmerzen.
*ikh hahba
baowkh-shmairtsen*

Ich habe
Rückenschmerzen.
*ikh hahba
rooken-shmairtsen*

after **nach** [+ dat] *nakh*
afternoon **der
Nachmittag(e)**
nakhmittahg(a)
afterwards **nachher**
nakh-hair
again **wieder** *veeder*, or
noch mal* *nokh mahl*
against **gegen** [+ acc]
gaigen
age **das Alter(-)** *alter*;
under age **minderjährig**
minder-yairikh
ago **vor** [+ dat] *for*, e.g. a
week ago **vor einer Woche**
to agree **einverstanden
sein** *ine-fair-shtanden
zyne*
aid **die Hilfe** *hilfa*
AIDS **AIDS** *aids*
air **die Luft** *looft*; in the
open air **im Freien** *im
fryen*; air-conditioned
airconditioned
airconditioned
airline **die Flug-
gesellschaft(en)**
*floog-gazell-
shafft(en)*
airport **der
Flughafen(̈)** *floog-
hahfen pl: flooghayfen*
alarm clock **der Wecker(-)**
vekker
album **das Album** *alboom
pl: Alben alben*
alcohol **der Alkohol**
alkawhawl
alcoholic (drink)
alkoholisch *alkawhawlish*
all **alle** *alla*, or (whole)
ganz *gants*; all day
den ganzen Tag
dain gantsen tahg;
all of it **alles** *alless*; all
right (I agree) **in Ordnung**
in ordnoong, or (it's OK) **es
geht** *ess gayt*

allergy **die Allergie(n)**
alairghee(yen)
alone **allein** *allyne*
already **schon** *shawn*
also **auch** *aowkh*
always **immer** *immer*
amazing (unbelievable)
unglaublich *oonglaowblikh*,
or (astonishing) **erstaunlich**
airshtaownlikh, or (fabulous)
toll* *tol*
ambulance **der**
Krankenwagen(-)
kranken-vahgen
America **Amerika [n]**
ah-maireekah
American **amerikanisch**
amaireekahnish, or **der**
Amerikaner(-)/die
Amerikanerin(nen)
amaireekahner/
amaireekahnerin(nen)
and **und** *oont*
angry **böse** *burza*, or
verärgert *fair-airgurt*
animal **das Tier(e)** *teer(a)*
ankle **das Fußgelenk(e)**
fooss-galenk(a)
to annoy **ärgern** *airgurn;*
to be/get annoyed **sich**
ärgern *zikh airgurn*
annoying **lästig** *lestikh*, or
(very) **ärgerlich** *airgurlikh*
answer **die Antwort(en)**
antvort(en)
to answer (someone)
antworten [+ dat] *antvorten*,
or (question) **beantworten**
ba-antvorten, or (phone)
ran'gehen* *ran-gayen*, or
(door) **hin'gehen** *hin-gayen*
answering machine **der**
Anrufbeantworter(-)
anroofba-antvorter
antibiotic **das**
Antibiotikum *anteebee-*
awteekoom pl: **Antibiotika**
anteebee-awteekah

antiseptic **antiseptisch**
anteeseptish
any (see not any)
anyone (as in "is anyone
there?") **jemand** *yamant*,
or (stressed, as in "is *anyone*
there?") **irgend jemand**
eergunt yaymant, or (any
old person, as in "anyone
will do") **jeder** *yaider*
f: jede *yaida* (see also
nobody)
anything (as in "do you
like anything?") **etwas**
etvass, or (stressed, as in
"do you like *anything*?")
irgend etwas *eergunt*
etvass (see also nothing)
anywhere **irgendwo**
eerguntvaw, or (no matter
where) **egal wo** *aygahl*
vaw (see also nowhere)
apple **der Apfel(¨)** *apfel* pl:
epfel (see also picture above)
appointment **die**
Verabredung(en) *fair-*
apraidoong(en), or (with
doctor, lawyer) **der**
Termin(e) *tairmeen(a)*
apricot **die Aprikose(n)**
ap-reekawza(n)
April **April [m]** *aprill*
arcade (amusement) **die**
Spielhalle(n) *shpeelhalla(n)*
area (region) **die**
Gegend(en) *gaigunt*
pl: *gaigunden*, or (in town)
das Viertel(-) *feertel*
argument **die**
Auseinandersetzung(en)
aowss-eye-nander-
zetsoong(en), or **der**
Streit(e) *shtryte(-a);* to
have an argument **sich**
streiten *zikh shtryte-en*
arm **der Arm(e)** *arm(a)*
to arrive **an'kommen** *an-*
kommen

apple **der Apfel**
der Stiel *shteel*
die Schale
shahla
das
Kerngehäuse
kairn-gehoyza

der Kern *kairn*

art **die Kunst** *koonst;* art
school **die**
Kunsthochschule(n)
koonst-hawkhshoola(n)
artist **der Künstler(-)/die**
Künstlerin(nen)
koonstler/koonstlerin(nen)
as (like) **wie** *vee;* (just)
as ... as **(genau)so ... wie**
(genaow)-zaw ... vee; as
usual **wie üblich** *vee*
oohblikh
ashtray **der Aschenbecher(-)**
ashenbekher
to ask **fragen** *frahgen;* to
ask a question **eine Frage**
stellen *ine-a frahga*
shtellen; to ask out
ein'laden *ine-lahden*
aspirin **die**
Schmerztablette(n)
shmairts-tabletta(n)
assistant (in shop) **der**
Verkäufer(-)/die
Verkaüferin(nen)
fairkoyfer/fairkoyferin(nen)
at (time) **um** *oom*, or (place,
as in "at the corner") **an** [+
dat] *an*, or (place, as in "at
the bank/school") **auf** [+
dat] *aowf*, or (as in "at
Anna's") **bei** [+ dat] *by*
attractive **reizvoll** *rites-*
foll, or **attraktiv** *atrakteef*

audience **das Publikum**
pooblikoom
August **August [m]** *aow-goost*
Australia **Australien [n]**
aow-strahleeyen
Australian **australisch**
aow-strahlish, or **der
Australier(-)/die
Australierin(nen)**
*aow-strahleeyer/
aow-strahleeyerin(nen)*
Austria **Österreich [n]**
urster-eye-kh
Austrian **österreichisch**
urster-eye-khish, or **der
Österreicher(-)/die
Österreicherin(nen)** *urster-eye-kher/urster-eye-kherin(nen)*
author **der Autor(en)/die
Autorin(nen)** *aow-tor(en)/
aow-torin(nen)*
autumn **der Herbst(e)**
hairpst(a)
avalanche **die Lawine(n)**
laveena(n)

average **durchschnittlich**
doorkh-shnittlikh, or
(neither good nor bad)
mittelmäßig *mittelmaissikh*
avocado **die Avocado(s)**
avawkahdaw(s)
to avoid **vermeiden** *fair-my-den*
away **weg** *vaig*
awful **furchtbar** *foorkhtbar*
back (part of body) **der
Rücken(-)** *rooken*, or (as in
"go/come back") **zurück**
tsoorook, or (not front) **die
Hinterseite(n)** *hinter-zyta(n)*
bad **schlecht** *shlekht*, or
schlimm *shlim*, or (naughty)
böse *burza*; too bad! **Pech!**
pekh
bag **die Tasche(n)** *tasha(n)*
baker's **die Bäckerei(en)**
bekka-rye(-n)
balcony **der Balkon(s)**
balkon(s), or (in theatre)
oberster Rang [m]
awbester rang
ball **der Ball(¨e)** *bal pl: bella*

banana **die Banane(n)**
banahna(n)
band (musical) **die Band(s)**
band(s) (see also picture
below)
bank (money) **die Bank(en)**
bank(en)
bar **die Bar(s)** *bahr(s)*, or
(counter) **die Theke(n)**
taika(n)
bargain: it's a bargain **das
ist (aber) günstig** *dass isst
(ahber) goonstikh*
bat (sport) **der Schläger(-)**
shlaiger
bath **das Bad(¨er)** *baht pl:
baider*, or (bath tub) **die
Badewanne(n)**
bahdevanna(n)
bathroom **das
Badezimmer(-)**
bahdetsimmer
battery **die Batterie(n)**
battairee(yen)
to be **sein** *zyne* (see also
Verbs, p. 58), or (as in "to be
right/hungry") **haben** *hahben*
beach **der Strand(¨e)**
shtrant pl: shtrenda
bean **die Bohne(n)**
bawna(n)
beard **der Bart(¨e)** *bart
pl: bairta*
beautiful **schön** *shurn*
because **weil** *vile*; because
of **wegen** [+ dat] *vaigen*
bed **das Bett(en)** *bet(en)*;
double bed **das
Doppelbett(en)** *doppel-bet(en)*
bedroom **das
Schlafzimmer(-)**
shlahftsimmer
beef **das Rindfleisch**
rintfly-sh
beer **das Bier(e)** *beer(a)*,
or (on tap) **das Fassbier(e)**
fassbeer(a)

band *die Band*

die Gitarristin
gitarristin
**Schlagzeug
[n]** *shlahg-tsoyg*
der Schlagzeuger
shlag-tsoyger
der Keyboarder
keeborder
**das
Saxophon**
zaxawfawn
die Gitarre
gitarra
der Saxophonist
zaxofonist
der Sänger *zenger*
**das
Keyboard**
keebort
**das
Mikro***
meekraw

beetle (insect) **der Käfer(-)** *kaifer*
before **vor** [+ dat] *for*, or (followed by a clause, as in "look before you go") **bevor** *befor*, or (beforehand) **vorher** *for-hair*
beggar **der Bettler(-)/ die Bettlerin(nen)** *betler/betlerin(nen)*
beginner **der Anfänger(-)/die Anfängerin(nen)** *anfenger/anfengerin(nen)*
beginning **der Anfang(̈e)** *anfang pl: anfeng-a*
behind **hinter** [+ acc or dat] *hinter*, or (at the back) **hinten** *hinten*
belt **der Gürtel(-)** *goohrtl*
bend (in the road) **die Kurve(n)** *koorva(n)*
best (person or thing, as in "the best film") **beste(n)** *besta(n)*, or (action, as in "Peter plays best") **am besten** *am besten*, or (most of all, as in "I like tennis best") **am liebsten** *am leepsten*
better **besser** *besser*
between **zwischen** [+ acc or dat] *tsvishen*
big **groß** *grawss*
bike **das Fahrrad(̈er)** *farraht pl: farraider*, or **das Rad(̈er)** *raht pl: raider*; racing bike **das Rennrad(̈er)** *renraht pl: renraider*; mountain bike **das Mountainbike(s)** (see also picture above)
bill (restaurant) **die Rechnung(en)** *rekhnoong(en)*; the bill please **zahlen bitte** *tsahlen bitta*

bike **das Fahrrad**

der Sattel *zattel*
der Reifen *rye-fen*
das Rad *raht*
die Kette *ketta*
das Pedal *pedahl*
die Luftpumpe *looft-poompa*
die Bremse *bremza*

bin **der Eimer(-)** *eye-mer*
binoculars **das Fernglas(̈er)** *fairnglass pl: fairnglayzer*
biodegradable **biologisch abbaubar** *bee-aw-lawgish apbaowbar*
bird **der Vogel(̈)** *fawgel pl: furgel*
birthday **der Geburtstag(e)** *geboorts-tahg(a)*; happy birthday **herzlichen Glückwunsch zum Geburtstag** *hairtslikhen glookvoonsh tsoom geboorts-tahg*
biscuit **der Keks(e)** *kaiks(a)*
bit (as in "a bit of cake") **das Stück(e)** *shtook(a)*, or (as in "a bit tired") **ein bisschen** *ine biss-khen*
to bite **beißen** *bye-ssen*, or (insect) **stechen** *shtekhen*
black **schwarz** *shvahrts*
blanket **die Decke(n)** *dekka(n)*
to bleed **bluten** *blooten*
blind **blind** *blint*

blister **die Blase(n)** *blahza(n)*
blond **blond** *blont*
blood **das Blut** *bloot*; blood pressure **der Blutdruck** *blootdrook*
blue **blau** *blaow*
to boast **an'geben** *angaiben*
boat (big) **das Schiff(e)** *shiff(a)*, or (small) **das Boot(e)** *bawt(a)* (see also sailing)
body **der Körper(-)** *kurper*
boiled **gekocht** *gekokht*
bone **der Knochen(-)** *knokh-en*, or (fish) **die Gräte(n)** *graita(n)*
book **das Buch(̈er)** *bookh pl: boohkher*
to book **buchen** *bookhen*
booked up **ausgebucht** *owssgebookht*
bookshop **die Buchhandlung(en)** *bookh-handloong(en)*
boot **der Stiefel(-)** *shteefel*
border (frontier) **die Grenze(n)** *grentsa(n)*
bored: to be bored **sich langweilen** *zikh langvye-len*
boring **langweilig** *langvye-likh*
to borrow **sich leihen** *zikh lye-un*
boss **der Chef(s)/die Chefin(nen)** *shef(s)/shefin(nen)*, or **der Boss*** *boss*
both **beide** *by-da*; both of them **die beiden** *dee by-dun*, or **alle beide** *allah by-da*
bottle **die Flasche(n)** *flasha(n)*; bottle opener **der Flaschenöffner(-)** *flashun-urfner*

bottom (not top) **der Boden** bawden, or (bum) **der Hintern(-)*** hintern, or **der Po(s)*** paw(z)
bowl **die Schüssel(n)** shoossel(n)
box office **die Kasse** kassa
boy **der Junge(n)** yoonga(n)
boyfriend **der Freund(e)** froynd(a)
bra **der BH(-)** bay hah
brake **die Bremse(n)** bremza(n)
brave **tapfer** tapfer
bread (or loaf of bread) **das Brot(e)** brawt(a); wholemeal bread **das Vollkornbrot(e)** folkorn-brawt(a)
to break **brechen** brekhen, or **kaputt'machen*** kapootmakhen; to break up (with someone) **Schluss machen*** shlooss makhen
breakfast **das Frühstück(e)** frooh-shtook(a); to have breakfast **frühstücken** frooh-shtooken
breast (bosom) **der Busen(-)** boozen, or (chest) **die Brust(̈e)** broost(a)
to breathe **atmen** ahtmen
bridge **die Brücke(n)** brooka(n)
bright (clever) **aufgeweckt** aowfgevekt, or (colour) **hell** hel
brilliant (fantastic) **genial** gaineeyahl, or **toll*** toll
to bring **bringen** bring-en
Britain **Großbritannien [n]** grawssbritannyen
broken **gebrochen** gebrokhen, or **kaputt*** kapoott
brother **der Bruder(̈)** brooder pl: brooh-der
brown **braun** braown

bruise **der blaue Fleck(en)** blaowa flek(en)
brush **die Bürste(n)** boohrsta(n), or (paintbrush) **der Pinsel(-)** pinzul
bug (germ) **der Bazillus** batsilooss pl: Bazillen batsillen, or (insect) **der Käfer(-)** kaifer
building **das Gebäude(-)** geboyda
bump (on head/body) **die Beule(n)** boyla(n), or (dent in car etc.) **die Delle(n)** della(n)
to bump into (something) **stoßen gegen** [+ acc] shtawssen gaigen, or (someone by chance) **zufällig treffen** tsoofellikh treffen
to burn **brennen** brennen
to burst **platzen** platsen
bus **der Bus(se)** booss(a); by bus **mit dem Bus** mit dem booss; bus station **der Busbahnhof(̈e)** boossbahn-hawf pl: boossbahn-hurfa; bus stop **die Bushaltestelle(n)** booss-halta-shtella(n)
busy **beschäftigt** besheftikht
but **aber** ahber
butcher's **die Metzgerei(en)** metsga-rye(-un)
butter **die Butter** bootter
to buy **kaufen** kaowfen
by (as in "by the station") **bei** [+ dat] by, or (as in "saved by someone") **von** [+dat] fon; by my/your/himself etc. **allein(e)** allyne(-a)
bye **tschüs*** tshooss, or **tschau*** tshaow
café **das Café(s)** kafay(s)

camera **der Fotoapparat**

der Film film
der Blitz blits
das Zoom tsoom
das Objektiv obyekteef
die Verschlussklappe fairshloossklappa
die Sonnenblende zonnenblenda

cake **der Kuchen(-)** kookhen, or (gâteau) **die Torte(n)** tawrta(n); cake shop **die Konditorei(en)** konditaw-rye(-un); it's a piece of cake **das ist ein Klacks*** dass ist ine klaks
calculator **der Taschenrechner(-)** tashen-rekhner
to call **rufen** roofen; to be called **heißen** hye-sen
calm **ruhig** roo-ikh
calorie **die Kalorie(n)** kaloree(yan); low-calorie **kalorienarm** kaloreeyanarm
camcorder **der Camcorder(-)** kamkorder
camera **der Fotoapparat(e)** fawtaw-apparaht(a), or **die Kamera(s)** kamairah(s) (see also picture above)
to camp **zelten** tselten
campsite **der Campingplatz(̈e)** kamping-plats pl: kamping-pletsa (see also picture right)

can (of fruit, drink) **die Dose(n)** *dawza(n)*; can opener **der Dosenöffner(-)** *dawzen-urfner*
can (be able to) **können** *kurnun*
to cancel **ab'sagen** *apzahgen*
cancelled (bus, train etc.) **gestrichen** *geshtrikhen*
candle **die Kerze(n)** *kairtsa(n)*
canoe **das Kanu(s)** *kahnoo(s)*
canoeing: to go canoeing **Kanu fahren** *kahnoo fahren*
cap (hat) **die Mütze(n)** *mootsa(n)*
capital (city) **die Hauptstadt(̈e)** *haowptshtat* pl: *haowptshtetta*
car **das Auto(s)** *aowtaw(s)*, or **der Wagen(-)** *vahgen*, or (banger) **die Kiste(n)*** *kissta(n)*; car park (open air) **der Parkplatz(̈e)** *parkplats* pl: *parkpletsa*, or (multi-storey) **das Parkhaus(̈er)** *parkhaowss* pl: *parkhoyzer*
card **die Karte(n)** *karta(n)*; credit card **die Kreditkarte(n)** *kredeet-karta(n)*; card game **das Kartenspiel(e)** *karten-shpeel(a)*

care: I don't care! **das ist mir egal!** *dass ist meer aygahl*, or **das ist mir wurscht!*** *dass ist meer voorsht*
careful **vorsichtig** *forzikhtik*
carnival **der Karneval(e)** *karnevahl(a)*, or **das Fest(e)** *fest(a)*
carrot **die Mohrrübe(n)** *mawroohba(n)*, or **die Karotte(n)** *karotta(n)*
to carry **tragen** *trahgen*
cartoon **der Cartoon(s)** *kartoon(s)*, or (film) **der Trickfilm(e)** *trickfilm(a)*
cash (money) **das Bargeld** *bar-ghelt*; to pay cash **bar bezahlen** *bar betsahlen*; cash desk **die Kasse(n)** *kassa(n)*; cash dispenser **der Geldautomat(en)** *ghelt-aowtawmaht(en)*
cassette **die Kassette(n)** *kassetta(n)*; cassette player **der Kassettenrecorder(-)** *kassetten-raikorder*
castle **das Schloss(̈er)** *shloss* pl: *shlursser*, or (fortified) **die Burg(en)** *boorg(en)*
casual **lässig** *lessikh*, or **cool*** *kool*

cat **die Katze(n)** *katsa(n)*
to catch **fangen** *fangen*
cathedral **der Dom(e)** *dawm(a)*
Catholic **katholisch** *katawlish*
cave **die Höhle(n)** *hurla(n)*
CD **die CD(s)** *tsee dee(s)*; CD-player **der CD-Player(-)** *tsee dee player*
to celebrate **feiern** *fye-ern*
cellar **der Keller(-)** *keller*
cemetery **der Friedhof(̈e)** *freedhawf* pl: *freedhurfa*
centre **das Zentrum** *tsentroom* pl: **Zentren** *tsentren*
century **das Jahrhundert(e)** *yarhoondert(a)*
cereal ask for it by name, e.g. cornflakes
certain **sicher** *sikher*
chair **der Stuhl(̈e)** *shtool* pl: *shtoohla*
championship **die Meisterschaft(en)** *mye-ster-shafft(en)*
chance (accident) **der Zufall(̈e)** *tsoofal* pl: *tsoofella*, or (possibility) **die Chance(n)** *shonsa(n)*, or (risk) **das Risiko** *reezikaw* pl: **Risiken** *reeziken*; by chance **zufällig** *tsoofellikh*

campsite **der Campingplatz**

die Sanitär-Anlagen *zanitair-anlahgun*
das Wohnmobil *vawn-mawbeel*
das Zelt *tselt*
der Wohnwagen *vawn-vahgun*
die Hängematte *henga-matta*
der Holzhammer *holts-hammer*
der Hering *hairing*
der Abfalleimer *apfal-eye-mer*
der Wasserkanister *vasser-kanister*
der Gaskocher *gahz-kokher*
die Anmeldung *anmeldoong*

climbing **Klettern [n]**

der Felsen
felzen

der Karabiner
karabeener

der Kletterer
kletterer

der Helm
helm

die Schlinge
shling-a

die Kreide
kry-da

der Sitzgurt
zitsgoort

der Kletterschuh
kletter-shoo

das Kletterseil
kletter-zyle

change **die Änderung(en)**
enderoong(en), or (money)
das Kleingeld *klyne-ghelt*
to change (alter) **ändern**
endern, or (money, wheel)
wechseln *vexeln*, or (train,
bus) **um'steigen** *oomshtye-
gen*, or (to get changed) **sich
um'ziehen** *zikh oomtseeyen*
changing-room (large) **der
Umkleideraum(¨e)**
oomklyda-raowm
pl: *oomklyda-royma*, or
(small, individual) **die
Umkleidekabine(n)**
oomklyda-kabeena(n)
channel (TV) **der Kanal(¨e)**
kanahl pl: *kanaila*; the
Channel **der Ärmelkanal**
airmel-kanahl
chaos **das Durcheinander**
doorkh-ine-ander, or **das
Chaos** *kah-oss*
character **der Charakter(e)**
karaktair pl: *karaktaira*, or
(personality) **die
Persönlichkeit(en)**
pairzurnlikh-kyte(n)
charity **die
Hilfsorganisation(en)**
hilfs-organeezatsee-yon(en)
charts (top records) **die
Charts** *charts*
to chat **plaudern**
plaowdern, or **sich
unterhalten** *zikh
oonterhalten*; to chat up
an'quatschen* *ankvatshen*
cheap **billig** *billikh*
to cheat **mogeln*** *mawguln*
to check (a fact, date)
überprüfen *oohber-
proohfen*, or **checken***
tsheken, or (a passport, ticket)
kontrollieren *kontrawleeren*
check-in (at airport) **die
Abfertigung(en)** *apfair-
tigoong(en)*

check-out (cash register)
die Kasse(n) *kassa(n)*
cheeky **frech** *frekh*
cheers **prost** *prawst*
cheer up! **Kopf hoch!** *kopf
hawkh*
cheese **der Käse** *kaiza*
cheesecake **der
Käsekuchen** *kaiza-kookhen*
chemist's **die Drogerie(n)**
droggeree(yun), or (for
prescriptions) **die
Apotheke(n)** *apawtaika(n)*
cheque **der Scheck(s)**
shek(s); cheque-book **das
Scheckbuch(¨er)** *shek-
bookh* pl: *shek-booh-kher*
cherry **die Kirsche(n)**
keersha(n)
chess **Schach [n]** *shahkh*
chest (part of body) **die
Brust(¨e)** *broost(a)*
chewing gum **das
Kaugummi** *kaowgoomee*
chicken (roast, grilled) **das
Hähnchen(-)** *hainkhen*, or
(live) **das Huhn(¨er)** *hoon*
pl: *hooh-ner*
child **das Kind(er)** *kint* pl:
kin-der
chips (French fries) **Pommes
frites** *pom frit*, or **Pommes***
pomuss
chocolate **die
Schokolade(n)**
shokawlahda, or (as in "a
box of chocolates") **die
Praline(n)** *prahleena(n)*
choice **die Wahl** *vahl*
choir **der Chor(¨e)** *kor* pl:
kur-a
to choose **wählen** *vailen*
chop (pork/lamb) **das
Kotelett(s)** *kotlet(s)*
Christian **christlich**
kristlikh
Christmas **Weihnachten [n]**
vye-nakhten

to chuck (throw) **schmeißen** *shmye-sen*, or (finish with a girl/boyfriend) **Schluss machen mit** *shlooss makhen mit*, e.g. she's chucked him **sie hat mit ihm Schluss gemacht**
church die Kirche(n) *keerkha(n)*
cider (apple wine) **der Apfelwein** *apfelvine*
cigarette die Zigarette(n) *tsiggaretta(n)*
cinema das Kino(s) *keenaw(s)*
circus der Zirkus(se) *tseerkooss(a)*
city die Großstadt(¨e) *grawshtat pl: grawshtetta*
classical klassisch *klassish*
clean sauber *zaowber*
clever klug *kloog*, or (crafty) **schlau** *shlaow*
cliff der Felsen(-) *felzun*
climber (rock) **der Kletterer(-)/die Klettererin(nen)** *kletterer/klettererin(nen)*, or (mountain) **der Bergsteiger(-) /die Bergsteigerin(nen)** *bairgshtye-ger/bairgshtye-gerin(nen)*
climbing (rock) **Klettern [n]** *klettern*, or (mountain) **Bergsteigen [n]** *bairg-shtygen* (see also picture left)
cloakroom die Garderobe(n) *gardarawba(n)*
close (physically) **in der Nähe** *in dair naya*, or (mentally) **eng** *eng;* close friends **eng befreundet** *eng bafroynded*
to close zu'machen *tsoomakhen*
closed geschlossen *geshlossen*, or **zu** *tsoo*

clothes Kleider *klyder,* or **Klamotten*** *klamotten*
cloud die Wolke(n) *volka(n)*
club der Verein(e) *fair-ine(-a)*, or **der Club(s)*** *kloob(s)*
clubbing: to go clubbing **in Clubs gehen** *in kloobs gayen*
coach (bus) **der Reisebus(se)** *ryzabooss(a)* or **der Bus(se)** *booss(a)*, or (trainer) **der Trainer(-)/die Trainerin(nen)** *trainer/trainerin(nen)*
coast die Küste(n) *koosta(n)*
coat der Mantel(¨) *mantel pl: mentel*
code der Code(s) *kawd(s)*, or (post/area code) **die Postleitzahl(en)** *posst-lite-tsahl(en)*, or (for phoning) **die Vorwahl(en)** *forvahl(en)*
co-ed (mixed) **gemischt** *gemisht*
coffee der Kaffee *kaffay,* or (coffee flavoured) **Mokka~** *mokkah*
coin die Münze(n) *moontsa(n)*
coincidence der Zufall(¨e) *tsoofal pl: tsoofella*
cold kalt *kalt*
cold (illness) **die Erkältung(en)** *airkeltoong(en);* to have a cold **erkältet sein** *airkeltet zyne*
to collect (stamps etc.) **sammeln** *zammeln*
colour die Farbe(n) *farba(n)*
colourful bunt *boont*
comb der Kamm(¨e) *kam pl: kemma*
to come kommen *kommen;* to come back **zurück'kommen** *tsoorook-kommen;* to come in **(he)rein'kommen** *(hair)rine-kommen*

comfortable bequem *bai-kvaim;* to feel comfortable **sich wohl fühlen** *zikh vawl foolen*
comic book der Comic(s) *komik(s)*
common (not unusual) **häufig** *hoyfikh*
compass der Kompass(e) *kom-pas(a)*
competition der Wettbewerb *vetbevairb,* or (people you are up against) ´ **die Konkurrenz** *konkoorents*
to complain sich beklagen *zikh beklahgen*
completely völlig *furlikh*
compulsory obligatorisch *obligatawrish,* or **Pflicht~** *pflikht*
computer der Computer(-) *kompyooter;* computer studies **die Informatik** *informahteek*
concert das Konzert(e) *kontsairt(a)*
condom das Präservativ(e) *prayzairvateef pl: prayzairvateeva,* or **das Kondom(e)** *kondawm(a),* or **der Gummi(s)*** *goomee(s)*
to confuse verwirren *fairvirrun*
to congratulate gratulieren *gratooleeren*
congratulations herzliche Glückwünsche *hairtslikha glookvoonsha*
connection (train, plane) **der Anschluss(¨e)** *anshlooss(a)*
conservation der Umweltschutz *oomvelt-shootts*
constipated verstopft *fairshtopft*
consulate das Konsulat(e) *konzoolaht(a)*

contact lens **die Kontaktlinse(n)** *kontaktlinza(n)*; soft/hard **weich/hart** *vye-kh/hart;* cleansing solution **Reinigungslösung** *rye-nigoongz-lerzoong;* rinsing solution **Abspüllösung** *apshpoohl-lerzoong*

contagious **ansteckend** *anshtekend*

contemporary (same age) **gleichaltrig** *glykh-altrikh,* or (people, things) **zeitgenössisch** *tsyte-genurssish*

to continue **weiter'machen** *vyter-makhen*

contraception **die Empfängnisverhütung** *empfengnis-fairhoohtoong*

conversation **das Gespräch(e)** *geshpraikh(a)*

to cook **kochen** *kokhen*

cookie **der Keks(e)** *kaiks(a)*

cool (trendy, relaxed) **cool*** *kool*

to cope **zurecht'kommen** *tsoorekht-kommen*

to copy **kopieren** *kopeeren*

cork (in bottle) **der Korken(-)** *korken*

corkscrew **der Korkenzieher(-)** *korken-tseeyer*

corner **die Ecke(n)** *ekke(n)*

correct **richtig** *rikhtikh*

cosmopolitan **kosmopolitisch** *kozmawpawleetish*

to cost **kosten** *kosten*

cotton (material) **die Baumwolle** *baowmvolla;* cotton wool **die Watte** *vatta*

to count **zählen** *tsailen*

country **das Land(̈er)** *lant pl: lender*

course (series of lessons) **der Kurs(e)** *koorss pl: koorza,* or (meal) **der Gang(̈e)** *gang pl: genga;* of course **natürlich** *natoohrlikh*

court (sports) **der Platz(̈e)** *plats pl: pletsa*

cousin **der Cousin(s)/die Cousine(n)** *koozang(s)/ koozeena(n)*

to cover **bedecken** *bedecken*

cow **die Kuh(̈e)** *koo pl: kooh-a*

coward **der Feigling(e)** *fye-gling(a)*

to crack (lose control, give in) **durch'drehen*** *doorkh-drayen;* to crack a joke **einen Witz reißen** *ine-un vits rye-ssen;* to crack up (laugh) **sich tot'lachen** *zikh tawt-lakhen*

cramp **der Krampf(̈e)** *krampf pl: krempfa*

crazy **verrückt** *fairookt,* or **irre** *irra;* to be crazy about (a person) **ganz wild auf** [+ acc] **sein** *gants vilt aowf ... zyne;* you must be crazy! **du bist wohl verrückt!** *doo bist vawl fairookt*

cream (on milk) **die Sahne** *zahna,* or (lotion) **die Creme** *kraim*

credit card (see card)

creepy **unheimlich** *oon-hyme-likh*

crime **das Verbrechen(-)** *fairbrekhen*

crisis **die Krise(n)** *kreeza(n)*

crisps **Chips** *tships*

to criticize **kritisieren** *kriteezeeren*

cross (angry) **böse** *burza,* or (annoyed) **sauer*** *zaower;* or (sign) **das Kreuz(e)** *kroyts(a)*

to cross **überqueren** *oohber-kvairen*

crossing (by sea) **die Überfahrt(en)** *oohberfahrt(en)* (see also pedestrian)

crossroads **die Kreuzung(en)** *kroytsoong(en)*

crossword **das Kreuzworträtsel(-)** *kroytsvort-raitsel*

cruel **grausam** *graowzahm*

to cry (weep) **weinen** *vye-nen*

cucumber **die Gurke(n)** *goorka(n)*

cultural **kulturell** *koolltoorell*

culture **die Kultur(en)** *koolltoor(en)*

cup **die Tasse(n)** *tassa(n)*

cupboard **der Schrank(̈e)** *shrank pl: shrenka*

curious (inquisitive) **neugierig** *noygeerikh*

custom **der Brauch(̈e)** *braowkh pl: broykha*

customs **der Zoll** *tsol*

to cut **schneiden** *shnyden*

Czech: the Czech Republic **die Tschechische Republik** *tshekhisha repoobleek*

damn! **verdammt noch mal!** *fairdamt nokh mahl*

to dance **tanzen** *tantsen*

dancer **der Tänzer(-)/die Tänzerin(nen)** *tentser/tentserin(nen)*

dangerous **gefährlich** *gefairlikh*

to dare (risk) **riskieren** *risskeeren,* or (be bold enough) **wagen** *vahgen;* I dare you! **Feigling!** *fye-gling*

dark **dunkel** *doonkel*

darts: to play darts **Pfeil werfen** *pfyle-vairfen*

date *das Datum* dahtoom *pl: Daten* dahten, or (meeting with boy/girlfriend) *die Verabredung(en)* fairupraidoong(en), or *das Date(s)*; date of birth *das Geburtsdatum* geboortsdahtoom; what's the date today? *den wievielten haben wir heute?* dain veefeelten hahben veer hoyta; up to date (current) *aktuell* aktoo-ell; out of date (no longer valid) *nicht mehr gültig* nikht mair gooltikh

day *der Tag(e)* tahg(a)

dead *tot* tawt

deaf *taub* taowp

dear *lieb* leeb

December *Dezember [m]* detsember

to decide *beschließen* beshleessen

deckchair *der Liegestuhl(̈e)* leega-shtool pl: leega-shtoohla

deep *tief* teef

degree *der Grad(e)* graht pl: grahda

delay *die Verspätung(en)* fair-shpaitoong(en)

delicious *köstlich* kurstlikh, or *lecker* lekker

democracy *die Demokratie* daymawkrahtee

demonstration *die Demonstration(en)* daimon-stratseeyawn(en), or *die Demo(s)** daimaw(s)

denim *der Jeansstoff(e)* jeanshtoff(a)

Denmark *Dänemark [n]* dainamark

dentist *der Zahnarzt(̈e)/ die Zahnärztin(nen)* tsahnartst pl: tsahnairt-sta)/ tsahnairtstin(nen)

deodorant *das Deodorant(s)* day-awdawrant(s), or *das Deo(s)**

department store *das Kaufhaus(̈er)* kaowf-haowss pl: kaowf-hoyzer

departure *die Abfahrt(en)* apfahrt(en), or (plane) *der Abflug(̈e)* apfloog pl: apflooh-ga; departure lounge (at airport) *die Abflughalle(n)* apflooghalla(n)

to depend: it depends *es kommt darauf an* ess komt dahraowf an

deposit (as guarantee) *die Kaution(en)* kaowtsee-awn(en), or (given in advance) *die Anzahlung(en)* antsahloong(en)

depressing *deprimierend* deprimeerend

to describe *beschreiben* be-shrye-ben

desk *der Schreibtisch(e)* shrype-tish(a)

dessert *der Nachtisch(e)* nahkh-tish(a)

detail *das Detail(s)* dai-tye(s)

detour (for traffic) *die Umleitung(en)* oomlyetoong(en), or (on foot) *der Umweg(e)* oomvaig(a)

diabetic *zuckerkrank* tsooker-krank

dialling tone *das Amtszeichen(-)* amtstsye-khen

diarrhoea *Durchfall [m]* doorkhfal

diary *der Terminkalender(-)* tairmeen-kalender, or *der Kalender(-),* or (private book) *das Tagebuch(̈er)* tahgabookh pl: tahgabooh-kher

dice *der Würfel(-)* voohrfel

dictionary *das Wörterbuch(̈er)* vurter-bookh pl: vurter-booh-kher

diesel (fuel) *der Diesel* deezel

diving *Tauchen [n]*

die Flossen *flossen*

der Bleigürtel *blye-goohrtel*

die Sauerstoffflasche *zaowershtof-flasha*

die Rettungsweste *rettoongz-vesta*

die Taucherin *taowkherin*

die Tauchermaske *taowkher-maska*

der Atemregler *ahtem-raigler*

der Taucheranzug *taowkher-antsoog*

der Schnorchel *shnorkhel*

der Druckmesser *drook-messer*

diet - drug

diet **die Diät(en)** *dee-ait(en)*
different **verschieden**
fairsheeden; different from/to
anders als *anders alts*
difficult **schwierig** *shveerikh*
dining room **das Eßzimmer(-)** *ess-tsimmer*
dinner (evening) **das Abendessen(-)** *ahbend-essen,* or (midday) **das Mittagessen(-)** *mittahg-essen*
direction **die Richtung(en)** *rikhtoong(en)*
director (of film) **der Regisseur(e)/die Regisseurin(nen)** *rayzhisur(a)/ rayzhisurin(nen)*
dirty **schmutzig** *shmootsikh*
disabled **behindert** *behindert*
disadvantage **der Nachteil(e)** *nakh-tyle(-a)*
disappointed **enttäuscht** *entoysht*
disaster **die Katastrophe(n)** *katastrawfa(n),* or (accident, tragedy) **das Unglück(e)** *oonglook(a)*
disco **die Disco(s)** *disskaw(s)*
discount **der Rabatt(e)** *rabatt(a)*
to discover **entdecken** *entdekken*
discrimination **die Diskriminierung** *diskrimineeroong*
to discuss **diskutieren** *diskooteeren*
disgusting **ekelhaft** *aikelhaft;* disgusting! **Schweinerei!*** *shvyna-rye*
dish (plate) **die Schüssel(n)** *shoossell(n),* or (meal) **das Gericht(e)** *gerikht(a)*
disk: floppy disk **die Diskette(n)** *disketta(n)*

distance **die Entfernung(en)** *entfairnoong(en)*
to disturb **stören** *shturen*
to dive (into water) **springen** *shpringen,* or (scuba) **tauchen** *taowkhen* (see picture p. 71)
divorced **geschieden** *gesheeden*
dizzy **schwindlig** *shvindlikh*
to do **machen** *makhen,* or **tun** *toon* (see also Verbs p. 58); to do up **zu'machen** *tsoo-makhen*
doctor **der Arzt(¨e)/die Ärztin(nen)** *artst pl: airtsta/airtstin(en)*
dodgy (dubious) **zweifelhaft** *tsvyfelhaft,* or (risky) **riskant** *risskant*
dog **der Hund(e)** *hoont pl: hoonda*
dole: to be on the dole **stempeln gehen*** *shtempeln gayen*
door **die Tür(en)** *toohr(en)*
double **Doppel~** *doppel* e.g. double bed **das Doppelbett**
down: to go/walk down **hinunter'gehen** *hinoonter-gayen*

draw (score) **unentschieden** *oonent-shee-den*
to draw (a picture) **zeichnen** *tsye-kh-nen*
dream **der Traum(¨e)** *traowm pl: troyma*
dress **das Kleid(er)** *klyde(-er)*
to dress (get dressed) **sich an'ziehen** *zikh an-tseeyen*
drink **das Getränk(e)** *getrenk(a)*
to drink **trinken** *trinken*
to drive **fahren** *fahren,* or (to go by car) **mit dem Auto fahren** *mit dem aowtaw fahren*
driver **der Fahrer(-)/die Fahrerin(nen)** *fahrer/fahrerin(nen)*
to drop (let fall) **fallen lassen** *falen lassen,* or (let go of) **los'lassen** *lawss-lassen;* to drop in (visit) **vorbei'kommen** *forbye-kommen;* to drop (someone) off **ab'setzen** *ap-zetsen*
drug **die Droge(n)** *drawga(n);* drug addict **der/die Drogensüchtige(n)** *drawgun-zookhtiga(n)*

egg **das Ei**

das hartgekochte Ei *hartgekokhta eye*

das weichgekochte Ei *vye-kh-gekokhta eye*

das Spiegelei *shpeegul-eye*

das Eigelb *eye-gelp*

das Eiweiß *eye-vice*

die Schale *shahla*

das Rührei *roor-eye*

das verlorene Ei *fairlorena eye*

der Eierbecher *eye-erbekher*

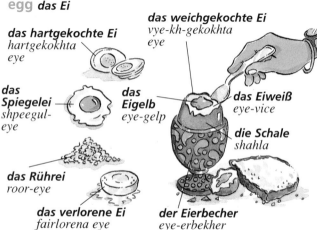

72

drunk **betrunken** betroonken, or **besoffen*** bezoffen; to get drunk **sich betrinken** zikh betrinken, or **blau werden*** blaow-vairden, or **sich besaufen*** zikh bezaowfen

dry **trocken** trocken

dubbed **synchronisiert** zoonkroneezeert

dump (for rubbish) **der Müllplatz(¨e)** murlplats pl: murlpletsa, or (dull/awful town) **das Kaff(¨er)*** kaf pl: keffer, or (dull/awful room) **das Dreckloch(¨er)*** dreklokh pl: dreklurkher

Dutch **holländisch** hollendish, or **der Holländer(-)/die Holländerin(nen)** hollender/hollenderin(nen)

duty-free **zollfrei** tsolfry

dying: to be dying to (do something) **darauf brennen (etwas) zu (tun)** dahraowf brennen (etvass) tsoo (toon); to be dying of thirst **vor Durst sterben** for doorst-shtairben

each (as in "each day/man") **jeder [m]** yaider, or **jede [f]** yaida, or **jedes [n]** yaidus, or (as in "they have two each") **je** yay, or (as in "they cost one mark each") **das Stück** dass shtook

ear **das Ohr(en)** awr(en) (see also to ache)

early **früh** frooh, or (ahead of time) **zu früh** tsoo frooh

to earn **verdienen** fair-deenen

earphones **die Kopfhörer** kopf-hur-er

east **der Osten** osten

Easter **Ostern [n]** awstern

easy **leicht** lye-kht

easy-going **ungezwungen** oon-getsvoongen

to eat **essen** essen or (guzzle) **fressen*** fressen

ecology **die Ökologie** urkolawghee

education (upbringing) **die Erziehung** airtseeyoong, or (studies) **die Ausbildung** aowssbildoong; higher education (academic) **der höhere Bildungsweg** hooera bildoongswek; further education **die Fortbildung** fortbildoong

egg **das Ei(er)** eye(-er) (see also picture below left)

elbow **der Ellenbogen(-)** ellenbawgen

election **die Wahl(en)** vahl(en)

electric **elektrisch** aylektrish

electricity **der Strom** shtrawm

else **sonst** zonst e.g. anything else? **sonst noch etwas?**

embarrassed **verlegen** fairlaigen

embarrassing **peinlich** pyne-likh

embassy **die Botschaft(en)** bawtshafft(en)

emergency **der Notfall(¨e)** nawt-fal pl: nawt-fella; emergency exit **der Notausgang(¨e)** nawt-aowssgang pl: nawt-aowssgeng-a

empty **leer** lair

end (of story) **der Schluss** shlooss, or (of road, month) **das Ende** enda, or (of finger, pen) **die Spitze(n)** shpitsa(n)

engine (of car) **der Motor(en)** mawtor(en)

England **England [n]** englant

English **englisch** english, or **der Engländer(-)/die Engländerin(nen)** englender/englenderin(nen); in English **auf Englisch**

to enjoy (yourself) **sich amüsieren** zikh-amoozeeren

enough **genug** ga-noog; that's enough **das reicht** dass rye-kht

entertainment **die Unterhaltung** oonter-halltoong

envelope **der Umschlag(¨e)** oomshlahg pl: oomshlaiga

environment **die Umwelt** oomvelt

equal **gleich** glye-kh

escalator **die Rolltreppe(n)** roltreppa(n)

essential **unbedingt erforderlich** oonbedinkt airforderlikh

EU **die EU** ay ooh

Europe **Europa [n]** oyrawpah

European **europäisch** oyrawpayish, or **der Europäer(-)/die Europäerin(nen)** oyrawpayer/oyrawpayerin(nen)

evening **der Abend(e)** ahbent pl: ahbenda

everybody **alle** alla, or (stressed, as in "everybody knows") **jeder** yaide

everything **alles** alluss

everywhere **überall** oohber-al

to exaggerate **übertreiben** oohber-try-ben

exam **die Prüfung(en)** proohfoong(en)

example **das Beispiel(e)** by-shpeel(a); for example **zum Beispiel**

excellent **ausgezeichnet** *aowss-getsye-kh-net*, or **exzellent** *ex-tsailent*
except **außer** [+ dat] *aowsser*
excess: excess weight **das Übergewicht** *oohber-gevikht;* excess fare **die Nachlösegebühr(en)** *nakhlurza-geboohr(en)*
exchange (holiday) **der Austausch** *aowsstaowsh;* foreign exchange office **die Devisen [pl]** *daiveezen,* or **die Wechselstube(n)** *vexel-shtooba(n)*
excited **aufgeregt** *aowfgayraykt;* to get excited **sich auf'regen** *zikh aowf-raygun*
exciting **aufregend** *aowfraygent*
excuse **die Entschuldigung(en)** *entshool-digoong(en);* excuse me! **Entschuldigung!**
exercise **die Übung(en)** *oohboong(en)*
exhausted **erschöpft** *airshurpft,* or **(total) kaputt*** *(tawtahl) kapoot*
exhibition **die Ausstellung(en)** *aowss-shtelloong(en)*
exit **der Ausgang(¨e)** *aowssgang pl: aowssgeng-a*
expensive **teuer** *toyer*
experience **die Erfahrung(en)** *airfahroong(en)*
to explain **erklären** *airklairen*
extra (additional) **zusätzlich** *tsoozetslikh,* or (spare or especially) **extra** *ekstrah*
eye **das Auge(n)** *aow-ga(n)*
fabulous **fabelhaft** *fahbel-haft*

face **das Gesicht(er)** *gezikht(er)*
to fail (exam) **durch'fallen** *doorkh-falun*
to faint **ohnmächtig werden** *awnmekhtikh vair-den;* I feel faint **mir wird schwach** *meer veert shvakh*
fair (just) **gerecht** *gayrekht,* or **fair** *fair*
faithful **treu** *troy*
to fall **fallen** *falun;* to fall for (a person) **sich in** [+ acc] **verlieben** *zikh in ... fairleeben,* or **sich in** [+ acc] **verknallen*** *zikh in ... fairknallen,* or (a trick) **herein'fallen auf** [+ acc] *hair-ine-falun aowf;* to fall out with (a person) **sich zerstreiten** *zikh tsair-shtryte-en*
family **die Familie(n)** *fameeleeya(n)*
famous (a star) **berühmt** *beroohmt,* or (well-known) **bekannt** *bekant*
fan (supporter, enthusiast) **der Fan(s)** *fan(s)*
to fancy (in German you say that "someone appeals to you") **gefallen** [+ dat] *gefalun,* e.g. he fancies Anna **Anna gefällt ihm**

fantastic **fantastisch** *fantastish*
far **weit** *vyte*
fare **der Fahrpreis(e)** *far-price pl: farprye-za;* full/half fare **zum vollen/halben Preis** *tsoom follen/halben price*
fashion **die Mode(n)** *mawda(n)*
fashionable **modern** *mawdairn*
fast **schnell** *shnell*
fat (on meat) **das Fett** *fet,* or (large) **dick** *dik*
father **der Vater(¨)** *fahter pl: faiter*
favourite **Lieblings~** *leeblings,* e.g. my favourite hat **mein Lieblingshut**
February **Februar [m]** *faibroo-ar*
fed: to be fed up **die Nase voll haben*** *dee nahza fol hahben*
to feel (as in "to feel happy/good") **sich fühlen** *zikh fooh-len*
feminist **die Feministin(nen)/der Feminist(en)** *feministin(en)/feminisst(en)*
ferry **die Fähre(n)** *faira(n)*
fever **das Fieber(-)** *feeber*

first aid kit das Erste-Hilfe-Set

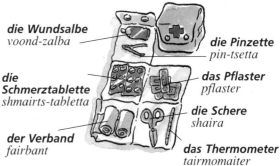

die Wundsalbe
voond-zalba

die Pinzette
pin-tsetta

das Pflaster
pflaster

die Schmerztablette
shmairts-tabletta

die Schere
shaira

der Verband
fairbant

das Thermometer
tairmomaiter

few (not many) **wenige** *vainiga;* a few (as in "I'd like a few") **ein paar** *ine par,* or (as in "a few cakes/people") **einige** *ine-iga*
fight (punch-up) **die Schlägerei(en)** *shlaiger-eye(-en)*
to fight **kämpfen** *kempfen*
to fill (bottle) **füllen** *foollen;* to fill up (with fuel) **voll tanken** *fol tanken*
film **der Film(e)** *film(a)*

fireworks (display) **das Feuerwerk** *foyer-vairk*
first (as in "the first book") **erste(n)** *airsta(n),* or (firstly) **zuerst** *tsoo-airst*
first aid **Erste Hilfe [f]** *airsta-hilfa* (see also picture below left)
fish **der Fisch(e)** *fish(a)*
to fish **fischen** *fishen,* or **angeln** *ang-eln*
fit (tantrum) **der Wutanfall(¨e)** *voot-an-fal* pl: *voot-an-fella,* or

flight **der Flug(¨e)** *floog* pl: *floohga*
floor (level) **der Stock(-)** *shtok,* or (ground) **der Boden** *bawden*
flower **die Blume(n)** *blooma(n)*
flu **die Grippe** *grippa*
fluently **fließend** *fleessent*
fly **die Fliege(n)** *fleega(n)*
to fly **fliegen** *fleegen*
to follow **folgen** [+ dat] *folgen*
food **das Essen** *essen*

football (soccer) Fußball
football (American) American Football

der Tormann *torman*
der Fan *fan*
Cheerleader *cheerleader*
das Schulterpolster *shoolter-polster*
der Helm *helm*
die Maske *maska*
das Tor *tor*
der Fußball *foossbal*
der Spieler *shpeeler*
der Schiedsrichter *sheeds-rikhter*
der Stollen *shtollen*
das Trikot *treekaw*

to find **finden** *finden;* to find out (information) **sich erkundigen** *zikh airkoon-digen,* or (discover) **heraus' finden** *hairaowss-finden*
fine **die Geldstrafe(n)** *gelt-shtrahfa(n),* or (OK) **gut** *goot,* or (weather) **schön** *shurn*
finger **der Finger(-)** *fing-er*
to finish **fertig'machen** *fairtikh-makhen*
fire **das Feuer(-)** *foyer;* fire brigade **die Feuerwehr** *foy-ervair;* fire exit **der Notausgang(¨e)** *nawt-aowss-gang* pl: *nawt-aowss-genga*

(on form) **fit** *fit;* to be in fits (laughter) **sich kaputt' lachen*** *zikh kapoot-lakhen*
to fit **passen** *pas-en*
to fix (mend) **in Ordnung bringen** *in ordnoong bringen,* or (arrange a time) **aus'machen** *aowss-makhen*
fizzy **mit Kohlensäure** *mit kawlen-zoyra*
flat **flach** *flakh,* or (apartment) **die Wohnung(en)** *vawnoong(en)*
flavour **der Geschmack(¨e)** *geshmak* pl: *geshmekka,* or (ice cream) **die Sorte(n)** *zorta(n)*

foot **der Fuß(¨e)** *fooss* pl: *fooh-sa;* on foot **zu Fuß** *tsoo fooss*
football (soccer) **Fußball [m]** *foossbal* (see picture above)
for **für** *foohr,* or (as in "I have been waiting for two hours") **seit** [+ dat] *zyte;* what for? **wozu?** *vaw-tsoo*
forbidden **verboten** *fairbawten*
foreigner **der Ausländer(-)/ die Ausländerin(nen)** *aowss-lender/ aowss-lenderin(nen)*
forest **der Wald(¨er)** *valt* pl: *velder*

to forget **vergessen** *fair-gessen*

to forgive **verzeihen** *fair-tsye-en*

fork **die Gabel(n)** *gahbel(n)*

fountain **der Brunnen(-)** *broonen*

France **Frankreich [n]** *frank-rye-kh*

to freak out (lose your cool) **durch'drehen*** *doorkh-drayen*, or **aus'flippen*** *aowss-flippen*

free **frei** *fry*

to freeze **frieren** *freeren*

French **französisch** *frantsurzish*

fresh **frisch** *frish*

Friday **Freitag [m]** *fry-tahg*

fridge **der Kühlschrank(¨e)** *koohl-shrank* pl: *koohl-shrenka*

fried **Brat~** *braht*, e.g. fried potatoes **Bratkartoffeln** (see also egg picture)

friend **der Freund(e)/die Freundin(nen)** *froynd(a)/froyndin(nen)*, or (acquaintance) **der/die Bekannte(n)** *bekanta(n)*, or (pal, mate) **der Kumpel(-)*** *koompel*

friendly **freundlich** *froyndlikh*

frightened: to be frightened **Angst haben** *angst-hahben*

from **von** [+ dat] *fon*, or (as in "I come from Bonn") **aus** [+ dat] *aowss*, or (with time/age, as in "from 6pm/ 13 years up") **ab** [+ dat] *ap*

front at/in the front **vorne** *forna*; in front of **vor** [+ acc or dat] for

fruit **das Obst** *awpst*

full **voll** *fol*, or (as in "I'm full") **satt** *zat*

fun **der Spaß** *shpahss*; it's fun **es macht Spaß** *ess makht shpahss*; to have fun **sich amüsieren** *zikh amoohzeeren*; to make fun of **sich über** [+ acc] **lustig machen** *zikh oohber ... loosstikh makhen*

funfair **die Kirmes(sen)** *keermes(sen)*, or **der Rummel** *roommel*

funny (amusing) **lustig** *loosstikh*, or (odd, amusing) **komisch** *kawmish*

fuss: to make a fuss **Theater machen*** *tay-ahter makhen*

gallery **die Galerie(n)** *gallairee(yun)*

game **das Spiel(e)** *shpeel(a)*, or (informal game of tennis, cards) **die Partie(n)** *partee(yun)*

garage (to get car mended) **die Werkstatt(¨en)** *vairk-shtatt* pl: *vairk-shtetten* (see also petrol station)

garden **der Garten(¨)** *garten* pl: *gairten*

garlic **der Knoblauch** *knawblaowkh*

gas **das Gas** *gahss*

gate (in airport) **der Flugsteig(e)** *floog-shtyge(-a)*

gear (car, bike) **der Gang(¨e)** *gang* pl: *gheng-a*

general **allgemein** *allga-mine*

generous **großzügig** *grawss-tsoog-ikh*

geography **die Geographie** *gai-aw-grafee*

German **deutsch** *doytsh*, or (man/woman) **Deutsche(n)** *doytsha(n)*; in German **auf Deutsch**

Germany **Deutschland [n]** *doytsh-lant*

to get (buy) **kaufen** *kaowfen*, or (fetch) **holen** *hawlen*, or (obtain) **bekommen** *bekommen*, or **kriegen*** *kreegun*, or (train/taxi) **nehmen** *naimen*, or (understand) **mit'bekommen** *mit-bekommen*, or **kapieren*** *kapeeren*; to get away (escape) **entkommen** *entkommen*; to get off (bus, train) **aus'steigen aus** [+ dat] *aowss-shtygen aowss*; to get on (bus, train) **ein'steigen in** [+ acc] *ine-shtygen in*; to get on (like) **sich verstehen** *zikh fair-shtayun*; to get up **auf'stehen** *aowf-shtayun*

girl **das Mädchen(-)** *mait-khean*

girlfriend **die Freundin(nen)** *froyndin(nen)*

to give **geben** *gaiben*, or (as a gift, treat) **schenken** *shenken* (see also Verbs, p. 58)

glass **das Glas(¨er)** *glass* pl: *glaizer*

glasses (spectacles) **die Brille(n)** *brilla(n)*

glove **der Handschuh(e)** *hant-shoo(-a)*

go: your go **du bist dran** *doo bist dran*; have a go! **versuch mal!** *fairzookh-mahl*

to go **gehen** *gayen* (see also Verbs, p. 58); go! **los!** *lawss*

god **der Gott(¨er)** *got* pl: *gurter*

good **gut** *goot*, or (weather) **schön** *shurn*; good-looking **gut aussehend** *goot aowss-sayend*; good morning **guten Morgen** *gooten mawrgun*; good afternoon **guten Tag** *gooten tahg*; good night **gute Nacht** *goota nakht* goodbye **(auf) Wiedersehen** (aowf) veeder-zain, or **tschüs*** tshooss, or (on the phone) **(auf) Wiederhören** (aowf) veeder-hur-un

gossip (scandal) **der Klatsch** klatsh

to gossip (natter) **schwätzen** shvetsen, or (tell tales) **klatschen*** klatshen

government **die Regierung(en)** rai-geeroong(en)

gram **das Gramm(e)** gramm(a)

grandfather **der Großvater(¨)** grawss-fahter pl: grawss-faiter, or (grandad) **Opa(s)** aw-pah(s)

grandmother **die Großmutter(¨)** grawss-mooter, or (granny) **Oma(s)** aw-mah(s)

grant (for studies) **das Stipendium** shtippen-deeyoom pl: **Stipendien** shtippen-deeyen

grapefruit **die Grapefruit(s)**

grape **die Traube(n)** traowba(n)

grass **das Gras(¨ er)** grass pl: graizer

grateful **dankbar** dankbar

great (terrific) **großartig** grawss-artikh, or **geil*** guile

green **grün** groohn

grey **grau** graow

grilled **gegrillt** gegrillt

gross (horrid) **fies*** feess

grotty **mies*** meess

ground **der Boden** bawden; on the ground **auf dem Boden** aowf dem bawden; ground floor **das Erdgeschoss** aird-geshoss

group **die Gruppe(n)** grooppa(n)

to grow **wachsen** vuxen

to guess **raten** rahten

guest **der Gast(¨ e)** gast pl: gesta; guest house **die Pension(en)** penzee-yawn(en)

guide **der Führer(-)/ die Führerin(nen)** foohrer/foohrerin(nen)

guilty **schuldig** shooldikh

guitar **die Gitarre(n)** gitarra(n)

guy **der Typ(en)*** toop(en), or **der Kerl(e)*** kairl(a)

gym **die Turnhalle(n)** toorn-halla(n) or **das Fitness-Center**; to do gym **turnen** toornen

gypsy **der Zigeuner(-)/ die Zigeunerin(nen)** tsigoyner/tsigoynerin(nen)

habit **die Gewohnheit(en)** gavawn-hite(-en)

hair **das Haar(e)** hahr(a) (see also picture below)

hair **die Haare**

hairdresser **der Friseur(e)/ die Friseuse(n)** frizur(a)/ frizurza(n)

hairstyle **die Frisur(en)** frizoor(en)

half **halb** halp, or (not whole, as in "half of it") **die Hälfte(n)** helfta(n)

ham **der Schinken(-)** shinken

hand **die Hand(¨ e)** hant pl: henda; handmade **handgearbeitet** hantga-arbye-tet; hands off! **Finger weg!** fing-er-vek

to hang (something up) **auf'hängen** aowf-hengen; to hang up (phone) **auf'legen** aowf-laigun

hangover **der Kater(-)** kahter

to happen **passieren** passeeren, or **geschehen** geshayen

happy **glücklich** glooklikh

lockig lokkikh
glatt glat
kraus kraowss
kurz koorts
der Schaumfestiger shaowmfestiger
der Haarspray hahrshpray
der Fön furn
das Gel gail
lang lang
blond blont
rot rawt
braun braown
schwarz shvarts
die Haarbürste hahrboohrsta
der Kamm kam
die Haarspange hahrshpanga

hard **hart** *hart*, or (difficult) **schwer** *shvair*

hat **der Hut(¨e)** *hoot pl: hooh-ta*

to hate **hassen** *hassen*

to have **haben** *hahben* (see also Verbs p. 58); to have to **müssen** *moossen* (see Useful irregular verbs p. 59)

he **er** *air*, or **der*** *dair*

head **der Kopf(¨e)** *kopf pl: kurpfa* (see also to ache)

health **die Gesundheit** *gazoont-hite*

healthy **gesund** *gazoont*

to hear **hören** *hur-un*

heart **das Herz(en)** *hairts(en);* heart-broken **todunglücklich** *tawt-oon-glooklikh*

heating **die Heizung** *hites-oong*

heavy **schwer** *shvair*

helicopter **der Hubschrauber(-)** *hoop-shraowber*

hell **die Hölle** *hurla*

hello **hallo** *hallaw*

helmet **der Helm(e)** *helm(a)*

help **die Hilfe** *hillfa*

to help **helfen** [+ dat] *helfen;* to help yourself **sich bedienen** *zikh badeenen*

her (as in her pen) **ihr [m, n]** *eer*, or **ihre [f, pl]** *eera*

her (as in "he's taller than her" and "I see her") **sie** *zee*, or (in dat. case) **ihr** *eer* (for more about cases, see p. 56)

here **hier** *heer*

hi **hallo** *hallaw*

hiccups: to have hiccups **Schluckauf haben** *shlookaowf hahben*

to hide (something) **verstecken** *fairshteken*, or (yourself) **sich verstecken** *zikh fairshteken*

hi-fi (system) **die Hi-fi-Anlage(n)** *hifi-anlahga(n)*

high **hoch** *hawkh*

hiking: to go hiking **wandern gehen** *vandern gayen*

hill **der Hügel(-)** *hoohgul*

him **er** *air*, or (in acc. case) **ihn** *een*, or (in dat. case) **ihm** *eem* (for more about cases, see p. 56)

Hindu **der/die Hindu(s)** *hindoo(s)*

hippy **der Hippie(s)** *hippee(s)*

his **sein [m, n]** *zyne*, or **seine [f, pl]** *zyne-a*

history **Geschichte [f]** *geshikhta*

hit (success) **der Erfolg(e)** *airfolg(a)*, or **der Knüller(-)*** *k-nooller*, or **der Hit(s)** *hit(s)*

to hit (strike) **schlagen** *shlahgun*, or (hit target) **treffen** *treffen*

hobby **das Hobby(s)** *hobbee(s)*

to hold **halten** *hall-ten*

hole **das Loch(¨er)** *lokh pl: lurkher*

holiday **der Urlaub(e)** *oorlaowb*, or (bank holiday) **der Feiertag(e)** *fire-tahg(a);* the holidays **die Ferien** *faireeyen*

Holland **Holland [n]** *hollant*

home: at home **zu Hause** *tsoo haowza;* to go home **nach Hause gehen** *nakh haowza gayen*

homeless **obdachlos** *obdakh-lawss*

homework **die Hausaufgaben [pl]** *haowss-aowf-gahben*

homosexual **homosexuell** *hawmaw-zexoo-el*, or **schwul** *shvool*

honest **ehrlich** *airlikh*

to hope **hoffen** *hoffen*

horn (of car) **die Hupe(n)** *hoopa(n)*

horoscope **das Horoskop(e)** *hawrawskawp(a)* (see also picture below)

horrible **furchtbar** *foorkht-bar*

horse **das Pferd(e)** *pfairt pl: pfairda*

horoscope
das Horoskop

Steinbock *shtyne-bok*

Wassermann *vasserman*

Schütze *shootsa*

Fische *fisha*

Skorpion *skorpeeyawn*

Widder *vidder*

Waage *vahga*

Stier *shteer*

Jungfrau *yoong-fraow*

Zwillinge *tsvillinga*

Löwe *lurva*

Krebs *kraips*

hospital **das Krankenhaus(̈er)** *kranken-haowss pl: kranken-hoyzer*
hot **heiß** *hysse*, or (spicy) **scharf** *sharf*; I am/feel hot **mir ist sehr warm** *meer isst zair vahrm*
hotel **das Hotel(s)** *hawtel(s)*
hour **die Stunde(n)** *shtoonda(n)*
house **das Haus(̈er)** *haowss pl: hoyzer*
hovercraft **das Hovercraft(s)** *hoverkraft(s)*
how **wie** *vee*; how are you? **wie geht's?** *vee gaits*; how much? **wie viel?** *vee feel*; how many? **wie viele?** *vee feela*
to hug (someone) **(jemanden) umarmen** *(yaymanden) oom-armen*
human **menschlich** *menshlikh*
hungry: to be hungry **Hunger haben** *hoong-er hahben*
hurry: to be in a hurry **es eilig haben** *ess eye-likh hahben*
to hurry **sich beeilen** *zikh ba-eye-len*
to hurt **weh tun** *vay toon* (see also to ache)
hypocritical **heuchlerisch** *hoykh-lerish*
I **ich** *ikh*
ice **das Eis** *ice*; ice cream **das Eis** *ice*; ice cube **der Eiswürfel(-)** *ice-voohrfel*; ice rink **die Eisbahn(en)** *ice-bahn(en)*
idea **die Idee(n)** *eeday(en)*
idiot **der Idiot(en)** *id-ee-awt(en)*, or **der Dummkopf(̈e)*** *doomm-kopf pl: doomm-kurpfa*
if **wenn** *ven*

ill **krank** *krank*
illegal **illegal** *illaygahl*
imagination **die Fantasie** *fan-ta-zee*
to imagine (to picture) **sich vor'stellen** *zikh forshtellen*, or (as in "you're just imagining it") **sich ein'bilden** *zikh ine-bilden*
immediately **sofort** *zawfort*
immigrant **der Einwanderer(-)/die Einwandererin(nen)** *ine-vanderer/inevandererin(nen)*
important **wichtig** *vikhtikh*
in **in** [+ dat or acc] *in*, or (here) **da** *dah*, or (trendy) **in*** *in*; in there (as in "it's in there") **da drin** *dah drin*, or (with motion, as in "go in there") **da rein*** *dah rine*
to include **ein'schließen** *ine-shleessen*
independent **unabhängig** *oonap-heng-ikh*
indoors **drinnen** *drinnen*
infection **die Entzündung(en)** *ent-tsoondoong(en)*
infectious **ansteckend** *an-shtekent*
information **die Auskunft(̈e)** *aowsskoonft pl: aowsskoohnfta*
injection **die Spritze(n)** *shpritsa(n)*
injury **die Verletzung(en)** *fairletsoong(en)*; injury time (in sports) **die Nachspielzeit** *nakh-shpeel-tsite*
innocent **unschuldig** *oonshooldikh*
insect **das Insekt(en)** *inzekt(en)*; insect bite **der Stich(e)** *shtikh(a)*; insect repellent **das Insektenschutzmittel(-)** *inzekten-shoots-mittel*

inside (as in "it's inside") **drin*** *drin*, or (with motion, as in "come inside") **(he)rein** *(hair)rine*; inside out **links herum** *links hairoom*
to insist on (something) **auf** [+ dat] **bestehen** *aowf (...) beshtayen*
instead **statt dessen** *shtat dessen*
instructor **der Lehrer(-)/die Lehrerin(nen)** *lairer/lairerin(nen)*
instrument **das Instrument(e)** *instrooment(a)* (see also picture below)
insult **die Beleidigung(en)** *ba-lye-digoong(en)*
insurance **die Versicherung(en)** *fair-zikheroong(en)*

instruments Instrumente

das Cello *tshellaw*
die Geige *guy-ga*
das Horn *horrn*
der Flügel *floohgul*
die Klarinette *klarinetta*
die Oboe *awbawa*
die Trompete *trompaita*
die Querflöte *kvair-flurta*
die Posaune *pawzaowna*

interested: to be interested in *sich interessieren für* [+ acc] *zikh interesseeren foohr*

interesting *interessant* *interessant*

international *international* *intair-natsee-awnahl*

interval *die Pause(n)* *paow-za(n)*

interview (job) *das Vorstellungsgespräch(e) forshtelloongs-geshpraikh(a)*, or (with reporter) *das Interview(s) intair-view(s)*

to introduce (people) *vor'stellen for-shtellen*

to invite *ein'laden ine-lahden*

Ireland *Irland [n] eerlant*

Irish *irisch eerish*, or *der Ire(n)/die Irin(nen) eera(n)/eerin(en)*

iron (for clothes) *das Bügeleisen(-) boohgul-eye-zen*

island *die Insel(n) inzel(n)*

it (when unclear what "it" refers to, as in "it's fine") *es ess*, or *das dass*, or (when you know the gender of "it") *er [m] air*, or *sie [f] zee*, or *es [n] ess*, or (slang) *der* [m] *dair*, or *die* [f] *dee*, or *das* [n] *dass*; with it *damit dahmit*; on it *darauf dahraowf*; about it *darüber dahroohber*

Italy *Italien [n] itahleeyen*

jacket *die Jacke(n) yakka(n)*, or (bomber-style) *der Blouson(s) bloozong(s)* (see picture below)

jam *die Marmelade(n) marma-lahda(n)*, or *die Konfitüre(n) konfitoohra(n)*

January *Januar [m] yanoo-ar*

jealous *eifersüchtig eye-fer-zookhtikh*

jeans *die Jeans [pl] jeens*

jellyfish *die Qualle(n) kvalla(n)*

jewellery *der Schmuck shmook* (see picture below)

Jewish *jüdisch yooh-dish*

job (employment) *die Stelle(n) shtella(n)*, or (task) *die Arbeit(en) arbite(-en)*, or *der Job(s)**

to join (become a member) *Mitglied werden mitgleed vairden*; to join in *mit'machen mit-makhen*

joke *der Witz(e) vits(a)*; for a joke *zum Spaß tsoom shpahss*

juice *der Saft(¨e) zaft pl: zefta*

July *Juli [m] yoolee*

to jump *springen shpringen*

June *Juni [m] yoonee*

junk *der Trödel trurdel*

just (as in "he's just gone" or "it's just right") *gerade garahda*

to keep *behalten behallten*; to keep on (doing something) *weiter'machen vyter-makhen*; to keep an eye on *auf'passen auf* [+ acc] *aowf-passen aowf*

key *der Schlüssel(-) shloossel*

kick *der Tritt(e) tritt(a)*

to kill *töten turten*

kilo *das Kilo(-) keelaw*

kilometre *der Kilometer(-) keelaw-maiter*

kind (nice) *nett net*

kiss *der Kuss(¨e) kooss(a)*

to kiss *küssen koossen*, or (one another) *sich küssen zikh koossen*

jacket *die Jacke* or *der Blouson*

jewellery *der Schmuck*

der Blouson *bloozong*

der Ohrring *or-ring*

der Kragen *krahgun*

die Jacke *yakka*

der Ärmel *airmul*

der Knopf *k-nopf*

die Tasche *tasha*

die Kette *ketta*

die Halskette *hals-ketta*

die Brosche *brosha*

der Ring *ring*

die Schnalle *shnalla*

der Armreifen *arm-rye-fen*

das Armband *armbant*

kite **der Drachen**

der Griff *griff*

die Schnur *shnoor*

der Schwanz *shvants*

kit (equipment) **die Ausrüstung(en)** *aowss-roosstoong(en)*, or **der Kram*** *krahm*
kitchen **die Küche(n)** *kookha(n)*
kite **der Drachen(-)** *drakhen* (see picture above)
knee **das Knie(-)** *k-nee(ya)*
knickers **der Slip(s)** *slip(s)*
knife **das Messer(-)** *messer*
to know (facts) **wissen** *vissen* (see also Verbs, p. 58), or (person) **kennen** *kennen*
lager **das Pils(-)** *pils*, or **das (helle) Bier(e)** *(hella) beer(a)*
laid-back **locker*** *lokker*, or **cool*** *kool*
lake **der See(n)** *zay(un)*
lamb (meat) **das Lammfleisch** *lamm-flyshe*
land **das Land(¨er)** *lant pl: lender*
language **die Sprache(n)** *shprah-kha(n)*
last (the last) **letzte(n)** *letsta(n)*; at last **endlich** *entlikh*; last night **gestern Abend** *gestern ahbent*
late (not early) **spät** *shpait*, or (not on time) **verspätet** *fair-shpaitet*
to laugh **lachen** *lakhen*; to laugh at (a person, thing) **sich über** [+ acc] **lustig machen** *zikh oohber (...) loosstikh makhen*

launderette **der Waschsalon(s)** *vash-zallong(s)*
lazy **faul** *fowl*
leaf **das Blatt(¨er)** *blat pl: bletter*
to learn **lernen** *lairnen*
leather **das Leder(-)** *laider*
to leave **lassen** *lassen*, or (a place/person) **verlassen** *fair-lassen*, or (go away) **weg'gehen** *vek-gayen*
left (as in "the left side/shoe) **linke(n)** *linka(n)*; on the left **links** *links*; left-handed **linkshändig** *links-hendikh*
leg **das Bein(e)** *byne(-a)*
lemon **die Zitrone(n)** *tsitrawna(n)*
to lend **leihen** *lye-un*, or (money) **verleihen** *fair-lye-un*
less **weniger** *vainiger*
lesson **die Stunde(n)** *shtoonda(n)*
letter **der Brief(e)** *breef(a)*, or (of alphabet) **der Buchstabe(n)** *bookh-shtahba(n)*
lettuce **der Kopfsalat(e)** *kopf-zallaht(a)*, or **der Salat(e)** *zallaht(a)*
liar **der Lügner(-)/die Lügnerin(nen)** *loohg-ner/loohg-nerin(nen)*
library **die Bibliothek(en)** *bibli-aw-taik(en)*
licence (permit) **die Erlaubnis(se)** *airlaowb-nis(sa)*; (driving) **der Führerschein(e)** *foohrer-shyne(-a)*
lie **die Lüge(n)** *looh-ga(n)*

life **das Leben(-)** *laiben*
lifeguard (at pool) **der Bademeister(-)/die Bademeisterin(nen)** *bahda-my-ster*, or (on beach) **der Rettungsschwimmer(-)** *rettoongs-shvimmer*
lifejacket **die Schwimmweste(n)** *shvim-vesta(n)*
lift (elevator) **der Lift(s)** *lift(s)*, or **der Fahrstuhl(¨e)** *farshtool pl: farshtooh-la*
light **das Licht(er)** *likht(er)*, or (not dark) **hell** *hell*, or (not heavy) **leicht** *lye-kht*
lighter **das Feuerzeug(e)** *foy-er-tsoyg(a)*
like **wie** *vee*; like this/that **so** *zaw*; what's he/she like? **wie ist er/sie?** *vee isst air/zee*
to like **mögen** [+ acc] *murgun* (see Useful irregular verbs p. 59), or **gern haben** [+ acc] *gairn hahben*, or (to like doing something) **gern** *gairn* e.g. I like swimming **ich schwimme gern;** I'd like **ich möchte** *ikh murkhta*, or **ich hätte gern** *ikh hetta gairn*
likely **wahrscheinlich** *vahr-shyne-likh*; not likely! **kommt nicht in Frage!** *kommt nikht in frahga*
line **die Linie(n)** *lee-nee-ya(n)*
lip **die Lippe(n)** *lippa(n)*
to listen **zu'hören** *tsoo-hur-un*
litre **der/das Liter(-)** *leeter*

litter - medium

litter **der Abfall(¨e)** *apfal pl: apfella*

little (small) **klein** *klyne;* a little **ein wenig** *ine vainikh*

live (broadcast) **live** *live*

to live **leben** *laiben,* or (dwell) **wohnen** *vawnen*

liver **die Leber** *laiber*

living room **das Wohnzimmer(-)** *vawn-tsimmer*

loads of **massenhaft** *massen-hafft*

to loathe **verabscheuen** *fair-ap-shoyen*

local **Orts~** *orts* e.g. local call **das Ortsgespräch**

to lock **ab'schließen** *apshleessen*

lonely **einsam** *ine-zahm*

long **lang** *lang,* or (a long time) **lange** *lang-a*

loo **das Klo(s)*** *klaw(s)* (see also toilet)

to look **schauen** *shaowen,* or **gucken*** *gooken,* or (as in to look good/ill) **aus'sehen** *aowss-zayen;* to look after (care for) **auf'passen auf** [+ acc] *aowf-passen aowf;* to look for **suchen** *zookhen;* to look forward to **sich freuen auf** [+ acc] *zich froyen aowf;* to look round (in shop, etc.) **sich um'sehen** *zikh oom-zayen*

to lose **verlieren** *fair-leeren*

lost **verloren** *fair-loren;* to get lost (on foot) **sich verlaufen** *zikh fair-laowfen,* or (in car) **sich verfahren** *zikh fair-fahren;* get lost! **hau ab!** *how ap;* lost property (office) **das Fundbüro(s)** *foond-boohraw(s)*

lot: a lot of **eine Menge** *ine-a meng-a*

loud **laut** *laowt*

lousy **lausig*** *laow-zikh,* or **fies*** *feess*

love **die Liebe** *leeba;* in love **verliebt** *fair-leept;* love-life **das Liebesleben** *leebus-laiben*

to love (doing something) **(...) sehr gern** *(...) zair gairn,* or (someone) **lieb haben** *leeb hahben,* or (adore) **lieben** *leeben*

lovely (beautiful) **schön** *shurn,* or (nice) **lieb** *leeb*

low **niedrig** *needrikh*

luck **das Glück** *glook;* bad luck! **Pech!** *pekh;* good luck! **viel Glück!** *feel glook*

luckily **glücklicherweise** *glook-likher-vyze-a,* or **zum Glück** *tsoom glook*

luggage **das Gepäck** *gepeck;* hand-luggage **das Handgepäck** *hant-gepeck*

lunch **das Mittagessen(-)** *mittahg-essen;* to have lunch **zu Mittag essen** *tsoo mittahg-essen*

machine **die Maschine(n)** *masheena(n)*

mad **verrückt** *fairookt,* or **wahnsinnig** *vahn-zinnikh*

magazine **die Zeitschrift(en)** *tsite-shrift(en)*

to make **machen** *makhen* (see also Verbs, p. 58); to make up (invent) **erfinden** *air-finden,* or (be friends again) **sich versöhnen** *zikh fair-zurnen*

make-up **das Make-up** *make-up* (see picture opposite)

man **der Mann(¨er)** *man pl: menner*

to manage (cope) **zurecht'kommen** *tsoo-rekht-kommen,* or (succeed) **es schaffen** *ess shaffen*

many **viele** *feela*

map **die Landkarte(n)** *lant-karta(n),* or (of town) **der Stadtplan(¨e)** *shtat-plahn pl: shtat-plaina*

March **März [m]** *mairts*

margarine **die Margarine** *mar-gareena*

mark (German currency) **die Mark(-)** *mark,* or (stain) **der Fleck(en)** *flek(en),* or (at school) **die Note(n)** *nawta(n)*

market **der Markt(¨e)** *markt pl: mairkta*

match (for a candle) **das Streichholz(¨er)** *shtry-kh-holts pl: shtry-kh-hurltser,* or (sport) **das Spiel(e)** *shpeel(a),* or **das Match(e)** *matsh(a)*

maths **Mathe* [f]** *matta*

matter: it doesn't matter **es macht nichts** *ess makht nikhts;* what's the matter? **was ist (denn) los?** *vass isst (den) lawss*

mature **reif** *ryfe*

May **Mai [m]** *my*

mayonnaise **die Mayonnaise** *my-on-aiza*

me **ich** *ikh,* or (in acc. case) **mich** *mikh,* or (in dat. case) **mir** *meer* (for more about Cases, see p. 56)

meal **das Essen(-)** *essen*

to mean (signify) **bedeuten** *bedoyten;* to mean to **beabsichtigen** *ba-apzikhtigen*

meat **das Fleisch** *fly-sh*

medicine (medication) **das Medikament(e)** *maydikah-ment(a),* or (science) **die Medizin** *mayditseen*

medium (size) **medium** *maydeeyum,* or **mittelgroß** *mittel-grawss,* or (medium-cooked) **halbdurch** *halp-doorkh*

make-up *das Make-up*

der Make-up-Entferner
make-up-entfairner

die Watte
vatta

der Lidschatten
leed-shatten

der Lidstift
leed-shtift

das Rouge
roosh

die Wimpern-tusche
vimpern-toosha

der Lippenkonturenstift
lippen-kontooren-shtift

der Lippenstift
lippenshtift

die Grundierung
groondeeroong

to meet **treffen** *treffen*, or
(to get to know)
kennen'lernen *kennen-lairnen*
melon **die Melone(n)**
melawna(n); watermelon
die Wassermelone(n)
vasser-melawna(n)
menu **die Speisekarte(n)**
shpyze-a-karta(n), or (a set
menu) **das Menü(s)** *menoo(s)*
mess **das Durcheinander**
doorkhine-ander, or
(untidiness) **die Unordnung**
oonordnoong
message **die Nachricht(en)**
nakh-rikht(en); to take a
message **etwas aus'richten**
etvass aowss-rikhten; to
get the message **kapieren***
kapeeren
metre **der Meter(-)** *maiter*
microwave **die Mikrowelle(n)** *meekraw-vella(n)*
middle **die Mitte(n)** *mitta(n)*

milk **die Milch** *milkh;* milk
shake **der Milchshake(s)**
milkh-shake(s)
mind: do you mind? (does it
bother you?) **stört es dich/
euch/Sie?** (see page 57)
shturt ess dikh/oykh/zee; I
don't mind (it doesn't bother
me) **es stört mich nicht** *ess
shturt mikh nikht,* or (it's all
the same to me) **es ist mir
egal** *ess ist meer aygahl*
minute (time) **die Minute(n)**
minoota(n)
mirror **der Spiegel(-)**
shpeegul
Miss **Fräulein** *froy-lyne*
to miss (a bus/train)
verpassen *fair-pas-en,* or
(to regret the absence of)
vermissen *fair-missen*
mistake **der Fehler(-)**
failer
to mix (muddle)
durcheinander bringen
doorkh-ine-ander bring-en

mixed up (in your mind)
durcheinander *doorkh-ine-ander*
to moan (complain)
meckern* *meckern*
mobile (phone) **das
Handy(s)** *handy(s)*
model (fashion) **das
Model(s)** *model(s)*
modern **modern** *modairn*
moment: in/just a moment!
Augenblick mal! *aowgen-blik mahl,* or **Moment
mal!** *mawment mahl*
Monday **Montag [m]**
mawn-tahg
money **das Geld** *ghelt,* or
die Kohle(n)* *kawla(n),* or
das Moos* *mawss*
month **der Monat(e)**
maw-naht(a)
monument **das
Denkmal(̈er)** *denk-mahl
pl: denk-mailer,* or (big)
das Monument(e)
monooment(a)
mood: in a good/bad mood
gut/schlecht gelaunt
goot/shlekht galaownt
moody (temperament)
launisch *laownish*
moon **der Mond(e)** *mawnt
pl: mawnda*
moped **das Moped(s)**
mawped(s), or (small) **das
Mofa(s)** *mawfah(s)*
more **mehr** *mair,* or
(additional) **noch mehr**
nokh mair
morning **der Morgen(-)**
morgen; in the morning
morgens *morgens*
mosquito (in Europe) **die
Mücke(n)** *mooka(n),* or (in
tropics) **der Moskito(s)**
mosskeetaw(s); mosquito
bite **der Mückenstich(e)**
mooken-shtikh(a)

83

most (most of all) **am meisten** *am my-sten*, or (the majority of) **die meisten** *dee my-sten*
mother **die Mutter(¨)** *mooter*
motorbike **das Motorrad(¨er)** *mawtor-raht pl: mawtor-raider*
motorway **die Autobahn(en)** *aowtaw-bahn(en)*
mountain **der Berg(e)** *bairg(a)*
mouth **der Mund(¨er)** *moont pl: moonder*
to move **bewegen** *bevaigun;* to move house **um'ziehen** *oomtseeyen;* move over! **rück mal!** *rook mahl*
Mr **Herr** *hair*
Mrs **Frau** *fraow*
much **viel** *feel*
mugged: to get mugged **überfallen werden** *oohber-falun vairden*
murder **der Mord(e)** *mort pl: morda*
muscle **der Muskel(n)** *moosskel(n)*
museum **das Museum** *moozayoom* **pl: Museen** *moozayen*
mushroom (button) **der Champignon(s)** *shompeen-yong(s),* or (wild) **der Pilz(e)** *pilts(a)*
music **die Musik** *moozeek*
musician **der Musiker(-)/ die Musikerin(nen)** *moozikker/moozikkerin(nen)*
Muslim **muslemisch** *moozlaimish*
must (to have to) **müssen** *moossen* (see also Useful irregular verbs p. 59)
mustard **der Senf(e)** *zenf(a)*

my **mein [m, n]** *mine,* or **meine** *mine-a* (see page 58)
naff **bescheuert*** *beshoyert*
naïve **naiv** *na-eef*
naked **nackt** *nakt*
name **der Name(n)** *nahma(n);* first name **der Vorname(n)** *for-nahma(n);* what's your name? **wie heißt du/ihr?** *vee hye-st doo/eer,* or **wie heißen Sie?** *vee hye-sen zee*
narrow **eng** *eng*
nasty **unangenehm** *oonangenaim,* or (person) **gemein** *ge-myne*
national **national** *natsee-awnahl*
nationality **die Staatsangehörigkeit(en)** *shtahts-an-gehurikh-kyte(en)*
natural **natürlich** *natoohr-likh*
nature **die Natur** *natoor*
near **in der Nähe von** [+ dat] *in dair naya fon*
nearest (as in "the nearest shop") **nächste(n)** *nexta(n)*
nearly **fast** *fast*
necessary **nötig** *nurtikh*
neck **der Hals(¨e)** *halts pl: heltsa*
to need **brauchen** *braowkhen*
needle **die Nadel(n)** *nahdel(n)*
negative **negativ** *naigateef*
neighbour **der Nachbar(n)/ die Nachbarin(nen)** *nakhbar(n)/nakhbarin(nen)*
neighbourhood **die Gegend** *gaigunt*
nerve **der Nerv(en)** *nairf(en);* nerve-racking **nervtötend** *nairf-turtent;* what a nerve! **so eine Frechheit!** *zaw ine-a frekh-hyte*

nervous **nervös** *nairvurz,* or (with excitement) **aufgeregt** *aowf-geraikt*
never **nie** *nee;* never mind! (it doesn't matter) **macht nichts!** *makht nikhts,* or (too bad) **ist doch egal!** *isst dokh aygahl*
new **neu** *noy;* New Year **Neujahr [n]** *noy yar;* New Year's Eve **Silvester [n]** *zilvester*
news **die Nachrichten [pl]** *nakh-rikhten;* news stand (kiosk) **der Kiosk(e)** *keeosk(a)*
newspaper **die Zeitung(en)** *tsye-toong(en)*
next (as in "who's next?") **am nächsten** *am nexten,* or (as in "the next film/road") **nächste(n)** *nexta(n);* next to **neben** [+ acc or dat] *naiben*
nice (likeable) **nett** *net,* or **sympathisch** *zoompahtish,* or (pretty) **hübsch** *hoopsh;* nice and ... (as in "nice and cold") **schön ...** *shurn ...*
nickname **der Spitzname(n)** *shpits-nahma(n)*
night **die Nacht(¨e)** *nakht pl: nekhta;* last night **gestern Abend** *gesstern ahbent*
nightmare **der Alptraum(¨e)** *alptraowm pl: alptroyma*
no **nein** *nine;* no entry **kein Eintritt** *kine ine-trit;* no smoking **Nichtraucher** *nikht-raowkher;* no way! **von wegen!*** *fon vaygen*
nobody **niemand** *neemant*
noise **der Lärm** *lairm,* or (din) **der Krach** *krakh*
normal **normal** *nor-mahl*
north **der Norden** *norden;* north of **nördlich von** [+ dat] *nurdlikh fon*
nose **die Nase(n)** *nahza(n)*

nosy **neugierig**
noygheerikh; to be nosy
**die Nase in alles
hinein'stecken*** *dee nahza
in alless hinyne-shtecken*
not **nicht** *nikht,* or (not
a/any or no, as in "I've no
money", "that's no joke")
kein [m, n] *kyne,* or **keine
[f, pl]** *kyne-a* (see Negatives
p. 60); not until **erst** *airst*
note (money) **der Schein(e)**
shyne(-a)
notebook **das Notizheft(e)**
nawteets-heft(a)
nothing **nichts** *nikhts*
novel **der Roman(e)**
rawmahn(a)
November **November [m]**
nawvember
now **jetzt** *yetst;* now then!
also! *alzaw*
nowhere **nirgends**
neerghents
nuclear **Kern~** *kairn,* or
Atom~ *attawm,* e.g. nuclear
power **die Kernkraft,** or
Atomkraft
number **die Nummer(n)**
noomer(n) (for numbers in
German see p. 53)
nuts **Nüsse**

nurse **der
Krankenpfleger(-)/
die Krankenschwester(n)**
*kranken-pflaiger/kranken-
shvester(n)*
nut **die Nuss(¨e)** *nooss(a)*
(see picture below)
obnoxious **widerlich**
veederlikh
obscene **obszön** *obs-tsern*
obsessed **besessen**
bezessen
obvious **offensichtlich**
offen-zikht-likh
o'clock **Uhr** *oor* (see picture
for time)
October **Oktober [m]**
oktawber
odd (strange) **eigenartig**
eye-genartikh
of **von** [+ dat] *fon,* or (made
of) **aus** [+ dat] *aowss*
off (TV, light, machine)
aus(geschaltet)
aowss(geshaltet), or (gas,
electricity) **abgeschaltet**
apgeshaltet
offended **beleidigt** *bel-
eye-dikht*
to offer **an'bieten** *an-
beeten*

office **das Büro(s)**
booh-raw(s)
official **offiziell** *offitsee-ell*
often **oft** *oft;* how often?
wie oft? *vee oft*
oil **das Öl(e)** *url(a)*
OK **in Ordnung** *in
ordnoong,* or **okay,** or
(I'm/it's OK) **es geht** *ess gayt*
old **alt** *alt;* how old are
you? **wie alt bist du?** *vee
alt bist doo,* or **... seid ihr?**
... zyte eer, or **... sind Sie?** *...
zind zee* (see I, you, he, she,
etc. p. 57); old-fashioned
altmodisch *alt-mawdish,* or
out* *aowt*
olive **die Olive(n)** *oleeva(n)*
omelette **das Omelett(s)**
om-let(s)
on **auf** [+ acc or dat] *aowf,*
or (on an upright surface, as
in "on the wall/door") **an** [+
acc or dat] *an,* or (switched
on) **an** *an;* what's on? (at the
cinema) **was läuft?** *vass loyft*
one-way: one way street
die Einbahnstraße(n) *ine-
bahn-shtrahssa(n)*
onion **die Zwiebel(n)**
tsvee-bul(n)

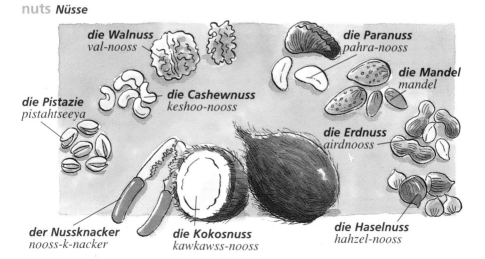

die Walnuss
val-nooss

die Paranuss
pahra-nooss

die Mandel
mandel

die Pistazie
pistahtseeya

die Cashewnuss
keshoo-nooss

die Erdnuss
airdnooss

der Nussknacker
nooss-k-nacker

die Kokosnuss
kawkawss-nooss

die Haselnuss
hahzel-nooss

only *nur noor*, or (with age or time, as in "he's only 11", "only yesterday") *erst airst;* only child *das Einzelkind(er) ine-tselkint pl: ine-tselkinder*
open *offen offen*, or *auf aowf;* in the open air *im Freien im fry-en*
to open **öffnen** *urfnen*, or *auf'machen aowf-makhen*
opera *die Oper(n) awper(n)*
opinion *die Meinung(en) mine-oong(en)*
opportunity *die Gelegenheit(en) galaigen-hyte(-en)*
opposite (facing) **gegenüber** *gaigen-oohber*, or (not the same) *das Gegenteil(e) gaigen-tile(-a)*
optimistic **optimistisch** *optimistish*
or **oder** *aw-der*
orange (colour) **orange** *orangsh*, or (fruit) *die Orange(n) orangsha(n)*
orchestra *das Orchester(-) orkester*
order (for food, drink) *die Bestellung(en) beshtelloong(en)*, or (sequence) *die Reihenfolge rye-enfolga*
to order (food, drink) **bestellen** *beshtellen*
ordinary **gewöhnlich** *gevurnlikh*
to organize **organisieren** *organeezeeren*
original **original** *origeenahl*, or (person, idea) **originell** *origeenell*, or (earliest) **ursprünglich** *oor-shproong-likh*
other (as in "the other shoe/side") **andere(n)** *andera(n)*

otherwise **sonst** *zonst*
our **unser [m, n]** *oonzer*, or **unsere [f, pl]** *oonzera*
out (not at home) **weg** *vek;* to be out of order (not working) **nicht funktionieren** *nikht foonk-tsee-yawn-eeren*
outrageous **unerhört** *oon-air-hurt*
outside (with motion, as in "I'm going outside") **nach draußen** *nakh draowssen*, or (without motion, as in "I'm outside") **draußen** *draowssen*, or (in front of, as in "outside the cinema") **vor** [+ dat] *for*
oven *der (Back)ofen(¨) (bak)awfen pl: (bak)urfen*
over (not under) **über** [+ acc or dat] *oohber*, or (as in "over here/there") **drüben** *droohben*, or (finished) **vorbei** *for-bye;* over the top **übertrieben** *oohber-treeben*
overrated **überschätzt** *oohber-shetst*
to overtake **überholen** *oohber-hawlen*
to owe **schulden** *shoollden*
own on your own **ganz allein** *gants al-ine*
owner **der Besitzer(-)/die Besitzerin(nen)** *bezitser/bezitserin(en)*
to pack (bags) **ein'packen** *ine-packen*
package tour *die Pauschalreise(n) paow-shahl-rye-za(n)*
padlock *das Vorhängeschloss(¨er) forheng-a-shloss pl: forheng-a-shlursser*
page *die Seite(n) zyte-a(n)*
to paint (a picture) **malen** *mahlen*

palace *der Palast(¨e) palasst pl: palesta*
pan (saucepan) *der Topf(¨e) topf pl: turpfa*, or (frying) *die (Brat)pfanne(n) (braht)-pfanna(n)*
panic *die Panik pahnik*
paper *das Papier papeer*
paperback (book) *das Taschenbuch(¨er) tashenbookh pl: tashenbooh-kher*
parcel *das Paket(e) pakait(a)*
pardon (what?) **wie bitte?** *vee bitta*
parents *die Eltern [pl] eltern*
park *der Park(s) park(s)*
to park **parken** *parken*
part (not all) *der Teil(e) tyle(-a)*, or (for bike etc.) *das Teil(e);* to take part **teil'nehmen** *tyle-naimen*
party *die Party(s) party(s)*, or *die Fete(n)* faita(n)*, or (political) *die Partei(en) par-tye(-en)*
to party **feiern** *fye-ern*
pass (identity card, permit) *der Ausweis(e) aowss-vysse pl: aowss-vyze-a;* day pass (travel) *die Tageskarte(n) tahgus-karta(n)*
to pass **vorbei'gehen an** [+ dat] *for-bye-gayen an ...*, or (an exam) **bestehen** *beshtayen*
passenger (plane, ship) *der Passagier(e) pas-asheer(a)*, or (train) *der/die Reisende(n) rye-zenda(n)*
passport *der Reisepass(¨e) rye-za-pass pl: rye-za-pessa*, or *der Pass(¨e) pass pl: pessa*
pasta *die Nudeln [pl] noodeln*

path **der Weg(e)** *vaig(a)*
patient: to be patient
Geduld haben *gedoold hahben*
pavement **der Bürgersteig(e)** *boohrger-shtyge(-a)*
to pay **bezahlen** *betsahlen*
peace **der Frieden** *freeden*
peaceful **friedlich** *freedlikh*
peach **der Pfirsich(e)** *pfeer-zikh(a)*
pear **die Birne(n)** *beer-na(n)*
pedestrian **der Fußgänger(-)/ die Fußgängerin(nen)** *fooss-genger/fooss-genger-in(nen)*; pedestrian crossing **der Fußgängerüberweg(e)** *foossgeng-er-oohbervaig(a)*
pen **der Stift(e)** *shtift(a)*, or (ball-point) **der Kuli(s)** *koo-lee(s)*
pencil **der Bleistift(e)** *blye-shtift(a)*
people **die Leute [pl]** *loyta*
pepper (vegetable) **die Paprikaschote(n)** *papreekah-shawta(n)*, or (spice) **der Pfeffer(-)** *pfeffer*
perfect **perfekt** *pairfekt*
performance (cinema) **die Vorstellung(en)** *forshtel-oong(en)*, or (theatre) **die Aufführung(en)** *aowf-foohroong(en)*
perhaps **vielleicht** *fee-lye-kht*
period (menstruation) **die Tage* [pl]** *tahga*, or **die Periode(n)** *pairee-awda(n)*
person **der Mensch(en)** *mensh(en)*
petrol **das Benzin** *bentseen*; lead-free petrol **das bleifreie Benzin** *blye-fry-a bentseen*; petrol station **die Tankstelle(n)** *tank-shtella(n)*

phone booth **die Telefonzelle**

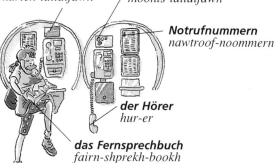

das Kartentelefon *karten-tailaifawn*
das Münztelefon *moonts-tailaifawn*
Notrufnummern *nawtroof-noommern*
der Hörer *hur-er*
das Fernsprechbuch *fairn-shprekh-bookh*
die Telefonkarte *tailaifawn-karta*

pharmacy **die Apotheke(n)** *ap-awtayka(n)*
philosophy **die Philosophie** *filo-zawfee*
phobia **die Phobie(n)** *faw-beeya(n)*
phone **das Telefon(e)** *tailai-fawn(a)*; phone booth **die Telefonzelle(n)** *tailai-fawn-tsella(n)*; phone call **der Anruf(e)** *an-roof(a)*; long-distance call **das Ferngespräch(e)** *fairn-geshpraikh(a)* (see also picture above)
to phone (make a call) **telefonieren** *tailai-fawneeren*, or (phone someone) **an'rufen** *an-roofen*
photo **das Foto(s)** *fawtaw(s)*
photographer **der Fotograf(en)** *fawtaw-grahf(en)*
to pick (choose) **aus'wählen** *aowss-vaylen*, or (gather) **pflücken** *pflooken*; to pick up (lift) **auf'heben** *aowf-hayben*
picnic **das Picknick(s)** *pik-nik(s)* (see also picture p. 88)

picture **das Bild(er)** *bilt* pl: *bilder*
pie **die Pastete(n)** *pastayta(n)*
piece **das Stück(e)** *shtook(a)*
pig **das Schwein(e)** *shvyne(-a)*
pill **die Tablette(n)** *tab-letta(n)*, or (contraceptive pill) **die (Antibaby)pille(n)** *(antee-baybee)-pilla(n)*
pineapple **die Ananas(-)** *an-an-as*
pink **rosa** *rawzah*
pity: it's a pity! **(wie) schade!** *(vee) shah-da*
place **der Ort(e)** *ort(a)*, or (seat) **der Platz(¨e)** *plats* pl: *pletsa*, or (position) **die Stelle(n)** *shtella(n)*; at my place **bei mir** *by meer*
plan **der Plan(¨e)** *plahn* pl: *play-na*
plane (aircraft) **das Flugzeug(e)** *floog-tsoyg(a)*
plant **die Pflanze(n)** *pflantsa(n)*
plaster (for cut or blister) **das Pflaster(-)** *pflaster*, or (cast) **der Gips(e)** *gips(a)*

picnic *das Picknick*

die Bank *bank*

der Abfalleimer
apfal-eye-mer
der Käse
kayza
das Wasser
vasser

das Brot
brawt

das Frisbee®
frizbee

Trauben [pl]
traowben
die Kühl-tasche
koohl-tasha

die Thermosflasche *zalahmee*
tairmoss-flasha

die Salami

der Korkenzieher
korken-tseeyer

das Taschenmesser
tashen-messer

die Küchenrolle
kookhen-rolla

plastic **Plastik~** *plastik,*
e.g. plastic bag **die Plastiktüte** *plastik-toota*
plate **der Teller(-)** *teller*
play (in theatre) **das Schauspiel(e)**
shaowshpeel(a)
to play **spielen** *shpeelen*
player **der Spieler(-)/die Spielerin(nen)**
shpeeler/shpeelerin(nen)
please **bitte** *bitta*
plug (water) **der Stöpsel(-)**
shturpsel, or (electrics) **der Stecker(-)** *shtekker*
plum **die Pflaume(n)**
pflaow-ma(n)
pocket **die Tasche(n)**
tasha(n); pocket-money **das Taschengeld** *tashen-ghelt*
poem **das Gedicht(e)**
gedikht(a)
to point (to/at) **zeigen auf**
[+ acc] *tsye-gun aowf*

police **die Polizei** *polit-sye;*
police officer **der Polizist(en)/ die Polizistin(nen)** *polits-isst(en)/politsistin(nen)*
polite **höflich** *hurflikh*
politics **die Politik** *politeek*
pollution **die Verschmutzung** *fair-shmootsoong*
poor **arm** *arm*
popular **beliebt** *beleept*
pork **das Schweinefleisch**
shvyne-a-flyshe
positive (not negative) **positiv** *paw-zit-eef*, or (sure)
völlig sicher *furlikh sikher*
possible **möglich** *murg-likh*
post (letters) **die Post**
posst; post-box **der Briefkasten(¨)** *breef-kasten pl: breef-kesten;*
post office **die Post** *posst,*
or **das Postamt(¨er)**
posstamt pl: posstemter

postcard **die Postkarte(n)**
posst-karta(n)
poster (picture) **das Poster(-)**
pawster, or (advertising) **das Plakat(e)** *plakaht(a)*
potato **die Kartoffel(n)**
kartoffel(n); mashed potato
der Kartoffelbrei *kartoffel-brye*, or **das Kartoffelpüree** *kartoffel-pooh-ray*
pound (UK money) **das Pfund(-)** *pfoond*
practical **praktisch** *praktish*
to practise **üben** *ooh-ben*
prawn (small) **die Krabbe(n)**
krabba(n), or (big) **die Garnele(n)** *garnayla(n)*
to prefer (something)
vor'ziehen *for-tsee-en*, or
(doing something) **... lieber**
... leeber, e.g. I prefer
painting **ich male lieber**
pregnant **schwanger**
shvanger
to prepare **vor'bereiten**
for-berye-ten
prescription **das Rezept(e)**
ray-tsept(a)
present (gift) **das Geschenk(e)** *gashenk(a)*
to press **drücken** *drooken*
to pretend **nur so tun** *noor zaw toon,* e.g. he's
pretending *er tut nur so*
pretty **hübsch** *hoobsh*
price **der Preis(e)** *price pl: prye-za*
printer **der Drucker(-)**
drooker
prison **das Gefängnis(se)**
gafengnis(sa), or **der Knast*** *k-nast*
private **privat** *preevaht*
prize **der Preis(e)** *price pl: prye-za*
problem **das Problem(e)**
praw-blaim(a)

programme **das Programm(e)** *prawgram(a)*, or (TV, radio) **die Sendung(en)** *zendoong(en)*
progress **der Fortschritt(e)** *fort-shritt(a)*
promise **das Versprechen(-)** *fair-shprekhen*
proof **der Beweis(e)** *bevice pl: bevyze-a*
prostitute (male) **der Strichjunge(n)** *strikh-yoong-a(n)*, or (female) **die Prostituierte(n)** *prostitoo-eerta(n)*
Protestant **evangelisch** *ayvangaylish*, or **protestantisch** *protestantish*
proud **stolz** *shtollts*
psychological **psychologisch** *psooh-khaw-law-gish*, or (in your mind) **psychisch** *psooh-khish*
pub **das Pub(s)** *pub(s)*, or **die Kneipe(n)** *k-nye-pa(n)*
public **öffentlich** *urfentlikh*
to pull **ziehen** *tseeyen*
puncture (flat tyre) **der Platten(-)** *platten*
pure **rein** *ryne*
purpose: on purpose **absichtlich** *ap-sikhtlikh*
purse **das Portemonnaie(s)** *port-monnay(s)*
to push **schieben** *sheeben*
to put **stellen** *shtellen*, or **tun*** *toon* (see also Verbs p. 58), or (in pocket/bag) **stecken** *shtekken*, or (in lying position) **legen** *laigen*; to put away **weg'räumen** *vaig-roymen*; to put down **hin'stellen** *hin-shtellen*; to put off (postpone) **verschieben** *fair-sheeben*, or (discourage) **ab'raten** *ap-rahten*, or (disgust) **an'ekeln**

an-aykeln, or (distract) **ab'lenken** *ap-lenken*; to put on (clothes) **an'ziehen** *an-tseeyen*; to put up with **sich ab'finden mit** [+ dat] *zikh ap-finden mit*
quality **die Qualität(en)** *kvalitayt(en)*
quantity **die Quantität(en)** *kvantitayt(en)*
to quarrel **sich streiten** *zikh shtrye-ten*
quarter **das Viertel(-)** *feertel* (see also time)
question **die Frage(n)** *frah-ga(n)*
queue **die Schlange(n)** *shlang-a(n)*
quick **schnell** *shnell*
quiet (calm) **ruhig** *roo-ikh*, or (not loud) **leise** *lye-za*; to be quiet **still sein** *shtill zyne*; Quiet! **Ruhe!** *roo-a*
quite (fairly) **ziemlich** *tseem-likh*, or (totally) **ganz** *gants*
race (running) **das Rennen(-)** *rennen*
racist **rassistisch** *rassistish*
racket (tennis etc.) **der Schläger(-)** *shlayger*
radiator (in car) **der Kühler(-)** *koohler*
radio **das Radio(s)** *rahdee-aw(s)*; radio cassette player **der (Radio) kassettenrecorder(-)** *(rahdee-aw)kassetten-raykorder*
railway **die Eisenbahn(en)** *eye-zun-bahn(en)*
rain **der Regen** *raygun*; it's raining **es regnet** *ess raygnet* (see also picture right)

rape **die Vergewaltigung(en)** *fair-gevaltigoong(en)*
rare (uncommon) **selten** *zelten*, or (steak) **blutig** *blootikh*
rash **der Ausschlag(̈e)** *aowss-shlahg pl: aowss-shlayga*
raw **roh** *raw*
razor **der Rasierer(-)** *raz-eerer*; razor blade **die Rasierklinge(n)** *razeer-kling-a(n)*
reaction **die Reaktion(en)** *ray-aktseeyawn(en)*
to read **lesen** *layzen*, or (aloud) **vor'lesen** *for-layzen*
ready **fertig** *fairtikh*
real **echt** *ekht*
really (truly) **wirklich** *veer-klikh*, or (extremely) **unheimlich*** *oon-hyme-likh*

rain **der Regen**

der Regenbogen *raigun-bawgun*
der Regenschirm *raigun-sheerm*

die Pfütze *pfootsa*
der Regenmantel *raigun-mantel*
der Regentropfen *raigun-tropfen*
der Gummistiefel *goommee-shteefel*

reason **der Grund(̈e)** *groont pl: groonda*
recently **neulich** *noylikh*
reception **der Empfang(̈e)** *emp-fang pl: emp-fenga*
recipe **das Rezept(e)** *ray-tsept(a)*
to recognize **erkennen** *airkennen*
to recommend **empfehlen** *emp-failen*
to record (tape) **auf'nehmen** *aowf-naimen*
red **rot** *rawt*
reduced (in sales) **herabgesetzt** *hair-ap-gazetst*
to refuse **ab'lehnen** *ap-lainen*
region **die Region(en)** *rayghee-awn(en)*
registered: by registered post **per Einschreiben** *pair ine-shrye-ben*
regular **regelmäßig** *raygul-may-ssikh*
rehearsal **die Probe(n)** *praw-ba(n)*
to relax **sich entspannen** *zikh ent-shpannen*

relaxed **entspannt** *ent-shpant*, or **locker*** *locker*
relieved **erleichtert** *air-lye-khtert*
religion **die Religion(en)** *rai-lighee-awn(en)*
to remember **sich erinnern an** [+ acc] *zikh air-innern an*
remote **abgelegen** *ap-galaigun*; remote control **die Fernbedienung(en)** *fairn-badeenoong(en)*
to rent **mieten** *mee-ten*; for rent **zu vermieten** *tsoo fair-mee-ten*
to repair **reparieren** *raipahreeren*
to repeat **wiederholen** *veeder-hawlen*
to reply **antworten** *ant-vorten*
research **die Forschung** *for-shoong*
reservation **die Reservierung(en)** *raizair-veeroong(en)*
reserved **reserviert** *raizair-veert*

responsible **verantwortlich** *fairant-vortlikh*
rest (break) **die Pause(n)** *paowza(n)*, or (remainder) **der Rest(e)** *rest(a)*
restaurant **das Restaurant(s)** *restawrang(s)*
result **das Ergebnis(se)** *air-gaybniss(a)*
return (ticket) **hin und zurück** *hin oont tsoorook*
revenge **die Rache** *rakha*
to reverse (car) **rückwärts fahren** *rook-vairts fahren*; to reverse charges (phone) **ein R-Gespräch führen** *ine air-geshpraikh foohren*
rice **der Reis** *rice*
rich **reich** *rye-kh*
rid: to get rid of (something) [acc +] **los'werden** *lawss-vairden*
ride: to go for a (bike/car) ride **eine Fahrt (mit dem Fahrrad/Auto) machen** *ine-a fart (mit daim far-raht/aowtaw) makhen*
ridiculous **lächerlich** *lekherlikh*

riding **Reiten [n]** *ryeten* (see picture left)
right (as in "the right side/shoe") **rechte(n)** *rekhta(n)*, or (correct) **richtig** *rikh-tikh*; to be right **recht haben** *rekht hahben*; that's right **das stimmt** *dass shtimmt*; on the right **rechts** *rekhts*; right-of-way **Vorfahrt** *for-fart*
riot **der Krawall(e)** *kra-val(a)*; to be a riot (scream) **zum Schießen sein*** *tsoom sheessen zyne*
to rip **reißen** *rye-sen*
ripe **reif** *rife*

riding **Reiten [n]**

der Schwanz *shvants*
die Reithose *ryte-hawza*
die Reitjacke *ryte-yakka*
der Sattel *zattel*
die Reitkappe *ryte-kappa*
die Satteldecke *zattel-dekka*
die Mähne *maina*
der Zaum *tsaowm*
die Zügel *tsoohgul*
der Huf *hoof*
die Reitpeitsche *ryte-pye-tsha*
der Steigbügel *shtyge-boohgul*
der Reitstiefel *ryte-shteefel*

rip-off it's a rip-off! **so ein Nepp!*** *zaw ine nep*
risk **das Risiko** *ree-zikaw* pl: **Risiken** *ree-zikun*
river **der Fluß pl: Flüsse** *flooss(a)*, or (large) **der Strom(¨e)** *shtrawm pl: shtrurma*
road **die Straße(n)** *shtrahssa(n);* road map **die Straßenkarte(n)** *shtrahssen-karta(n)*
roll (bread) **das Brötchen(-)** *brurt-khen*
romance (love affair/story) **die Liebesgeschichte(n)** *leebess-geshikhta(n)*
romantic **romantisch** *raw-man-tish*
roof **das Dach(¨er)** *dahkh* pl: *dekher;* roof rack **der Dachgepäckträger(-)** *dahkh-gepeck-traiger*
room **das Zimmer(-)** *tsimmer;* single/double room **das Einzel~/ Doppelzimmer** *ine-tsel-/ doppel-tsimmer;* twin room **das Zweibettzimmer** *tsvye-bet-tsimmer*
rope **das Seil(e)** *zyle(-a)*
rotten (off) **verdorben** *fair-dorben*, or (mean, unfair) **gemein** *ge-mine*
round (shape) **rund** *roont*, or (of drinks) **die Runde(n)** *roonda(n)*
roundabout **der Kreisverkehr(e)** *kryse-fairkahr(a)*
route **die Route(n)** *roota(n)*, or (bus) **die Linie(n)** *leeneeya(n)*
to row (a boat) **rudern** *roodern*
rubber band **das Gummiband(¨er)** *goomee-bant pl: goomee-bender*

sailing boat **das Segelboot**

der Spinnaker *shpinna-ker*

der Mast *mast*

das Hauptsegel *haowpt-zaigul*

der Baum *baowm*

die Kabine *kabeena*

der Anker *anker*

das Ruderboot *rooder-bawt*

der Fender *fender*   **der Riemen** *reemun*

die Schwimmweste *shvimvesta*

die Ruderpinne *rooderpinna*

das Ruder *rooder*

das Fall *fal*

der Klüver *kloohver*

die Boje *baw-ya*

rubbish (litter) **der Abfall(¨e)** *apfal pl: apfella*, or (garbage) **der Müll** *murl;* rubbish bin **der Abfalleimer(-)** *apfal-eye-mer*, or **der Mülleimer(-)** *murl-eye-mer;* to talk rubbish **Quatsch reden*** *kvatsh raiden*
rude **unhöflich** *oonhurflikh*, or (crude) **grob** *grawb*
ruin **die Ruine(n)** *roo-eena(n)*
rule **die Regel(n)** *raigul(n)*
rumour **das Gerücht(e)** *gerookht(a)*
to run **laufen** *laowfen*, or **rennen** *rennen;* to run away **weg'laufen** *vek-laowfen;* to run out (expire) **ab'laufen** *ap-laowfen*
rush hour **die Stoßzeit(en)** *shtawss-tsyte(-en)*

sad **traurig** *traow-rikh*
safe (out of danger) **sicher** *zikher*, or (for valuables) **der Safe(s)** *safe(s)*
safety **die Sicherheit** *zikher-hyte;* safety belt **der Sicherheitsgurt(e)** *zikher-hytes-goort;* safety pin **die Sicherheitsnadel(n)** *zikher-hytes-nahdel(n)*
sailing: sailing boat **das Segelboot(e)** *zaigul-bawt(a);* to go sailing **segeln** *zaigeln* (see picture above)
salad **der Salat(e)** *zalaht(a);* salad dressing (French dressing) **die Vinaigrette** *vinaigrett*
sale (reduced prices) **der Ausverkauf(¨e)** *aowss-fairkaowf pl: aowss-fairkoyfa;* for sale **zum Verkauf** *tsoom fair-kaowf*

salmon **der Lachs(e)** *lax(a)*
salt **das Salz(e)** *zalts(a)*
same **derselbe [m]** *dairzelba*, or **dieselbe [f]** *deezelba*, or **dasselbe [n]** *dasselba* , or **dieselben [pl]** *deezelben*
sand **der Sand** *zant*
sandwich **das Sandwich(es)** *zantvitsh(es)*, or **das Brot(e)** *brawt(a)*
sanitary towel **die Damenbinde(n)** *dahmen-binda(n)*
sarcastic **sarkastisch** *zahrkasstish*
Saturday **Samstag [m]** *zams-tahg*, or **Sonnabend [m]** *zonn-ahbent*
sauce **die Soße(n)** *zawssa(n)*
sausage (large) **die Wurst(̈e)** *voorst pl: voohrsta*, or (small) **das Würstchen(-)** *voohrst-khen*
to save (lives) **retten** *retten*, or (money, energy) **sparen** *shpahren*
savoury (not sweet) **nicht süß** *nikht zoohss*
to say **sagen** *zahg-en*
scared: to be scared (stiff) **(fürchterliche) Angst haben** *(foohrkh-terlikha) angst hahben*
scarf **der Schal(s)** *shahl(s)*
scary **gruslig** *groozlikh*
scenery (countryside) **die Landschaft(en)** *lant-shafft(en)*
school **die Schule(n)** *shoola(n)*
science **die Wissenschaft(en)** *vissen-shafft(en)*
scissors **die Schere(n)** *shaira(n)*
score (in a match) **der Spielstand** *shpeelshtant*

Scotland **Schottland [n]** *shot-lant*
Scottish **schottisch** *shottish*, or **der Schotte(n)/die Schottin(nen)** *shotta(n)/shottin(en)*
to scratch **kratzen** *kratsen*
to scream **schreien** *shrye-en*
screen (cinema) **die Leinwand** *lyne-vant*, or (TV, computer) **der Bildschirm(e)** *bilt-sheerm(a)*
scruffy **schlampig** *shlampikh*
sea **das Meer(e)** *mair(a)*, or **die See** *zay*
seafood **die Meeresfrüchte [pl]** *maires-frookhta*
seasick **seekrank** *zay-krank*
season **die Jahreszeit(en)** *yahres-tsyte(-en)*
seat (place) **der Platz(̈e)** *plats pl: pletsa*
second-hand **gebraucht** *gaibraowkht*
secret **das Geheimnis(se)** *ga-hyme-niss(a)*
secretary **der Sekretär(e)/die Sekretärin(nen)** *zekra-tair(a)/zekra-tairin(en)*
to see **sehen** *zayen*; to see again **wieder'sehen** *veeder-zayen;* see you soon **bis bald** *biss balt*
to seem **scheinen** *shy-nen*
selfish **egoistisch** *ego-istish*
self-service **die Selbstbedienung** *zelbst-badeenoong*
to sell **verkaufen** *fair-kaowfen*
to send **schicken** *shikken*
sense **der Sinn(e)** *zinn(a);* it doesn't make sense **es ist Unsinn** *ess ist oon-zin;* common sense **der Verstand** *fair-shtant*
sensible **vernünftig** *fair-noonftikh*

sensitive **empfindlich** *empfintlikh*
September **September [m]** *zeptember*
serious **ernst** *airnst*
service (in shop) **die Bedienung** *badeenoong*
sex (gender) **das Geschlecht(er)** *geshlekht(er),* or (intercourse) **der Verkehr** *fairkair,* or **der Sex*** *zex*
sexist **sexistisch** *zexistish*
sexy **sexy*** *zexee*
shade **der Schatten** *shatten*
shame what a shame! **(wie) schade!** *(vee) shahda*
shampoo **das Shampoo(s)** *shampoo(s)*
shape **die Form(en)** *form(en)*
to share **teilen** *tyle-en*
shattered (tired) **erledigt** *air-lay-dikht,* or (stunned) **platt*** *plat*
to shave **sich rasieren** *zikh razeeren*
shaving foam **der Rasierschaum** *razeer-shaowm*
she **sie** *zee*, or **die*** *dee*
sheet **das Bettlaken(-)** *betlahken*
shirt **das Hemd(en)** *hemt pl: hemden*
shock **der Schock(s)** *shok(s)*
shoe **der Schuh(e)** *shoo(-a);* athletics shoes **die Sportschuhe [pl]** *shport-shoo-a*
shop **das Geschäft(e)** *gesheft(a),* or (small) **der Laden(̈)** *lahden pl: layden*
shopping: to go shopping **einkaufen gehen** *ine-kaowfen gayen;* window shopping **einen Schaufensterbummel machen** *ine-en shaow-fenster-boommel makhen*

short **kurz** *koorts;* short cut **die Abkürzung(en)** *apkoohr-tsoong(en);* shortsighted **kurzsichtig** *koortszikhtikh*

shorts **die Shorts [pl]** *shorts*

shoulder **die Schulter(n)** *shoollter(n)*

to shout **schreien** *shrye-en,* or (call out) **rufen** *roofen,* or (yell) **brüllen** *broollen*

to show **zeigen** *tsye-gen;* to show off **an'geben** *angaiben*

shower **die Dusche(n)** *doosha(n);* to have a shower **sich duschen** *zikh dooshen*

shut **geschlossen** *geshlossen,* or **zu** *tsoo;* shut up! **halt den Mund!*** *halt dain moont*

shy **schüchtern** *shookh-tern*

sick (ill) **krank** *krank;* I feel sick **mir ist schlecht** *meer isst shlekht*

side **die Seite(n)** *zyte-a(n)*

sign (with hand etc.) **das Zeichen(-)** *tsye-khen,* or (on road etc.) **das Schild(er)** *shilt pl: shilder*

signature **die Unterschrift(en)** *oonter-shrift(en)*

Sikh **der/die Sikh(s)** *zeek(s)*

silent **still** *shtill;* to be silent (quiet) **still sein** *shtill zyne,* or (not to talk) **schweigen** *shvye-gun*

silly **albern** *albern,* or **doof*** *dawf*

simple **einfach** *ine-fakh*

since **seit [+ dat]** *zyte,* or (since then) **seitdem** *zyte-daim*

to sing **singen** *zing-en*

singer **der Sänger(-)/die Sängerin(nen)** *zeng-er/zeng-erin(nen)*

single (not double) **Einzel~** *ine-tsel* e.g. a single room **das Einzelzimmer,** or (not return) **einfach** *ine-fakh,* or (unmarried) **ledig** *laidikh,* or **single**

sister **die Schwester(n)** *shvesster(n)*

to sit (to sit down) **sich hin'setzen** *zikh hin-zetsen,* or (to be sitting down) **sitzen** *zitsen*

size **die Größe(n)** *grurssa(n)*

skate **der Schlittschuh(e)** *shlit-shoo(a)*

skating (on ice) **Eislaufen [n]** *ice-laowfen;* roller skating **Rollschuhlaufen [n]** *rolshoo-laowfen*

to ski **Ski laufen** *shee laowfen*

skiing **Skilaufen [n]** *shee-laowfen;* water-skiing **Wasserskilaufen [n]** *vasser-shee-laowfen;* ski resort **der Skiort(e)** *shee-ort(a)* (see also picture)

skin **die Haut** *haowt*

skirt **der Rock(¨e)** *rok pl: rooka*

sky **der Himmel(-)** *himmel*

slang **der Slang** *zleng*

to sleep **schlafen** *shlahfen*

skiing **Skilaufen [n]**

der Kabinenlift *kabeenenlift*

der Sessellift *zessellift*

der Schlitten *shlitten*

das Snowboard *snowboard*

der Monoski *monnaw-shee*

die Piste *pissta*

die Brille *brilla*

der Handschuh *hantshoo*

der Schlepplift *shlepplift*

der Skianzug *shee-antsoog*

der Skipass *shee-pas*

der Stock *shtok*

die Daunenjacke *daownen-yakka*

der Ski *shee*

der Skistiefel *shee-shteefel*

sleeper (bunk) *der Schlafplatz(¨e) shlahf-plats pl: shlahf-pletsa*
sleeping bag *der Schlafsack(¨e) shlahf-zak pl: shlahf-zekka*
slice *die Scheibe(n) shy-ba(n)*
to slip *aus'rutschen aowss-rootshen*
slob *der Schlamper(-)*/ die Schlamperin(nen) shlamper/shlamperin(nen)*
slowly *langsam lang-zam*
small *klein klyne*
smart (cunning) *raffiniert raffeeneert*, or (elegant) *schick shik*
smell *der Geruch(¨e) gerookh pl: gerooh-kha*, or (good) *der Duft(¨e) dooft(a)*, or (bad) *der Gestank geshtank*
to smell *riechen reekhen*
smile *das Lächeln lekheln*
to smoke *rauchen raowkhen*
smoking (sign) *Raucher raowkher*; non-smoking *Nichtraucher nikht-raowkher*
snack bar *die Imbissstube(n) imbiss-shtooba(n)*
snake *die Schlange(n) shlang-a(n)*
sneaky (cunning) *raffiniert raffeeneert*
to sneeze *niesen neezen*
snooty *hochnäsig hawkh-naizikh*
snow *der Schnee shnai* (see also weather)
so (as in "it's so easy") *so zaw*, or (as in "so, be quick") *also alzaw*; so-so (not great) *soso zaw-zaw*; so what? *na und? na-oont*

soap *die Seife(n) zye-fa(n)*; soap opera *die Serie(n) zaireeya(n)*, or *die Soap(s)* zoap(s)*
sober *nüchtern nooktern*
society *die Gesellschaft(en) gezell-shafft(en)*
sock *die Socke(n) zokka(n)*
soft *weich vye-kh*; soft drink *das alkoholfreie Getränk alkawhawl-fry-a getrenk*
software *die Software(s) zoft-vair(s)*
soldier *der Soldat(en)/die Soldatin(nen) zol-daht(en)/ zol-dahtin(nen)*
some (a few) *einige ine-iga*, or (certain, as in "some people") *manche mancha*
somebody *jemand yaimant*; somebody else *jemand anders yaimant anders*
something *etwas etvass*; something else *etwas anderes etvass anderes*
sometimes *manchmal manch-mahl*
somewhere *irgendwo eer-ghent-vaw*; somewhere else *woanders vaw-anders*
song *das Lied(er) leet pl: leeder*
soon *bald balt*
sorry (forgive me) *Verzeihung fair-tsye-oong*; I'm sorry *es tut mir Leid ess toot meer lyte*
sort *die Art(en) art(en)*, or *die Sorte(n) zorta(n)*
sound *der Laut(e) laowt(a)*, or (noise) *das Geräusch(e) geroysh(a)*, or (musical) *der Klang(¨e) klang pl: kleng-a*, or (TV, stereo) *der Ton(¨e) tawn pl: turna*
soup *die Suppe(n) zooppa(n)*

south *der Süden zoohden*; south of *südlich von* [+ dat] *zoohdlikh fon*
souvenir *das Souvenir(s) zoo-veneer(s)*
space (room) *der Platz plats*, or (outer space) *der Weltraum velt-raowm*
Spain *Spanien* [n] *shpahneeyen*
spare *übrig oohbrikh*; spare part *das Ersatzteil(e) airzats-tyle*; spare time *die Freizeit fry-tsyte*
to speak *sprechen shprekhen*
speaker (loudspeaker) *der Lautsprecher(-) laowt-shprekher*, or (with hi-fi) *die Box(en) box(en)*
speciality *die Spezialität(en) shpetsee-alitait(en)*
speed *das Tempo tempaw*; at full speed *mit vollem Tempo mit follem tempaw*
to spend (money) *aus'geben owss-gaiben*, or (time) *verbringen fair-bring-en*
spice *das Gewürz(e) gevoohrts(a)*
spicy *würzig voohrtsikh*
spider *die Spinne(n) shpinna(n)*
spinach *der Spinat shpinaht*
to spit *spucken shpooken*
to split (share out) *auf'teilen owf-tyle-en*, or (leave) *ab'hauen* ap-haowen*; to split up (relationship) *sich trennen zikh trennen*
to spoil (ruin) *verderben fair-dairben*, or (to damage) *beschädigen beshai-digen*
spontaneous *spontan shpon-tahn*
spoon *der Löffel(-) lurfel*

sport **der Sport** *shport;* sports centre **das Sportzentrum** *shport-tsentroom* **pl: Sportzentren** *shport-tsentren*

sporty (athletic) **sportlich** *shportlikh*

spot (pimple) **der Pickel(-)** *pickel,* or (place) **die Stelle(n)** *shtella(n)*

sprain (wrist/ankle) **die Verstauchung(en)** *fair-shtaowkh-oong(en)*

spring (season) **der Frühling** *froohling,* or (water) **die Quelle(n)** *kvella(n)*

spy **der Spion(e)/die Spionin(nen)** *shpee-yawn(a)/shpee-yawnin(en)*

square (in town) **der Platz(¨e)** *plats* pl: *pletsa*

stairs **die Treppe(n)** *treppa(n)*

stamp **die Briefmarke(n)** *breef-marka(n)*

to stand **stehen** *shtayen,* or (bear) **aus'stehen** *aowss-shtayen,* e.g. I can't stand ... **ich kann ... nicht ausstehen;** to stand up for **verteidigen** *fair-tye-digen*

star (in sky) **der Stern(e)** *shtairn(a),* or (person) **der Star(s)** *star(s)*

start **der Anfang(¨e)** *anfang* pl: *anfeng-a,* or (of race) **der Start(s)** *shtart(s)*

starter (first course) **die Vorspeise(n)** *for-shpye-za(n)*

station (train) **der Bahnhof(¨e)** *bahn-hawf* pl: *bahn-hurfa,* or (underground) **die Station(en)** *shtats-yawn(en),* or (radio) **der Sender(-)** *zender*

statue **die Statue(n)** *shtahtoo-a(n)*

to stay (remain) **bleiben** *blye-ben,* or (overnight) **übernachten** *oohber-nakhten,* or (several nights) **wohnen** *vawnen*

steak **das Steak(s)** *shtaik(s)*

to steal **stehlen** *shtailen*

step (footstep) **der Schritt(e)** *shritt(a),* or (stair) **die Stufe(n)** *shtoofa(n)*

stereotyped **stereotyp** *shtairayaw-toop*

stiff **steif** *shtyfe*

still (even now) **noch** *nokh,* or (stressed as in "he's *still* there") **immer noch** *immer-nokh*

to sting (insect) **stechen** *shtekhen,* or (jelly fish, nettles) **verbrennen** *fair-brennen*

stingy (not generous) **geizig** *guy-tsikh*

to stink **stinken** *shtinken*

to stir **um'rühren** *oom-roohren,* or (cause trouble) **auf'hetzen** *aowf-hetsen*

stomach **der Magen(¨)** *mahgen* pl: *maigen,* or (tummy) **der Bauch(¨e)** *baowkh* pl: *boykha;* upset stomach **der verdorbener Magen** *fair-dorbener mahgen* (see also ache picture)

stone **der Stein(e)** *shtyne(a)*

to stop (doing something) **auf'hören** *aowf-hur-en,* or (come to a halt) **an'halten** *an-halten,* or (prevent) **verhindern** *fair-hindern*

storm **der Sturm(¨e)** *shtoorm* pl: *shtoohrma,* or (with lightning) **das Gewitter(-)** *gevitter*

story **die Geschichte(n)** *geshikhta(n),* or (plot) **die Handlung(en)** *hantloong(en),* or (in paper) **der Artikel(-)** *arteekel*

straight (not curved) **gerade** *gerahda,* or (directly) **direkt** *deerekt,* or (old-fashioned) **konventionell** *konventsee-awnell;* straight ahead **geradeaus** *gerahda-aowss;* straight away **sofort** *zawfort*

strange **seltsam** *zelt-zahm*

street **die Straße(n)** *shtrahssa(n)*

stress **der Stress** *shtress*

strict **streng** *shtreng*

strike **der Streik(s)** *shtryke*

string **die Schnur(¨e)** *shnoor* pl: *shnoohra*

striped **gestreift** *geshtrye-ft*

strong **stark** *shtark*

stubborn **stur** *shtoor*

stuck-up **eingebildet** *ine-gebildet*

student **der Student(en)/ die Studentin(nen)** *shtoodent(en)/ shtoodentin(en)*

to study **studieren** *shtoodeeren*

stuff **das Zeug** *tsoyg,* or **der Kram*** *krahm*

stuffy (no air) **stickig** *shtickikh,* or (straight, old-fashioned) **angestaubt** *angeshtaowbt*

stunning (amazing) **verblüffend** *fair-blooffent,* or (gorgeous, terrific) **toll*** *toll*

stupid **dumm** *doomm,* or **blöd*** *blurd*

style **der Stil(e)** *shteel(a)*

subconsciously **im Unterbewusstsein** *im oonter-bevoosst-zyne*

subject **das Thema** *taimah* **pl: Themen** *taimen,* or (at school) **das Fach(¨er)** *fakh* pl: *fekher*

subtitle **der Untertitel(-)** *oonter-teetel*

suburbs **der Vorort(e)** *for-ort(a);* in the suburbs **am Stadtrand** *am shtatrant*
to succeed **Erfolg haben** *airfolg hahben*
success **der Erfolg(e)** *airfolg(a)*
suddenly **plötzlich** *plurtslikh*
to suffer **leiden** *lye-den*
sugar **der Zucker** *tsooker*
to suggest **vor'schlagen** *for-shlahgen*
suit **der Anzug(̈e)** *antsoog pl: antsoohga*
to suit: it suits you **es steht dir gut** *ess shtait deer goot*
suitcase **der Koffer(-)** *koffer*
summer **der Sommer(-)** *zommer*
sun **die Sonne(n)** *zonna(n);* sun block **der Sunblocker(-)** *zunblokker;* sun cream **die Sonnencreme(s)** *zonnen-kraim(s)*
to sunbathe **sich sonnen** *zikh zonnen* (see also picture below)

sunburned **sonnenverbrannt** *zonnen-fairbrant*
Sunday **Sonntag [m]** *zonntahg*
sunglasses **die Sonnenbrille(n)** *zonnen-brilla(n)*
sunny **sonnig** *zonnikh*
sunset **der Sonnenuntergang(̈e)** *zonnen-oontergang pl: zonnen-oontergenga*
sunstroke **der Sonnenstich** *zonnen-shtikh*
superficial **oberflächlich** *awber-flekhlikh*
supermarket **der Supermarkt (̈e)** *zoopermarkt pl: zoopermairkta*
superstitious **abergläubisch** *ahbergloybish*
supper **das Abendessen(-)** *ahbent-essen*
supplement **der Zuschlag(̈e)** *tsooshlahg pl: tsooshlayga*
to suppose **an'nehmen** *an-naimen*

supposed: to be supposed to **sollen** *zollen*
sure **sicher** *zikher*
to surf **surfen** *zoorfen* (see also picture below)
surprise **die Überraschung(en)** *oohber-rashoong(en)*
suspense **die Spannung** *shpannoong*
to swallow **schlucken** *shlooken*
to swap **tauschen** *taowshen*
to swear (promise) **schwören** *shvuren,* or (say bad words) **fluchen** *flookhen*
swearword **das Schimpfwort(̈er)** *shimfvort pl: shimfvurter*
to sweat **schwitzen** *shvitsen*
sweater **der Pullover(-)** *pull-awver,* or **der Pulli(s)*** *poolee(s)*
sweatshirt **das Sweatshirt(s)** *svet-shurt(s)*
sweet **die Süßigkeit(en)** *zoohssikh-kyte(-en),* or (sugary, cute) **süß** *zoohss*

to sunbathe *sich sonnen*   **to surf** *surfen*

das Badetuch *bahda-tookh*
der Sand *zant*
die Sonnenliege *zonnen-leega*
der Surfer *zoorfer*
der Sonnenschirm *zonnen-sheerm*
die Düne *doohna*
das Meer *mair*
der Windschutz *vint-shoots*
das Surfbrett *zoorf-brett*
die Sonnencreme *zonnen-kraim*
der Liegestuhl *leega-shtool*
die Sonnenbrille *zonnen-brilla*
die Welle *vella*
die Luftmatratze *looft-matratsa*
der Sonnenhut *zonnenhoot*

to swim *schwimmen*
shvimmen (see also picture below)

swimming *Schwimmen* [n]
shvimmen; swimming pool
das Schwimmbad(̈er)
shvimmbaht pl:
shvimmbayder

Switzerland *die Schweiz*
shvye-ts

swollen *geschwollen*
geshvollen

synagogue *die*
Synagoge(n) *zoona-*
gawga(n)

table *der Tisch(e)* *tish(a)*;
table football *Tischfußball*
[m] *tishfooss-bal*; table
tennis *Tischtennis* [n] *tish-*
tennis

to take *nehmen* *naimen* or
(to accompany) *bringen*
bring-en; to take away
weg'nehmen *vaig-naimen*,
or (food) *mit'nehmen* *mit-*
naimen; to take off (clothes)
aus'ziehen *owss-tseeyen*

to talk *sprechen*
shprekhen

tall *groß* *grawss*

tampon *der Tampon(s)*
tampon(s)

tanned *braun* brown

tap *der Wasserhahn(̈e)*
vasserhahn pl: *vasserhaina*

tape (cassette) *die*
Kassette(n) *kassetta(n)*

tart *die Torte(n)* *torta(n)*,
or *der Kuchen(-)* *kookhen*,
or (small) *das Törtchen(-)*
turtkhen

taste *der Geschmack(̈e)*
geshmak pl: *geshmekka*

to taste (as in "taste it")
probieren *probeeren*, or (as
in "it tastes sweet")
schmecken *shmekken*

tax *die Steuer(n)*
shtoyer(n)

taxi *das Taxi(s)* *taxee(s)*;
taxi stand *der Taxistand(̈e)*
taxee-shtant pl: *taxee-*
shtenda

tea (drink) *der Tee* *tay*, or
(afternoon snack of coffee
and cake) *Kaffee und*
Kuchen *kaffay oont*
kookhen, or (evening meal)
das Abendessen(-) *ahbent-*
essen

to teach *unterrichten*
oonter-rikhten, or (as in "it
teaches us") *lehren* *lairen*

teacher *der Lehrer(-)/die*
Lehrerin(nen) *lairer/*
lairerin(en)

team *das Team(s)* *teem(s)*,
or (sport) *die*
Mannschaft(en) *man-*
shafft(en)

to tease *necken* *necken*, or
(to be joking) *Spaß machen*
shpahss makhen

teenager *der Teenager(-)*
teenager, or *der Teen(s)**,
or *der/die Jugendliche(n)*
yoogunt-likha(n)

telephone (see phone)

television *der Fernseher(-)*
fairn-zayer; on television
im Fernsehen *im fairn-*
zayen

to tell (say) *sagen* *zahgun*,
or (recount) *erzählen* *air-*
tsailen; to tell off
aus'schimpfen *aowss-*
shimpfen

temperature *die*
Temperatur(en) *tempera-*
toor(en); to have a
temperature *Fieber haben*
feeber hahben

temporary *vorübergehend*
for-oohber-gayent

tennis *Tennis* [n] *tennis*

tense *gespannt* *gushpant*

tent *das Zelt(e)* *tselt(a)*

term (school) *das*
Halbjahr(e) *halp-yar(a)*, or
(six-month university term)
das Semester(-) *zay-mester*

terrible *schrecklich* *shrek-*
likh

terrific *sagenhaft* *zahgun-*
haft, or *super** *zoo-pair*

than *als* *alts*

to thank *danken* [+ dat]
danken

to swim *schwimmen*

die Bademütze
bahda-mootsa

die Badehose
bahda-hawza

Rückenschwimmen [n]
rooken-shvimmen

Kraul [n]
kraowl

der Schwimmflügel
shvimm-floogel

Brustschwimmen [n]
broost-shvimmen

der Badeanzug
bahda-antsoog

die Badeshorts
bahda-shorts

der Schwimmreifen
shvimm-rye-fen

der Bikini
beekeenee

97

thankful **dankbar** *dankbar*
thanks **danke** *danka*
thank you **danke** *danka*
that (as in "that's good")
das *dass;* that one
der/die/das da
dair/dee/dass dah (These
words change with gender
and case, see p. 56.)

what time is it?
wieviel Uhr ist es?

Viertel nach
neun
*feertel nakh
noyn*

drei Uhr
dry oor

zehn vor
acht
*tsain for
akht*

elf Uhr zwanzig
elf oor tsvantsikh

Viertel vor eins
feertel for ine-ts

halb elf†
halp elf

Mittag *mittahg*
Mitternacht *mitternakht*

the **der [m]** *dair,* or **die [f,
pl]** *dee,* or **das [n]** *dass*
(These words change with
gender and case, see p.56.)
theatre **das Theater(-)**
tay-ahter
their **ihr [m, n]** *eer,* or **ihre
[f, pl]** *eera* (**ihr/ihre** change
according to gender and
case in the same way as
ein/eine, see p. 57.)
then **dann** *dan*
there **dort** *dort,* or **da** *dah,*
or (with motion, as in "she
went there") **dorthin** *dorthin,* or **dahin** *dah-hin;*
there is/are **da ist/sind** *dah
isst/zint,* or **es gibt** [+ acc]
ess ghipt
these **diese** *deeza,* or **die
hier*** *dee heer* (These
words change with gender
and case, in the same way
as **die [pl]**, see p. 56.)
they **sie** *zee,* or **die*** *dee*
thick **dick** *dik,* or (stupid)
blöd* *blurd*
thief **der Dieb(e)/
die Diebin(nen)**
deeb(a)/deebin(en)
thin **dünn** *doon,* or (slim)
schlank *shlank*
thing **die Sache(n)**
zakha(n), or (object) **das
Ding(e)** *ding(a)*
things (belongings) **die
Sachen [pl]** *zakhan*
to think (believe) **glauben**
glaowben, or (consider)
denken *dengken,* or
(reckon) **meinen** *my-nen*
thirsty: to be thirsty **Durst
haben** *doorst hahben*
this **dieser [m]** *deezer,* or
diese [f] *deeza,* or **dieses
[n]** *deezess;* this one
der/die/das hier)
dair/dee/dass heer (These

words change with gender
and case, see p. 56.); this
morning/evening **heute
Morgen/Abend** *hoyta
morgan/ahbent*
those **die da** *dee dah* (**die**
changes with gender and
case, see p.56.)
thread **der Faden(¨)**
fahden pl: faiden
threat **die Bedrohung(en)**
bedrawoong(en)
to threaten **bedrohen**
bedrawen
thrill **der Nervenkitzel(-)**
nairven-kitsel
throat **die Kehle(n)**
kaila(n); sore throat
Halsschmerzen [pl] *halts-
shmairtsen*
through **durch** [+ acc]
doorkh
to throw **werfen** *vairfen;* to
throw away/out **weg'werfen**
vek-vairfen; to throw up (be
sick) **brechen** *brekhen*
thug **der Schlägertyp(en)**
shlaigertoop(en)
Thursday **Donnerstag [m]**
donnerstahg
ticket **die Karte(n)** *karta(n),*
or (travel) **die Fahrkarte(n)**
far-karta(n), or (plane) **der
Flugschein(e)** *floog-shyne(a)*
(travel) ticket machine **der
Fahrkartenautomat(en)**
farkarten-aowtaw-maht(en);
ticket office (theatre) **die
Kasse(n)** *kassa(n),* or (travel)
der Fahrkartenschalter(-)
farkarten-shallter
to tickle **kitzeln** *kitseln*
tie **die Krawatte(n)**
kravatta(n)
to tie **binden** *binden;* to tie
a knot **einen Knoten
machen** *ine-en k-nawten
makhen*

†In German you say "half before eleven" rather than "half past ten", e.g. **elf** = eleven but **halb elf** = half past ten.

tights *die Strumpfhose(n)* *shtroomf-hawza(n)*
till *die Kasse kassa(n)*
time *die Zeit(en) tsyte(-en),* or (occasion) *das Mal(e) mahl(a);* on time **pünktlich** *poonkt-likh;* what time is it? **wieviel Uhr ist es?** *veefeel oor isst es* (see also picture left)
timetable (transport) *der Fahrplan(̈e) far-plahn* pl: *far-plaina*
tiny winzig *vintsikh*
tip (end) *die Spitze(n) shpitsa(n),* or (money) *das Trinkgeld(er) trink-gelt* pl: *trink-gelder*
tissue (hanky) *das Papiertaschentuch(̈er) papeer-tashen-tookh* pl: *papeer-tashen-tooh-kher*
to (towards) *zu* [+ dat] *tsoo,* or (into, and with [f], [m] or [pl] countries) *in in,* or (with [n] countries) *nach nakh,* or (as in "ten to four") *vor for*
toast *der Toast(e) tawst(a)*
today heute *hoyta*
together zusammen *tsoo-zammen*
toilet *die Toilette(n) twaletta(n);* ladies/gents **Damen/Herren** *dahmen/hairen;* toilet paper *das Toilettenpapier twaletten-papeer*
toll *der Zoll(̈e) tsol* pl: *tsurla*
tomato *die Tomate(n) tawmahta(n);* tomato sauce *die Tomatensoße tawmahten-zawssa*
tomorrow morgen *morgan;* tomorrow morning **morgen früh** *morgan-frooh*

tongue *die Zunge(n) tsoong-a(n)*
tonight heute Abend *hoyta-ahbent*
tonsil *die Mandel(n) mandel(n)*
too (too much) *zu tsoo,* or (also) **auch** *aowkh*
tool *das Werkzeug(e) vairk-tsoyg(a)* (see picture below)
tooth *der Zahn(̈e) tsahn* pl: *tsaina* (see also ache picture)

tour (trip) *die Tour(en) toor(en),* or (music) *die Tournee(n) toor-nay(en);* package tour *die Pauschalreise(n) paow-shahl-rye-za(n)*
tourist *der Tourist(en)/ die Touristin(nen) toorist(en)/tooristin(nen);* tourist office *die Tourist-Information(en) toorist-informatsyown(en)*
tow schleppen *shleppen*

tools Werkzeug [n]

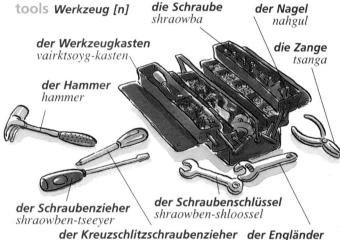

die Schraube *shraowba*
der Nagel *nahgul*
der Werkzeugkasten *vairktsoyg-kasten*
die Zange *tsanga*
der Hammer *hammer*
der Schraubenzieher *shraowben-tseeyer*
der Schraubenschlüssel *shraowben-shloossel*
der Kreuzschlitzschraubenzieher *kroyts-shlits-shraowben-tseeyer*
der Engländer *englender*

toothbrush *die Zahnbürste(n) tsahn-boohrsta(n)*
toothpaste *die Zahnpasta tsahn-pasta*
top (highest part) *die Spitze(n) shpitsa(n),* or (lid) *der Deckel(-) deckel,* or (clothing) *das Top(s) top(s)*
topic *das Thema(s) taima(s)*
torch (pocket) *die Taschenlampe(n) tashen-lampa(n),* or (flaming) *die Fackel(n) fakkel(n)*
to touch an'fassen *an-fassen*

towel *das Handtuch(̈er) hant-tookh* pl: *hant-toohkher*
town *die Stadt(̈e) shtat* pl: *shtetta;* town centre *die Stadtmitte shtat-mitta;* old town *die Altstadt alt-shtat;* town hall *das Rathaus(̈er) raht-haowss* pl: *raht-hoyzer*
toy(s) *das Spielzeug shpeel-tsoik(a)*
tracksuit *der Trainingsanzug(̈e) trainings-antsoog* pl: *trainings-antsoohga*

train **der Zug**

die Abfahrtstafel
apfahrts-tahfel
die Ankunftstafel
ankoonfts-tahfel

die Ankunftstafel | die Abfahrtstafel

der Fahrkartenschalter
farkarten-shalter

der Büfettwagen *boofett-vahgun*

der Wagen *vahgun*

Nichtraucher *nikhtraowkher*

der Speisewagen *shpy-za-vahgun*

der Liegewagen *leega-vahgun*

der Gepäckwagen
gepek-vahgun

der Bahnhofsvorsteher
bahnhawfs-forshtayer

traffic **der Verkehr**
fairkair; traffic jam **der
Stau(s)** *shtaow(s);* traffic
lights **die Ampel(n)**
ampel(n)
train **der Zug(̈e)** *tsoog*
pl: *tsooh-ga* (see also
picture above)
to train (for sport)
trainieren *traineeren*

trainers **die
Sportschuhe [pl]**
shport-shoo-a
tram **die
Straßenbahn(en)**
shtrahssenbahn(en);
tram stop **die
Straßenbahnhaltestelle
(n)** *shtrahssenbahn-
halta-shtella(n)*
tramp **der Tramp(s)**
tremp(s)
to translate
übersetzen *oohber-
zetsen*
to travel **reisen** *rye-zen*
travel agency **das
Reisebüro(s)** *rye-za-
boohraw(s)*
traveller **der/die
Reisende(n)** *rye-
zenda(n);* traveller's
cheque **der
Reisescheck(s)** *rye-za-
shek(s)*
tree **der Baum(̈e)**
baowm pl: *boyma*
trip (long) **die Reise(n)**
rye-za(n), or (short) **der
Ausflug(̈e)** *owss-floog*
pl: *owss-floohga*
trolley (for baggage)
der Gepäckwagen(-)
gepekvahgun, or
(supermarket) **der
Einkaufswagen(-)** *ine-
kaowfs-vahgun*
trouble **der Kummer**
koommer
trousers **die Hose(n)**
hawza(n)
true **wahr** *var*
to trust **vertrauen** [+ dat]
fair-traowen
to try (attempt) **versuchen**
fair-zookhen, or (test)
probieren *prawbeeren*
T-shirt **das T-Shirt(s)**

Tuesday **Dienstag [m]**
deens-tahg
tuna **der Thunfisch(e)**
toon-fish(a)
tunnel **der Tunnel(-)**
toonnel
to turn (rotate) **drehen**
drayen, or (to turn left/right
in car) **ab'biegen** *ap-
beegun;* to turn around/back
sich um'drehen *zikh oom-
drayen;* to turn down
(volume) **leiser stellen** *lye-
zer shtellen;* to turn off
(light/TV) **aus'machen**
owss-makhen; to turn on
(light/TV) **an'machen** *an-
makhen;* to turn up
(volume) **lauter stellen**
laowter shtellen, or (arrive)
auf'tauchen *owf-taowkhen*
twin (brother/sister) **der
Zwilling(e)** *tsvilling(a)*
typical **typisch** *toopish*
tyre **der Reifen(-)** *rye-fen;*
tyre pressure **der
Reifendruck** *rye-fen-drook*
ugly **hässlich** *hesslikh*
umbrella **der
Regenschirm(e)** *raigun-
sheerm(a)*
under **unter** [+ acc or dat]
oonter
underground (trains) **die
U-Bahn** *oo-bahn*
to understand **verstehen**
fair-shtayen
underwear **die
Unterwäsche** *oontervesha*
unemployed **arbeitslos**
arbytes-lawss
unemployment **die
Arbeitslosigkeit** *arbytes-
lawzikh-kyte*
unfortunately **leider** *lye-der*
United States **die
Vereinigten Staaten [pl]**
fair-ine-igten shtahten

university **die Universität(en)** *oo-nee-vair-zitait(en)*, or **die Uni(s)*** *oo-nee(s)*
unusual **ungewöhnlich** *oon-gevurnlikh*, or (exceptional) **außergewöhnlich** *owsser-gevurnlikh*
up: to go/walk up **hinauf'steigen** *hinaowf-shtye-gun*
urgent **dringend** *dring-ent*
us **wir** *veer*, or (in acc. and dat. case) **uns** *oonts* (for more about Cases, see p. 56)
to use **benutzen** *benootsen*
used: to be used to **an** [+acc] **gewöhnt sein an** (...) *gevurnt zyne*
useful **nützlich** *noots-likh*
useless (of no use) **nutzlos** *noots-lawss;* he/she is useless **er/sie ist zu nichts nütze** *air/zee ist tsoo nikhts nootsa*
usual **gewöhnlich** *gevurnlikh*
vacation **die Ferien [pl]** *faireeyen*
vaccination **die Impfung(en)** *imp-foong(en)*

valid **gültig** *gooltikh*
valuables **die Wertsachen [pl]** *vairt-zakhen*
vanilla **Vanille [f]** *vaneelya*
vegetables **das Gemüse** *gamoohza*
vegetarian **vegetarisch** *ve-get-ahrish*
very **sehr** *zair*, or **unheimlich*** *oon-hyme-likh*
video **das Video(s)** *vidai-aw(s)*
view (sight) **die Aussicht** *aow-sikht*
village **das Dorf(¨er)** *dorf* pl: *durfer*
vineyard **der Weinberg(e)** *vyne-bairg(a)*
to visit **besuchen** *bezookhen*
vital **unbedingt notwendig** *oonbedinkt nawt-vendikh*
volleyball **Volleyball [m]** *vollay-bal*
to vote **wählen** *vailen*
wacky **verrückt** *fair-rookt*
to waffle **schwafeln** *shvahfeln*
wage **der Lohn(¨e)** *lawn* pl: *lurna*
waist **die Taille(n)** *tie-ya(n)*

waistcoat **die Weste(n)** *vesta(n)*
to wait **warten** *varten*
waiter **der Kellner(-)** *kellner*
waiting room (station) **der Wartesaal** *varta-zahl* pl: **Wartesäle** *varta-zaila*, or (doctor's, dentist's) **das Wartezimmer(-)** *varta-tsimmer*
waitress **die Kellnerin(nen)** *kellnerin(en)*
to wake up (yourself) **auf'wachen** *owf-vakhen*, or (someone else) **auf'wecken** *owf-vekken*
Wales **Wales [n]** *vales*
walk **der Spaziergang(¨e)** *shpatseergang* pl: *shpatseergeng-a*, or (stroll) **der Bummel(-)** *boommel*, or (hike) **die Wanderung(en)** *vanderoong(en)*
to walk **gehen** *gayen*, or **laufen** *laowfen*
Walkman® **der Walkman(s)®** *vawkman(s)*
wallet **die Brieftasche(n)** *breef-tasha(n)*

water **das Wasser**

das Mineralwasser ohne Kohlensäure *minairahl-vasser awna kawlen-zoyra*

der Wasserfall *vasserfal*

das Mineralwasser mit Kohlensäure *minairahl-vasser mit kawlenzoyra*

ein Glas Wasser *ine glahss vasser*

wine **der Wein**

der Eiswürfel *ice-voohrfel*

der Rotwein *rawt-vine*

der Weißwein *vice-vine*

der Rosé *rawzay*

der Korkenzieher *korken-tseeyer*

der Korken *korken*

der Weinberg *vine-bairg*

ein Glas Wein *ine glahss vine*

101

to want **wollen** *vollen*
war **der Krieg(e)** *kreeg(a)*
warm **warm** *vahrm*
warning **die Warnung(en)** *vahrnoong(en)*
to wash **waschen** *vashen*, or (yourself) **sich waschen** *zikh vashen*; to wash up **ab'spülen** *ap-shpoohlen*
washing: washing machine **die Waschmaschine(n)** *vash-masheena(n)*; washing powder **das Waschpulver(-)** *vash-poolver*; washing-up liquid **das Spülmittel(-)** *shpoohl-mittel*
wasp **die Wespe(n)** *vesspa(n)*
waste (of time/money etc.) **die Verschwendung(en)** *fair-shvendoong(en)*
to waste **verschwenden** *fairshvenden*
watch **die Armbanduhr(en)** *armbant-oor(en)*, or **die Uhr(en)** *oor(en)*
to watch (look at) **zu'schauen** *tsoo-shaowen*
water **das Wasser** *vasser* (see also picture p. 101)
waterproof **wasserdicht** *vasserdikht*
way (direction) **die Richtung(en)** *rikhtoong(en)*, or (route) **der Weg(e)** *vaig(a)*, or (manner) **die Art und Weise** *art oont*

vye-za; no way! **auf keinen Fall!** *owf kye-nen fal;* get out of the way! **weg da*!** *vek dah;* by the way **übrigens** *ooh-brigents*
we **wir** *veer*
to wear **tragen** *trahgen;* to wear out (exhaust) **erschöpfen** *air-shurpfen*, or (overuse) **ab'nutzen** *ap-nootsen*
weather **das Wetter** *vetter;* what's the weather like? **wie ist das Wetter?** *vee isst dass vetter;* weather forecast **die Wettervorhersage(n)** *vetter-forhair-zahga(n)* (see also picture below)
Wednesday **Mittwoch [m]** *mitvokh*
week **die Woche(n)** *vokha(n)*
weekend **das Wochenende(n)** *vokhen-enda(n)*
weight **das Gewicht(e)** *gevikht(a);* to lose weight **ab'nehmen** *ap-naimen;* to put on weight **zu'nehmen** *tsoo-naimen*
weird (strange) **seltsam** *zeltzahm*, or (creepy) **unheimlich** *oon-hyme-likh*
welcome **willkommen** *villkommen;* you're welcome! **bitte sehr!** *bitta zair*

well **gut** *goot;* well-cooked **durch(gebraten)** *doorkh(gebrahten);* well-known **bekannt** *bekant;* to feel well **sich wohl fühlen** *zikh vawl foohlen*
Welsh **walisisch** *valeezish*, or **der Waliser(-)/ die Waliserin(nen)** *valeezer/valeezerin(en)*
west **der Westen** *vesten*
wet **nass** *nass*
what **was** *vass;* what for? **wozu?** *vawtsoo;* what about? **worüber?** *vawroohber*
wheel **das Rad(̈er)** *raht* pl: *raider;* steering wheel **das Lenkrad(̈er)** *lenkraht* pl: *lenkraider*
wheelchair **der Rollstuhl(̈e)** *rol-shtool* pl: *rol-shtooh-la*
when (at what time?) **wann?** *van,* or (if, whenever) **wenn** *ven*
where **wo** *vaw;* where from? **woher?** *vawhair;* where to? **wohin?** *vawhin*
which **welcher [m]** *velkher,* or **welche [f, pl]** *velkha,* or **welches [n]** *velkhess* (These words change according to gender and case in the same way as **der, die** and **das**, see 56.)
while (at same time) **während** *vairent*

what's the weather like?
wie ist das Wetter?

es regnet *ess raignet*

es ist bedeckt *ess isst bedekt*

es ist sonnig *ess isst zonnikh*

es schneit *ess shnyte*

white **weiß** *vice*
who **wer** *vair*, or (in acc. case) **wen** *vain*, or (in dat. case) **wem** *vaim*
whole **ganz** *gants*
why **warum** *vahroomm*
wide **breit** *bryte*
wild (not tame) **wild** *vilt*, or (angry) **wütend** *voohtent*
to win **gewinnen** *gavinnen*
wind **der Wind(e)** *vint pl: vinda* (see also picture below)
window **das Fenster(-)** *fenster*
windscreen **die Windschutzscheibe(n)** *vintshoots-shy-ba(n)*
windsurfer (board) **das Surfbrett(er)** *zoorf-bret(er)*
wine **der Wein(e)** *vine(-a)* (see also picture p. 101)
winter **der Winter(-)** *vinter*
wish **der Wunsch(̈e)** *voonsh(a)*; best wishes **herzliche Grüße** *hairtslikha groohssa*
to wish (hope for) **wünschen** *voontschen*
with **mit** [+ dat] *mit*
without **ohne** [+ acc] *awna*
woman **die Frau(en)** *fraow(en)*, or (lady) **die Dame(n)** *dahma(n)*
wonderful **wunderbar** *voonderbar*

wood (material) **das Holz (̈er)** *hollts pl: hurltser*, or (forest) **der Wald(̈er)** *valt pl: velder*
wool **die Wolle(n)** *volla(n)*
word **das Wort(̈er)** *vort pl: vurter*; word processing **die Textverarbeitung** *textfair-ar-bye-toong*
work **die Arbeit(en)** *ar-byte(-en)*
to work **arbeiten** *ar-byte-en*, or (function) **funktionieren** *foonktsee-aw-neeren*, or (go well) **klappen*** *klappen*
world **die Welt(en)** *velt(en)*
worried **besorgt** *bezorkt*
worry **die Sorge(n)** *zorga(n)*; not to worry! **keine Sorge!** *kye-na zorga*
worse **schlimmer** *shlimmer*
to write **schreiben** *shrye-ben*
writer **der Schriftsteller(-)/ die Schriftstellerin(nen)** *shrift-shteller/shrift-shtellerin(en)*
wrong (incorrect) **falsch** *falsh*, or (unfair) **ungerecht** *oon-gerekht*; to be wrong (not right) **Unrecht haben** *oon-rekht hahben*, or (mistaken) **sich täuschen** *zikh toyshen*; what's wrong? **was ist los?** *vass isst lawss*

year **das Jahr(e)** *yar(a)*
yellow **gelb** *gelp*
yes **ja** *yah*, or (after negative) **doch** *dokh*
yesterday **gestern** *guess-tern*; the day before yesterday **vorgestern** *for-guesstern*
yet: not yet **noch nicht** *nokh nikht*
yogurt **der Joghurt(-)** *yogoort*
you (casual) **du** *doo*, or (casual [pl]) **ihr** *eer*, or (polite) **Sie** *zee*, or (in acc. case) **dich** *dikh*, or **euch** *oykh*, or **Sie** *zee*, or (in dat. case) **dir** *deer*, or **euch** *oykh*, or **Ihnen** *eenen* (for more about Cases, see p. 56)
you (one, as in "you/one can never tell") **man** *man*
young **jung** *yoong*; young people **die Jugend** *yoogent*
your (casual) **dein [m, n]** *dine*, or **deine [f, pl]** *dine-a*, or (casual plural) **euer [m, n]** *oyer*, or **eure [f, pl]** *oyra*, or (polite) **Ihr [m, n]** *eer*, or **Ihre [f, pl]** *eera* (These words change in the same way as **ein/eine**, see p. 57.)
youth hostel **die Jugendherberge(n)** *yoogunt-hairbairga(n)*
zip **der Reißverschluss(̈e)** *rice-fairshlooss(a)*

es gibt ein Gewitter *ess gipt ine gevitter*

es ist kalt *ess isst kalt*

es ist sehr warm *es isst zair vahrm*

es ist windig *ess isst vindikh*

ab *from*

ab'biegen *to turn*

der Abend(e) *evening;* **zu Abend essen** *to have dinner*

das Abendessen(-) *supper*

das Abenteuer(-) *adventure*

aber *but, or however*

abergläubisch *superstitious*

ab'fahren *to leave*

die Abfahrt(en) *departure*

die Abfahrtstafel(n) *departure board*

der Abfall(¨e) *rubbish, or litter, or waste*

die Abfallbeseitigung *rubbish/garbage disposal*

der Abfalleimer(-) *rubbish bin*

die Abfertigung (airport) *check-in*

sich ab'finden mit *to put up with*

ab'fliegen (plane) *to take off*

der Abflug(¨e) *departure*

die Abflughalle(n) *departure lounge*

abgeschaltet *(switched) off*

ab'hauen* *to clear off, or to split (leave);* **hau ab!*** *get lost!*

das Abitur *German exams taken at end of secondary/high school*

die Abkürzung(en) *short cut, or abbreviation*

ab'laufen *to run out* (expire)

ab'lehnen *to refuse*

ab'lenken *to distract*

ab'nehmen *to lose weight*

ab'nutzen *to wear out* (overuse)

ab'raten *to put off, or to warn*

ab'sagen *to cancel*

ab'schließen *to lock*

ab'setzen *to take off* (hat), *or to drop off* (a person)

absichtlich *on purpose*

ab'spülen *to wash up*

die Abspüllösung(en) (contact lens) *rinsing solution*

adoptiert *adopted*

die Adresse(n) *address*

ähnlich (wie) *similar (to)*

aktuell *up to date*

der Akzent(e) *accent*

akzeptieren *to accept*

albern *silly*

das Album (pl: Alben) *album*

der Alkohol *alcohol*

alkoholfrei *non-alcoholic*

alkoholisch *alcoholic*

alle *all, or everybody*

allein *alone, or by yourself*

die Allergie(n) *allergy*

alles *all of it, or everything*

allgemein *general*

der Alltag *everyday life*

der Alptraum(¨e) *nightmare*

als *when, or than*

also *so, or therefore, or right*

alt *old;* **wie alt ...?** *how old ...?*

das Alter(-) *age*

der Altglascontainer(-) *bottle bank*

altmodisch *old-fashioned*

die Altstadt *old town*

Amerika [n] *America*

der Amerikaner(-)/die Amerikanerin(nen) *American*

amerikanisch *American*

die Ampel(n) *traffic lights*

das Amtszeichen *dialling tone*

sich amüsieren *to have fun*

an *on, or at*

die Ananas(-) *pineapple*

an'bieten *to offer*

andere (or **anderer** or **anderes**) *other*

ändern *to change*

anders als *different from/to*

anderswo *somewhere else*

die Änderung(en) *change*

an'ekeln *to put off* (disgust)

der Anfall(¨e) *fit;* **der epileptische Anfall** *epileptic fit*

der Anfang(¨e) *start, or beginning*

der Anfänger(-)/die Anfängerin(nen) *beginner*

an'fassen *to touch*

an'geben *to show off, or to boast, or* (sport) *to serve*

angeln *to fish*

an'greifen *to attack*

die Angst(¨e) *fear;* **Angst haben** *to be scared*

an'halten *to stop*

der Anhänger(-)/die Anhängerin(nen) *supporter, or* [m] (car) *trailer, or* [m] (jewellery) *pendant*

der Anker(-) *anchor*

an'kommen *to arrive;* **es kommt darauf an** *it depends*

die Ankunftstafel(n) *arrivals board*

an'machen *to switch on, or* (slang) *to chat up*

die Anmeldung(en) *registration*

an'nehmen *to accept, or to suppose*

die Annonce(n) *advertisement*

an'quatschen* *to chat up*

der Anruf(e) *phone call*

der Anrufbeantworter(-) *answering machine*

an'rufen *to phone*

der Anschluß *connection*

die Ansichtskarte(n) *postcard (with picture)*

ansteckend *contagious, or infectious*

der Anstecker(-) *badge*

die Antibabypille(n) *contraceptive pill*

das Antibiotikum
(pl: Antibiotika) *antibiotic*
antiseptisch *antiseptic*
die Antwort(en) *answer*
antworten *to reply*
die Anzahlung(en) *deposit*
die Anzeige(n)
advertisement, or (police)
report, or (computer) *display*
sich an'ziehen *to get dressed*
der Anzug("e) *suit*
der Apfel(") *apple*
der Apfelkuchen(-) *apple
cake,* or *apple tart*
die Apfelsine(n) *orange*
der Apfelstrudel(-) *apple
strudel* (apple in puff pastry)
der Apfelwein *cider*
die Apotheke(n) *pharmacy*
die Aprikose(n) *apricot*
April [m] *April*
die Arbeit(en) *job,* or *work*
arbeiten *to work*
arbeitslos *unemployed*
die Arbeitslosigkeit
unemployment
ärgerlich *annoying*
ärgern *to annoy;* **sich
ärgern** *to be/get annoyed*
arm *poor*
der Arm(e) *arm*
das Armband("er) *bracelet*
die Armbanduhr(en)
watch
der Ärmel(-) *sleeve*
der Ärmelkanal *the Channel*
der Armreifen(-) *bangle*
die Art(en) *sort,* or *way,* or
manner
der Artikel(-) *article*
**der Arzt("e)/die
Ärztin(nen)** *doctor*
der Aschenbecher(-)
ashtray
Asien [n] *Asia*
**der Asylant(en)/die
Asylantin(nen)** *asylum
seeker*

der Atem *breath*
der Atemregler(-)
regulator
atmen *to breathe*
attraktiv *attractive*
auch *also,* or *too*
auf *on,* or *up,* or *open;*
auf ... zu *towards*
die Aufführung(en)
(theatre) *performance*
aufgeregt *excited,* or *nervous*
aufgeweckt *bright* (clever)
auf'hängen *to hang* (up)
auf'heben *to keep,* or *to
pick up* (lift)
auf'hetzen *to stir* (up)
auf'hören *to stop*
der Aufkleber(-) *sticker*
auf'legen *to hang up*
(phone)
auf'machen *to open*
die Aufnahme(n) *photo,*
or *recording*
auf'nehmen *to record*
auf'passen *to pay attention;*
auf'passen auf *to watch,* or
to keep an eye on, or *to look
after*
sich auf'regen *to get
excited*
aufregend *exciting*
auf'stehen *to get up*
auf'tauchen *to turn up*
(arrive)
auf'teilen *to split* (share
out)
auf'wachen *to wake up*
auf'wärmen *to warm up*
auf'wecken *to wake*
(someone) *up*
auf Wiederhören *goodbye*
(on the phone)
auf Wiedersehen *goodbye*
der Aufzug("e) *lift*
das Auge(n) *eye*
der Augenblick(e)
moment; **Augenblick mal!**
just a moment!

augenscheinlich *evident(ly)*
August [m] *August*
aus *from,* or *of;* **von mir aus**
I don't mind
aus'bilden *to train,* or *to
educate*
die Ausbildung *education*
(studies), or *training*
die Ausfahrt(en)
motorway exit
aus'flippen* *to flip,* or *to
freak out*
der Ausflug("e) *trip*
der Ausgang("e) *result,* or
exit, or (airport) *departure
gate*
aus'geben *to spend*
(money)
ausgebucht *booked up*
ausgeschaltet (switched)
off
ausgezeichnet *excellent*
die Auskunft("e)
information, or *inquiries*
**das Ausland: im/ins
Ausland** *abroad*
**der Ausländer(-)/die
Ausländerin(nen)**
foreigner
aus'machen *to switch off,*
or *to arrange,* or *to fix*
aus'nutzen *to take
advantage of*
aus'richten *to tell;* **etwas
aus'richten** *to take a
message*
sich aus'ruhen *to rest*
die Ausrüstung(en)
equipment
aus'schimpfen *to tell off*
der Ausschlag("e) *rash*
aus'sehen *to look* (as in "to
look good/ill")
außer *except*
außergewöhnlich *unusual*
die Aussicht *view*
der Austausch *exchange*
(holiday)

aus'stehen to stand (endure), e.g. **ich kann ... nicht ausstehen** I can't stand ...
aus'steigen aus to get off (bus, train), or to drop out of (college/a competition)
die Ausstellung(en) exhibition
Australien [n] Australia
der Australier(-)/die Australierin(nen) Australian
australisch Australian
der Ausverkauf("e) sale
aus'wählen to pick (choose)
der Ausweis(e) pass, or identity card
aus'ziehen to take off (clothes), or to move out
das Auto(s) car
die Autobahn(en) motorway
der Autor(en)/die Autorin(nen) author
die Avocado(s) avocado

die Bäckerei(en) baker's
der Backofen(˙) oven
das Bad("er) bath
der Badeanzug("e) swimming costume
die Badehose(n) swimming trunks
der Bademeister(-)/die Bademeisterin(nen) lifeguard
die Bademütze(n) swimming cap
die Badeshorts [pl] bermuda swimming trunks
das Badetuch("er) bath towel
das Badezimmer(-) bathroom
die Bahn railway
der Bahnhof("e) station (train)

der Bahnhofsvorsteher(-) station master
bald soon
der Balkon(e) balcony
der Ball("e) ball
das Ballett ballet
die Banane(n) banana
die Band(s) band
die Bank(en) bank
die Bank("e) bench
die Bar(s) bar
das Bargeld cash (money)
der Bart("e) beard
die Batterie(n) battery
der Bauch("e) stomach
Bauchschmerzen [pl] stomach ache
der Baum("e) tree, or (sailing) boom
die Baumwolle cotton
der Bazillus (pl: Bazillen) bug (germ)
beabsichtigen to intend
beantworten to answer
bedecken to cover
bedeckt (weather) overcast
bedeuten to mean
bedienen to serve; **sich bedienen** to help yourself
die Bedienung service
bedrohen to threaten
die Bedrohung(en) threat
sich beeilen to hurry
der Befehl(e) order, or (computer) command
behalten to keep
behindert disabled
bei at, e.g. **bei Anna** at Anna's, or near, e.g. **bei Bonn** near Bonn
beide both
das Bein(e) leg
das Beispiel(e) example
beißen to bite
bekannt famous, or well-known
der/die Bekannte(n) friend
sich beklagen to complain

bekommen to get (obtain)
beleidigt offended
die Beleidigung(en) insult
beliebt popular
benutzen to use
das Benzin petrol
bequem comfortable
der Berg(e) mountain
das Bergsteigen mountain climbing
berühmt famous
sich besaufen* to get drunk
beschädigen to damage
beschäftigt busy
beschimpfen to swear at
beschließen to decide
beschreiben to describe
besessen obsessed
die Besichtigungstour(en) sightseeing tour
der Besitzer(-)/die Besitzerin(nen) owner
besoffen* drunk
besorgt worried
besser better
beste (or bester or bestes) best
bestehen to pass (an exam); **auf (...) bestehen** to insist on (something); **bestehen aus** to consist of
bestellen to order
die Bestellung(en) order
der Besuch(e) visit, or visitor(s)
besuchen to visit
sich betrinken to get drunk
betrunken drunk
das Bett(en) bed
das Bettlaken(-) sheet
der Bettler(-)/die Bettlerin(nen) beggar
die Beule(n) bump
bevor before
bewegen to move
der Beweis(e) proof
bezahlen to pay

der BH(-) *bra*
die Bibliothek(en) *library*
das Bier(e) *beer;* **helles Bier** *lager*
der Bikini(s) *bikini*
das Bild(er) *picture*
die Bildhauerei *sculpture*
der Bildschirm(e) *screen* (TV, computer)
billig *cheap*
die Binde(n) *sanitary towel*
binden *to tie;* **sich binden** *to commit yourself*
die Bindung(en) *binding*
der Bioladen(¨) *health food shop*
biologisch abbaubar *biodegradable*
die Birne(n) *pear*
bis bald *see you soon*
bißchen: ein bißchen *a bit,* or *a little*
bitte *please,* or *you're welcome;* **wie bitte?** *pardon?*
bitter *bitter* (taste)
die Blase(n) *blister,* or *bladder,* or *bubble*
das Blatt(¨er) *leaf,* or *sheet* (of paper)
blau *blue,* or (slang) *drunk*
bleiben *to stay* (remain)
bleifrei *lead-free*
der Bleigürtel(-) *weight belt*
der Bleistift(e) *pencil*
blind *blind*
der Blitz(e) *lightning,* or (camera) *flash*
blöd* *stupid*
blond *blond*
der Blouson(s) *jacket* (bomber-style)
die Blume(n) *flower*
das Blut *blood*
der Blutdruck *blood pressure*
bluten *to bleed*
blutig *bloody,* or (steak) *rare*

Bock: keinen Bock haben* *not to feel like* (doing something)
der Boden *ground*
die Bohne(n) *bean*
die Boje(n) *buoy*
das Boot(e) *boat*
der Boss(e)* *boss*
böse *angry,* or *bad,* or *evil*
die Botschaft(en) *embassy*
das Bowling *bowling*
die Box(en)* *speaker* (hi-fi)
Brat~ *fried* e.g. **Bratwurst** *fried sausage*
der Brauch(¨e) *custom*
brauchen *to need*
braun *brown*
brechen *to break,* or *to throw up* (be sick)
breit *wide*
die Bremse(n) *brake*
brennen *to burn*
der Brief(e) *letter*
der Brieffreund(e)/die Brieffreundin(nen) *pen pal*
der Briefkasten(¨) *post-box*
die Briefmarke(n) *stamp*
die Brieftasche(n) *wallet*
die Brille(n) *glasses*
bringen *to bring,* or *to take*
die Brosche(n) *brooch*
das Brot *bread,* or *loaf*
das Brötchen(-) *(bread) roll*
die Brücke(n) *bridge*
der Bruder(¨) *brother*
brüllen *to shout*
der Brunnen(-) *fountain*
die Brust(¨e) *breast,* or *chest*
Brustschwimmen [n] *breast-stroke*
das Buch(¨er) *book*
buchen *to book*
die Buchhandlung(en) *bookshop*
der Buchstabe(n) *letter* (of alphabet)

der Buckel(-) *bump,* or *hump*
der Büfettwagen(-) *buffet car*
das Bügeleisen(-) *iron* (for clothes)
der Bummel(-) *walk,* or *stroll*
bunt *colourful*
die Burg(en) *castle*
der Bürgersteig(e) *pavement*
das Büro(s) *office*
die Bürste(n) *brush*
der Bus(se) *bus*
der Busbahnhof(¨e) *bus station*
der Busen(-) *bosom*
die Bushaltestelle(n) *bus stop*
die Butter *butter*

das Café(s) *café*
der Campingplatz(¨e) *campsite*
die Cashewnuss(¨e) *cashew nut*
das Cello(s) *cello*
der Champignon(s) *mushroom*
die Chance(n) *chance*
das Chaos *chaos*
der Charakter(e) *personality*
checken* *to check*
Cheerleader *cheerleader*
der Chef(s)/die Chefin(nen) *boss*
Chips *crisps*
der Chor(¨e) *choir*
christlich *Christian*
der Code(s) *code*
der Comic(s) *comic book*
cool* *cool,* or *laid-back,* or *trendy,* or *casual*
der Cousin(s)/die Cousinin(nen) *cousin*
die Creme(s) *cream*

da *there;* **da ist/sind** *there is/are;* **der/die/das da** *that one*
das Dach(¨er) *roof*
der Dachgepäckträger(-) *roof rack*
daheim *at home*
dahin *there*
dahinter kommen* *to get the low-down*
die Dame(n) *lady*
Damen *ladies*
Dänemark [n] *Denmark*
dankbar *grateful*
danke *thanks*
danken *to thank*
dann *then*
das *the, or it, or that*
das Date(s)* *date (meeting with boy/girlfriend)*
das Datum (pl: Daten) *date*
die Daunenjacke(n) *quilted jacket*
DB (Deutsche Bahn) [f] *German railways*
das Deck(s) *deck*
die Decke(n) *blanket*
der Deckel(-) *top, or lid*
dein (or **deine**) *your* (casual)
die Demokratie *democracy*
die Demonstration(en) *demonstration*
denken *to think* (consider)
das Denkmal(¨er) *monument*
denn *because*
der Deodorant(s) *deodorant*
deprimierend *depressing*
der *the, or* (slang) *it, or he, or her, or him*
deutsch *German;* **auf Deutsch** *in German*
der/die Deutsche(n) *German*
Deutschland [n] *Germany*
Devisen [pl] *foreign exchange*

Dezember [m] *December*
das Dia(s) *(photographic) slide*
der Dialekt(e) *dialect*
die Diät(en) *diet*
dich *you*
dick *fat, or thick*
die *the, or* (slang) *her, or she, or them, or they, or it;* **die da** *those*
der Dieb(e)/die Diebin(nen) *thief*
Dienstag [m] *Tuesday*
diese (or **dieser** or **dieses**) *this, or these*
der Diesel *diesel*
das Ding(e) *thing*
direkt *direct, or straight*
die Diskette(n) *floppy disk*
die Diskriminierung(en) *discrimination*
diskutieren *to discuss*
doch *yes*
der Dom(e) *cathedral*
Donnerstag [m] *Thursday*
doof* *stupid*
Doppel~ *double, e.g.* **das Doppelbett** *double bed*
das Dorf(¨er) *village*
dort *there*
die Dose(n) *can*
der Dosenöffner(-) *can opener*
der Drachen(-) *kite*
Drachenfliegen [n] *hang-gliding*
dran: du bist dran *it's your go*
draußen *outside*
das Dreckloch(¨er)* *dump*
drehen *to turn, or* (film) *to shoot*
drin* *inside*
dringend *urgent*
drinnen *indoors*
die Droge(n) *drug*
der/die Drogensüchtige(n) *drug addict*

die Drogerie(n) *chemist's*
drüben *over there, or on the other side*
drücken *to press*
der Drucker(-) *printer*
der Druckmesser(-) *pressure gauge*
du *you* (see also p. 57)
der Duft(¨e) *smell* (good)
duften *to smell* (good)
dumm *stupid*
Dummkopf(¨e)* *idiot*
die Düne(n) *dune*
dunkel *dark*
dünn *thin, or* (drink) *weak*
durch *through, or* (caused) *by*
durch'drehen* *to crack, or to freak out*
durcheinander *mixed up*
das Durcheinander *chaos, or mess*
durcheinander bringen *to mix up, or to confuse*
Durchfall [m] *diarrhoea*
durch'fallen *to fail* (exam)
durchgebraten *well-cooked*
durchschnittlich *average*
Durst: Durst haben *to be thirsty*
die Dusche(n) *shower*
sich duschen *to have a shower*

echt *real*
die Ecke(n) *corner*
egal: es ist mir egal *I don't mind/care;* **ist doch egal!** *never mind!;* **egal wo** *anywhere*
egoistisch *selfish*
ehrlich *honest*
das Ei(er) *egg;* **das hartgekochte Ei** *hard-boiled egg;* **das verlorene Ei** *poached egg;* **das weichgekochte Ei** *soft-boiled egg*

der Eierbecher(-) *eggcup*
eifersüchtig *jealous*
das Eigelb(-) *egg yolk*
eigenartig *odd* (strange)
eilig *urgent;* **es eilig haben**
to be in a hurry
ein (or **eine**) *a, an*
die Einbahnstraße(n) *one
way street*
sich ein'bilden *to imagine*
einfach *simple,* or *single*
der Eingang(̈e) *entrance*
eingebildet *stuck-up*
einige *some,* or *a few*
einkaufen gehen *to go
shopping*
der Einkaufswagen(-)
(supermarket) *trolley*
ein'laden *to invite,* or *to ask
out*
die Einladung(en)
invitation
ein'packen *to pack*
einsam *lonely*
ein'schließen *to lock up,* or
to include
das Einschreiben(-)
recorded delivery letter
ein'steigen in *to get onto*
der Eintritt *entry,* or
admission
einverstanden sein *to
agree*
**der Einwanderer(-)/die
Einwandererin(nen)**
immigrant
Einzel~ *single e.g.* **das
Einzelzimmer** *single room*
das Eis *ice,* or *ice cream*
die Eisbahn(en) *ice rink*
die Eisdiele(n) *ice cream
parlour*
die Eisenbahn(en) *railway*
Eis'laufen [n] *ice skating*
der Eiswürfel(-) *ice cube*
das Eiweiß *egg white*
ekelhaft *disgusting*
elektrisch *electric*

der Ellenbogen(-) *elbow*
die Eltern [pl] *parents*
der Empfang(̈e) *reception*
die Empfängnisverhütung
contraception
empfehlen *to recommend*
empfindlich *sensitive*
das Ende(n) *end*
endlich *at last*
eng *narrow,* or (clothes)
tight, or (friends) *close*
eng befreundet *close
friends*
England [n] *England*
**der Engländer(-)/die
Engländerin(nen)** *English*
or [m] *adjustable spanner*
englisch *English*
entdecken *to discover*
die Entfernung(en)
distance
entkommen *to get away*
die Entschuldigung(en)
excuse, or *apology;*
Entschuldigung! *excuse me!,*
or *sorry!*
sich entspannen *to relax*
entspannt *relaxed*
enttäuscht *disappointed*
die Entzündung(en)
infection
epileptisch *epileptic*
er *he,* or *him,* or *it*
die Erbse(n) *pea*
die Erdbeere(n) *strawberry*
das Erdgeschoss *ground
floor*
die Erdnuss (pl: Erdnüsse)
peanut
die Erfahrung(en)
experience
erfinden *to invent*
der Erfolg(e) *hit,* or
success; **Erfolg haben** *to
succeed*
erforschen *to explore*
das Ergebnis(se) *result*
sich erholen *to recover*

erinnern *to remind;* **sich
erinnern an** *to remember*
erkältet sein *to have a cold*
die Erkältung *cold* (illness)
erkennen *to recognize*
erklären *to explain*
sich erkundigen *to find
out,* or *to get information*
die Erlaubnis(se)
permission, or *permit*
erledigt *finished,* or (slang)
shattered
erleichtert *relieved*
ernst *serious*
erotisch *erotic*
das Ersatzteil(e) *spare part*
erschöpfen *to wear out*
erschöpft *exhausted*
erschreckt *startled,* or
frightened
erst *not until,* or *only*
erstaunlich *amazing*
erste(n) *first;* **Erste Hilfe [f]**
first aid; **das Erste-Hilfe-Set**
first aid kit
der/die Erwachsene(n)
adult
erzählen *to tell*
die Erziehung *education,*
or *upbringing*
erzielen *to score*
es *it*
das Essen *food,* or *meal*
essen *to eat*
der Essig *vinegar*
das Esszimmer(-) *dining
room*
etwas *something,* or
anything, or *a little;* **etwas
anderes** *something else*
Europa [n] *Europe*
**der Europäer(-)/die
Europäerin(nen)** *European*
europäisch *European*
evangelisch *Protestant*
exotisch *exotic*
extra *extra*
exzellent *excellent*

fabelhaft *fabulous*
das Fach("er) (school) *subject*
der Faden(") *thread*
die Fähre(n) *ferry*
fahren *to drive, or to ride* (bike), or *to go* (by car/train)
der Fahrer(-)/die Fahrerin(nen) *driver*
die Fahrkarte(n) *ticket*
der Fahrkartenschalter(-) *ticket office*
der Fahrplan("e) *timetable*
der Fahrpreis(e) *fare*
das Fahrrad("er) *bike*
der Fahrschein(e) *ticket*
der Fahrstuhl("e) *lift, or elevator*
die Fahrt(en) *journey, or trip*
fair *fair* (just)
der Fall("e) *fall, or case;* **auf keinen Fall!** *no way!;* **für alle Fälle** *just in case*
das Fall(en) (sailing) *sheet*
fallen *to fall;* **fallen lassen** *to drop*
der Fallschirm(e) *parachute*
falsch *wrong* (incorrect)
die Familie(n) *family*
der Fan(s) *fan, or supporter*
fangen *to catch*
die Fantasie *imagination*
fantastisch *fantastic*
die Farbe(n) *colour*
Fasching [m] *Shrovetide carnival*
das Fassbier(e) *beer* (on tap)
fast *nearly*
faul *lazy*
Februar [m] *February*
Federball [m] *badminton*
der Fehler(-) *mistake*
feiern *to celebrate, or to party*
der Feiertag(e) *holiday* (bank holiday)

der Feigling(e) *coward;* **Feigling!** *I dare you!*
feilschen *to haggle*
der Feind(e)/die Feindin(nen) *enemy*
das Feinkostgeschäft(e) *delicatessen*
der Felsbrocken(-) *rock, or boulder*
der Felsen(-) *cliff, or rock-face*
der Feminist(en)/die Feministin(nen) *feminist*
das Fenster(-) *window*
die Ferien [pl] *holidays*
die Fernbedienung(en) *remote control*
die Ferne *distance*
das Ferngespräch(e) *long-distance phone call*
das Fernglas("er) *binoculars*
der Fernseher(-) *television*
das Fernsprechbuch("er) *telephone directory*
fertig *ready, or finished, or* (slang) *exhausted*
fertig machen *to finish*
das Fest(e) *festival, or party*
die Fete(n)* *party*
das Fett *fat*
das Feuer(-) *fire*
die Feuerwehr *fire brigade*
das Feuerwerk *fireworks*
das Feuerzeug(e) *lighter*
das Fieber *fever;* **Fieber haben** *to have a temperature*
fies* *gross* (horrid), or *lousy, or nasty*
der Film(e) *film*
finden *to find, or to think*
der Finger(-) *finger;* **Finger weg!** *hands off!*
der Fisch(e) *fish, or* (star sign) *Pisces*
fischen *to fish*
fit *fit*
flach *flat*

die Flasche(n) *bottle*
der Flaschenöffner(-) *bottle opener*
der Fleck(en) *mark, or spot;* **der blaue Fleck** *bruise*
das Fleisch *meat*
die Fleischerei(en) *butcher's*
die Fliege(n) *fly*
fliegen *to fly*
fließend *fluent*
Flipper [m] *pinball*
flirten *to flirt*
der Flohmarkt("e) *flea market*
das Floß("e) *raft*
die Flosse(n) (diving) *flipper*
fluchen *to swear*
der Flug("e) *flight*
der Flügel(-) *wing, or grand piano*
die Fluggesellschaft(en) *airline*
der Flughafen(") *airport*
der Flugschein(e) *plane ticket*
der Flugsteig(e) *airport gate*
das Flugzeug(e) *plane*
der Fluss ("e) *river*
folgen *to follow, or to obey*
der Fön(e) *hair-dryer*
Football: American Football [m] *American football*
die Form(en) *shape*
die Forschung *research*
die Fortbildung *further education*
der Fortschritt(e) *progress*
das Foto(s) *photo*
der Fotoapparat(e) *camera*
der Fotograf(en)/die Fotografin(nen) *photographer*
die Frage(n) *question;* **das kommt nicht in Frage!** *no way!* or *it's out of the question*

fragen to ask
Frankreich [n] France
französisch French
Frau Mrs, or Ms
die Frau(en) woman, or wife
Fräulein Miss
frech cheeky
die Frechheit(en) cheek, or impudence; **so eine Frechheit!** what a nerve!
frei free; **im Freien** in the open air
Freitag [m] Friday
die Freizeit spare time
fressen (animals) to eat, or (slang) to scoff
sich freuen to be happy; **sich freuen auf** to look forward to
der Freund(e) friend (male), or boyfriend
die Freundin(nen) friend (female), or girlfriend
freundlich friendly
der Frieden peace
der Friedhof(¨e) cemetery
friedlich peaceful
frieren to freeze
das Frisbee(s) frisbee
frisch fresh
der Friseur(e)/die Frieseurin(nen) hairdresser
die Frisur(en) hairstyle
früh early
der Frühling spring (season)
das Frühstück(e) breakfast
frühstücken to have breakfast
fühlen to feel
der Führer(-)/die Führerin(nen) guide, or [m] guide book
der Führerschein(e) driving licence
füllen to fill
das Fundbüro(s) lost property (office)

funktionieren to work
für for
furchtbar awful, or horrible
der Fuß(¨e) foot
Fußball [m] football
der Fußball football (the ball)
der Fußgänger(-)/die Fußgängerin pedestrian
der Fußgängerüberweg(e) pedestrian crossing
das Fußgelenk(e) ankle

die Gabel(n) fork
gähnen to yawn
die Galerie(n) gallery
der Gang(¨e) corridor, or (meal) course, or (car, bike) gear
die Gangschaltung gears
ganz all (whole), or quite (totally), or whole; **ganz allein** on your own; **ganz wild auf ... sein** to be crazy about; **den ganzen Tag** all day
die Garage(n) garage
die Garderobe(n) cloakroom
die Garnele(n) king prawn
der Garten(¨) garden
das Gas gas
der Gaskocher(-) camping stove
der Gast(¨e) guest
der Gastarbeiter(-)/die Gastarbeiterin(nen) guest worker (from abroad)
der Gastgeber(-)/die Gastgeberin(nen) host
das Gebäude(-) building
geben to give
das Gebiss(e) (riding) bit
gebraucht second-hand
gebrochen broken
das Geburtsdatum date of birth
der Geburtstag(e) birthday

das Gedicht(e) poem
die Geduld patience
gefährlich dangerous
gefallen to like, or to fancy (in German you say that "someone appeals to you") e.g. **Anna gefällt ihm** he fancies Anna
das Gefängnis(se) prison
das Gefühl(e) feeling
gegen against
die Gegend(en) area, or neighbourhood
das Gegenteil(e) opposite
gegenüber opposite (facing)
gegrillt grilled
das Geheimnis(se) secret
gehen to go, or to walk
geht: wie geht es? how are you?; **es geht** all right; **geht das?** is that possible?
die Geige(n) violin
geil* great, or terrific
geizig stingy
gekocht boiled
das Gel(s) gel
gelaunt: gut/schlecht gelaunt in a good/bad mood
gelb yellow
das Geld money
der Geldautomat(en) cash dispenser
die Geldstrafe(n) fine
die Gelegenheit(en) opportunity
gemein nasty, or rotten
gemischt mixed, or co-ed
das Gemüse vegetables
genial brilliant (fantastic)
genug enough
geöffnet open
das Gepäck luggage
der Gepäckwagen(-) baggage trolley
gerade just (as in "just right"), or straight (not curved)
geradeaus straight ahead

das Geräusch(e) - halt!

das Geräusch(e) *sound*
gerecht *fair* (just)
das Gericht(e) *dish* (meal)
gern (or **gern haben**) *to like,*
e.g. **ich hätte gern** *I'd like,*
ich schwimme gern *I like
swimming*
der Geruch("e) *smell*
das Gerücht(e) *rumour*
das Geschäft(e) *shop*
geschehen *to happen*
das Geschenk(e) *present*
die Geschichte(n) *story,* or
history
geschieden *divorced*
das Geschlecht(er) *sex*
(gender)
geschlossen *closed,* or *shut*
der Geschmack("e) *taste,*
or *flavour*
die Geschwindigkeit(en)
speed
die Geschwister [pl]
brothers and sisters
geschwollen *swollen*
die Gesellschaft(en) *society*
das Gesicht(er) *face*
das Gespräch(e)
conversation
der Gestank *stink*
das Gestell(e) (glasses)
frame
gestern *yesterday;* **gestern
Abend** *last night*
gestreift *striped*
gestrichen *cancelled*
gesund *healthy*
die Gesundheit *health*
das Getränk(e) *drink;* **das
alkoholfreie Getränk** *soft
drink*
die Gewalt *violence*
das Gewicht(e) *weight*
gewinnen *to win*
das Gewitter(-) *storm*
die Gewohnheit(en) *habit*
gewöhnlich *ordinary,* or
usual

**gewöhnt: an ... gewöhnt
sein** *to be used to*
das Gewürz(e) *spice*
gibt: es gibt *there is/are*
der Gips(e) *plaster* (cast)
die Gitarre(n) *guitar*
**der Gitarrist(en)/die
Gitarristin(nen)** *guitarist*
das Glas("er) *glass;* **ein
Glas Wasser/Wein** *a glass of
water/wine*
glatt *smooth,* or *slippery,* or
(hair) *straight*
glauben *to think,* or *to
believe*
gleich *equal,* or *the same*
gleichzeitig *simultaneous*
das Glück *luck;* **zum Glück**
luckily
glücklich *happy*
glücklicherweise *luckily*
der Gott("er) *god*
der Grad *degree*
das Gramm(e) *gram*
das Gras("er) *grass*
die Gräte(n) *fish bone*
gratulieren *to congratulate*
grau *grey*
grausam *cruel*
die Grenze(n) *border,* or
frontier
der Griff(e) *handle*
die Grippe *flu*
grob *coarse,* or *rude,* or
gross
groß *big,* or *tall,* or *great*
großartig *terrific*
Großbritannien [n] *Britain*
die Größe(n) *size*
die Großmutter(¨)
grandmother
die Großstadt("e) *city*
der Großvater(¨)
grandfather
großzügig *generous*
grün *green*
der Grund("e) *reason*
die Gruppe(n) *group*

gruslig *scary*
gucken* *to look*
gültig *valid;* **nicht mehr
gültig** *out of date*
der Gummi(s)* *condom*
das Gummiband("er)
rubber band
der Gummistiefel(-)
wellington boot
günstig *convenient,* or
reasonably priced
die Gurke(n) *cucumber*
der Gurt(e) (riding) *girth,* or
(climbing) *sling*
der Gürtel(-) *belt*
die Gürteltasche(n) *bum
bag*
gut *good,* or *well,* or *fine* (OK)
gut aussehend *good-
looking*
**das Gymnasium
(pl: Gymnasien)**
secondary/high school

das Haar(e) *hair*
die Haarbürste(n) *hairbrush*
die Haarspange(n) *hair-
slide*
der Haarspray(s) *hairspray*
haben *to have*
das Hähnchen(-) *chicken*
(for roasting, grilling)
halb *half,* or (with time) *half
before,* e.g. **halb elf** *half past
ten* (half before 11)
halbdurch *medium(-cooked)*
das Halbjahr(e) (school)
term
die Hälfte(n) *half*
hallo *hello,* or *hi*
der Hals("e) *neck*
die Halskette(n) *necklace*
Halsschmerzen [pl] *sore
throat*
das Halstuch("er) (neck)
scarf
halt! *stop!;* **halt den
Mund!*** *shut up!*

halten to hold, or to keep, or to stop
der Hamburger(-) hamburger
das Hammelfleisch mutton
der Hammer(¨) hammer
die Hand(¨e) hand
handgearbeitet handmade
das Handgepäck hand-luggage
die Handlung(en) plot
der Handschuh(e) glove
das Handtuch(¨er) towel
die Hängematte(n) hammock
hart hard
die Haselnuss(¨e) hazelnut
hassen to hate
hässlich ugly
häufig common, or frequent
das Hauptsegel(-) main sail
die Hauptstadt(¨e) capital city
das Haus(¨er) house; **zu Hause** at home
die Hausaufgaben [pl] homework
die Haut skin
das Heimspiel(e) home game
heiß hot
heißen to be called; **wie heißen Sie?,** or **wie heißt du/ihr?** what's your name?
der Heizkörper(-) radiator
die Heizung heating
helfen to help
hell bright, or light
der Helm(e) helmet
das Hemd(en) shirt
herabgesetzt reduced
heraus'finden to find out
der Herbst autumn
herein'fallen auf to fall for (a trick)
herein'kommen to come in

der Hering(e) herring, or (camping) tent peg
Herr Mr, or gentleman
Herren gents
sich herum'treiben to hang around/out
das Herz(en) heart
herzlich warm; **herzliche Glückwünsche** congratulations; **herzlichen Glückwunsch zum Geburtstag** happy birthday; **herzliche Grüße** best wishes
heuchlerisch hypocritical
Heuschnupfen [m] hayfever
heute today; **heute Morgen/Abend** this morning/evening
hier here; **die hier*** these; **der/die/das hier** this one
die Hilfe help, or aid
die Hilfsorganisation(en) charity
die Himbeere(n) raspberry
der Himmel(-) sky
hin there; **hin und zurück** return (there and back)
hinauf'steigen to go/walk up
der Hindu(s) Hindu
sich hin'setzen to sit down
hin'stellen to put (down)
hinten behind, or at the back
der Hintern(-)* bottom (bum)
hinunter'gehen to go/walk down
hinzu'fügen to add
hoch high
hochnäsig snooty
hoffen to hope
höflich polite
der höhere Bildungsweg higher education
die Höhle(n) cave
die Höhlenforschung caving

holen to fetch
Holland [n] Holland
der Holländer(-)/die Holländerin(nen) Dutch
holländisch Dutch
die Hölle hell
das Holz(¨er) wood
der Holzhammer(¨) mallet
der Honig honey
hören to hear
der Hörer(-) (phone) receiver
das Horn(¨er) horn
das Horoskop(e) horoscope
die Hose(n) trousers
das Hotel(s) hotel
das Hovercraft(s) hovercraft
hübsch pretty, or nice
der Hubschrauber(-) helicopter
der Huf(e) hoof
der Hügel(-) hill
das Huhn(¨er) chicken (live)
der Humor humour
der Hund(e) dog
Hunger [m] hunger; **Hunger haben** to be hungry
die Hupe(n) horn (of car)
husten to cough
der Hut(¨e) hat
hysterisch hysterical

ich I, or me
die Idee(n) idea
der Idiot(en) idiot
illegal illegal
die Imbissstube(n) snack bar
immer always
die Impfung(en) vaccination
in in, or to, or (slang) trendy
inbegriffen inclusive
Indien [n] India
die Informatik computer studies
das Insekt(en) insect

das Insektenschutzmittel(-) *insect repellent*
die Insel(n) *island*
das Instrument(e) *instrument*
interessant *interesting*
sich interessieren für *to be interested in*
international *international*
das Interview(s) *interview*
der Ire(n)/die Irin(nen) *Irish*
irgend~ *any,* e.g. **irgendwo** *anywhere*
irisch *Irish*
Irland [n] *Ireland*
irre *crazy*
Italien [n] *Italy*

ja *yes*
die Jacke(n) *jacket*
das Jahr(e) *year*
die Jahreszeit(en) *season*
das Jahrhundert(e) *century*
Januar [m] *January*
je *each;* **je nach** *depending on*
die Jeans [pl] *jeans*
der Jeansstoff(e) *denim*
jede (or **jeder** or **jedes**) *each,* or *everybody,* or *anyone*
jemand *anyone,* or *somebody;* **jemand anders** *somebody else*
jetzt *now*
joggen *to jog*
der Joghurt(-) *yogurt*
jonglieren *to juggle*
jüdisch *Jewish*
Judo [n] *judo*
die Jugendherberge(n) *youth hostel*
der/die Jugendliche(n) *young person*
Juli [m] *July*
jung *young*
der Junge(n) *boy*

Jungfrau [f] (star sign) *Virgo*
Juni [m] *June*

die Kabine(n) *cabin* (boat), or *changing-cubicle*
der Kabinenlift(s) *cable car*
der Käfer(-) *bug* (insect), or *beetle*
das Kaff(s)* *dump* (dull, awful town)
der Kaffee *coffee;* **Kaffee und Kuchen** *afternoon snack of coffee and cake*
der Kalender(-) *calendar,* or *business diary*
kalorienarm *low-calorie*
kalt *cold;* **es ist kalt** *it is cold;* **kalte Füße kriegen** *to have cold feet* (about something)
die Kamera(s) *camera*
der Kamm(¨e) *comb*
kämpfen *to fight*
der Kanal(¨e) *canal,* or (TV) *channel*
das Kanu(s) *canoe;* **Kanu fahren** *to go canoeing*
kapieren* *to get the message* (understand)
der Kapitän(e) *captain*
kaputt* *broken,* or *exhausted;* **sich kaputt lachen*** *to be in fits* (of laughter); **kaputt machen*** *to break*
der Karneval(e) *carnival*
die Karotte(n) *carrot*
die Karriere(n) *career*
die Karte(n) *card,* or *ticket,* or *map,* or (restaurant) *menu*
das Kartenspiel(e) *card game*
das Kartentelefon(e) *card phone*
die Kartoffel(n) *potato*
der Kartoffelbrei *mashed potato*

das Kartoffelpüree *mashed potato*
der Käse *cheese*
der Käsekuchen(-) *cheesecake*
die Kasse(n) *check-out* (cash desk), or *ticket office*
die Kassette(n) *cassette,* or *tape*
der Kassettenrecorder(-) *cassette player*
die Katastrophe(n) *disaster*
der Kater(-) *tomcat,* or (slang) *hangover*
die Kathedrale(n) *cathedral*
katholisch *Catholic*
die Katze(n) *cat*
kaufen *to buy*
das Kaufhaus(¨er) *department store*
das Kaugummi(s) *chewing gum*
die Kaution(en) *deposit*
Kegeln [n] *bowling*
die Kehle(n) *throat*
kein (or **keine**) *not,* or *not a(n),* or *no,* or *nobody*
der Keks(e) *biscuit*
der Keller(-) *cellar*
der Kellner(-) *waiter*
die Kellnerin(nen) *waitress*
kennen *to know;* **kennen lernen** *to meet,* or *to get to know*
das Kennzeichen(-) *car registration number*
der Kerl(e)* *bloke,* or *guy*
der Kern(e) *pip*
Kern~ *nuclear,* e.g. **die Kernkraft** *nuclear power*
das Kerngehäuse(-) *core*
die Kerze(n) *candle*
die Kette(n) *chain*
das Keyboard(s) *keyboard*

der Keyboarder(-)/die Keyboarderin(nen) *keyboard player*
das Kilo(-) *kilo*
der Kilometer(-) *kilometre*
das Kind(er) *child*
das Kino(s) *cinema*
der Kiosk(e) *kiosk*
die Kirche(n) *church*
die Kirmes(sen) *funfair*
die Kirsche(n) *cherry*
die Kiste(n) *box*, or *chest*, or (slang) *old banger* (car)
kitzeln *to tickle*
Klacks: das ist ein Klacks* *it's a piece of cake*
Klamotten* [pl] *clothes*
der Klang(˘e) *sound*
klappen* *to work* (go well)
die Klarinette(n) *clarinet*
klassisch *classical*
der Klatsch *gossip*
klatschen *to gossip*, or *to applaud*
das Kleid(er) *dress*
die Kleider [pl] *clothes*, or *dresses*
klein *little*, or *small*
das Kleingeld *change* (money)
der Kletterer(-)/die Kletterin(nen) *rock climber*
Klettern [n] *rock climbing*
der Kletterschuh(e) *climbing shoe*
das Kletterseil(e) *climbing rope*
klingeln *to ring*
das Klo(s)* *loo*
klug *clever*
der Knast* *prison*
das Knie(-) *knee*
der Knoblauch *garlic*
der Knochen(-) *bone*
der Knopf(˘e) *button*
der Knoten(-) *knot*
der Knüller(-)* *hit* (success)

kochen *to cook*
koffeinfrei *decaffeinated*
der Koffer(-) *suitcase*
die Kohle(n)* *dosh* (money)
Kohlensäure: mit/ohne Kohlensäure *fizzy/still*
die Kokosnuss(˘e) *coconut*
komisch *funny*
kommen *to come*
der Kompass(e) *compass*
die Konditorei(en) *cake shop*
das Kondom(e) *condom*
die Konfitüre(n) *jam*
die Konkurrenz(en) *competition*
können *can* (to be able to), or *to know*
das Konsulat(e) *consulate*
die Kontaktlinse(n) *contact lens*
der Kontrolleur(e)/die Kontrolleurin(nen) *ticket collector*
kontrollieren *to check*
konventionell *straight*, or *conventional*
das Konzert(e) *concert*
der Kopf(˘e) *head*; **Kopf hoch!** *cheer up!*
der Kopfhörer(-) *earphones*
der Kopfsalat(e) *lettuce*
Kopfschmerzen [pl] *headache*
das Kopftuch(˘er) (head) *scarf*
kopieren *to copy*
der Korb(˘e) *basket*
der Korken(-) *cork*
der Korkenzieher(-) *corkscrew*
der Körper(-) *body*
koscher *kosher*
kosmopolitisch *cosmopolitan*
kosten *to cost*
köstlich *delicious*

das Kotelett(s) (meat) *chop*
die Krabbe(n) *prawn* (small)
der Krach *noise*
der Kragen(-) *collar*
der Kram* *stuff*, or *kit*
der Krampf(˘e) *cramp*
krank *ill*, or *sick*
das Krankenhaus(˘er) *hospital*
der Krankenpfleger(-) *nurse* (man)
die Krankenschwester(n) *nurse* (woman)
der Krankenwagen(-) *ambulance*
kratzen *to scratch*
Kraul [n] (swimming) *crawl*
kraus (hair) *frizzy*, or (clothes) *crinkly*
der Krawall(e) *riot*
Krebs [m] (star sign) *Cancer*
die Kreditkarte(n) *credit card*
die Kreide(n) *chalk*
der Kreisverkehr(e) *roundabout*
das Kreuz(e) *cross* (sign)
der Kreuzschlitz-schraubenzieher(-) *Phillips® screwdriver*
die Kreuzung(en) *crossroads*
das Kreuzworträtsel(-) *crossword*
der Krieg(e) *war*
kriegen* *to get*
der Krimi(s)* *thriller*
die Krise(n) *crisis*
kritisieren *to criticize*
der Krug(˘e) *jug*
die Küche(n) *kitchen*
der Kuchen(-) *cake*
die Küchenrolle(n) *kitchen paper*
die Kuh(˘e) *cow*
der Kühler(-) (car) *radiator*
der Kühlschrank(˘e) *fridge*

die Kühltasche(n) *cool box*, or *cool bag*
der Kuli(s) (ball-point) *pen*
der Kult(e) *cult*
die Kultur *culture*
kulturell *cultural*
der Kummer *trouble*, or *grief*
der Kumpel(-) *mate*, or *pal*
die Kunst *art*
die Kunsthochschule(n) *art school*
der Künstler(-)/die Künstlerin(nen) *artist*
der Kurs(e) *course* (series of lessons), or *exchange rate*
die Kurve(n) *bend*
kurz *short*
kurzsichtig *short-sighted*
der Kuss(¨e) *kiss*
küssen *to kiss*
die Küste(n) *coast*

lächeln *to smile*
das Lächeln *smile*
lachen *to laugh*
lächerlich *ridiculous*
der Lachs(e) *salmon*
der Laden(¨) *shop*
das Lamm(¨er) *lamb* (animal)
das Lammfleisch *lamb* (meat)
das Land(¨er) *country*, or *land*, or (German) *state*
die Landkarte(n) *map*
die Landschaft(en) *scenery* (countryside)
lang (or **lange**) *long*, or *for a long time*
langsam *slow*, or *slowly*
sich langweilen *to be bored*
langweilig *boring*
der Lärm *noise*
der Laser(-) *laser*
lassen *to leave*, or *to let*
lässig *casual*

lästig *annoying*
die Latzhose(n) *dungarees*
laufen *to run*, or *to walk*
launisch *moody*
lausig* *lousy*
laut *loud*
der Laut(e) *sound*
der Lautsprecher(-) *(loud)speaker*
die Lawine(n) *avalanche*
leben *to live*
das Leben(-) *life*
der Lebensstil *lifestyle*
die Leber(n) *liver*
lecker *delicious*
das Leder(-) *leather*
ledig *single* (unmarried)
leer *empty*
legen *to lay down*, or *to put*
lehren *to teach*
der Lehrer(-)/die Lehrerin(nen) *teacher*, or *instructor*
leicht *easy*, or *light* (not heavy)
Leid: es tut mir Leid *I'm sorry*
leiden *to suffer*
leider *unfortunately*
leihen *to lend*; **sich ... leihen** *to borrow*
die Leinwand (cinema) *screen*, or (art) *canvas*
leise *quiet* (not loud)
das Lenkrad(¨er) *steering wheel*
die Lenkstange(n) *handlebars*
lernen *to learn*
lesen *to read*
letzte (**letzter**, or **letztes**) *last* (the last), or *the latest*
die Leute [pl] *people*
das Licht(er) *light*
der Lidschatten(-) *eye shadow*
der Lidstift(e) *eyeliner pencil*

lieb *dear*, or *lovely* (nice)
die Liebe *love*
lieben *to love*
lieber (in letter) *dear*, or *prefer* (doing something), e.g. **ich male lieber** *I prefer painting*
die Liebesgeschichte(n) *romance*
das Liebesleben *love-life*
lieb haben *to love* (someone)
Lieblings~ *favourite*, e.g. **mein Lieblingshut** *my favourite hat*
liebsten: am liebsten *best*
das Lied(er) *song*
der Liegestuhl(¨e) *deck chair*
der Liegewagen(-) *couchette*
der Lift(s) *lift*
die Linie(n) *line*, or *route*
linke (or **linken**) *left*(hand)
links *on the left*; **links herum** *inside out*;
linkshändig *left-handed*
die Lippe(n) *lip*
der Lippenkonturenstift(e) *lip liner*
der Lippenstift(e) *lipstick*
der/das Liter(-) *litre*
das Loch(¨er) *hole*
locker* *relaxed*, or *laid-back*
lockig *curly*
der Löffel(-) *spoon*
der Lohn(¨e) *wage*
sich lohnen *to be worthwhile*
los! *come on!*, or *go!*; **was ist (denn) los?** *what's the matter?*; **was ist los?** *what's wrong?*
los'lachen *to burst out laughing*
los'lassen *to let go*
los'werden *to get rid of*
Löwe [m] (star sign) *Leo*
die Luft *air*

die Luftmatratze(n) *Lilo®,*
Luftpost [f] *airmail*
die Luftpumpe(n) *pump*
die Lüge(n) *lie* (fib)
lügen *to lie* (fib)
der Lügner(-)/die
Lügnerin(nen) *liar*
die Lust *pleasure,* or *desire;*
hast du Lust ...? *do you*
fancy (doing something)?
lustig *funny,* or *cheerful;*
sich über (...) lustig machen
to laugh at, or *to make fun of*

machen *to do,* or *to make*
macho *macho*
macht: macht nichts! *never*
mind!, or *it doesn't matter*
das Mädchen(-) *girl*
der Magen(¨) *stomach*
die Mähne(n) *mane*
Mai [m] *May*
das Make-up *make-up*
der Make-up-Entferner
make-up remover
das Mal(e) *time* (occasion)
malen *to paint*
man *you,* or *one (as in "you*
can't tell")
manche *some,* or *certain*
manchmal *sometimes*
die Mandel(n) *almond*
der Mann(¨er) *man,* or
husband
die Mannschaft(en) *team*
der Mantel(¨) *coat*
die Margarine *margarine*
die Mark(-) *mark* (German
currency)
der Markt(¨e) *market*
die Marmelade(n) *jam*
März [m] *March*
die Maschine(n) *machine*
die Maske(n) *mask*
massenhaft *loads of*
der Mast(en) *mast*
Mathe* [f] *maths*
die Mauer(n) *wall*

die Mayonnaise
mayonnaise
meckern* *to moan*
die Medien [pl] *media*
das Medikament(e)
medicine (medication)
die Medizin *medicine*
(science)
das Meer(e) *sea*
Meeresfrüchte [pl] *seafood*
mehr *more*
mein (or meine) *my*
meinen *to reckon*
die Meinung(en) *opinion;*
meiner Meinung nach *in my*
opinion
die meisten *most* (the
majority)
der Meister(-)/die
Meisterin(nen) *champion*
die Meisterschaft(en)
championship
die Melone(n) *melon*
die Menge *amount;* eine
Menge *a lot of*
der Mensch(en) *person*
die Menschenrechte [pl]
human rights
menschlich *human*
das Menü(s) *set menu*
das Messer(-) *knife*
der Meter(-) *metre*
die Methode(n) *method*
die Metzgerei(en)
butcher's
mies* *grotty*
mieten *to rent*
das Mikro(s)* *microphone*
die Mikrowelle(n)
microwave
die Milch *milk*
der Milchshake(s) *milk*
shake
minderjährig *under age*
das Mineralwasser
mineral water; mit
Kohlensäure *sparkling;* ohne
Kohlensäure *still*

die Minute(n) *minute*
mit *with*
mit'bekommen *to*
understand
das Mitglied(er) *member;*
Mitglied werden *to join*
mit'machen *to join in*
mit'nehmen *to take*
Mittag [m] *midday;* zu
Mittag essen *to have lunch*
das Mittagessen *lunch*
die Mitte(n) *middle*
mittelgroß *medium* (size)
mittelmäßig *average*
Mitternacht [f] *midnight*
Mittwoch [m] *Wednesday*
möchte: ich möchte *I'd like*
die Mode(n) *fashion*
das Model(s) *model*
modern *fashionable*
das Mofa(s) *moped*
mogeln* *to cheat*
mögen *to like*
möglich *possible*
die Mohrrübe(n) *carrot*
Mokka~ *coffee flavoured*
der Moment(e) *moment;*
Moment mal! *just a*
moment!
momentan *at the moment*
der Monat(e) *month*
der Mond(e) *moon*
Montag [m] *Monday*
das Monument(e)
monument
Moos* [n] *dosh* (money)
das Moped(s) *moped*
der Mord(e) *murder*
der Mörder(-)/die
Mörderin(nen) *murderer*
morgen *tomorrow*
der Morgen(-) *morning;*
Morgen früh *tomorrow*
morning
morgens *in the morning*
die Moschee(n) *mosque*
das Motorrad(¨er)
motorbike

117

die Mücke(n) *midge,* or *mosquito*
der Mückenstich(e) *midge/mosquito bite*
der Müll *rubbish*
der Mülleimer(-) *rubbish bin*
der Müllplatz("e) *(rubbish/garbage) dump*
die Mülltonne(n) *dustbin*
der Mund("er) *mouth*
die Münze(n) *coin*
das Münztelefon(e) *coin phone*
das Museum (pl: Museen) *museum*
die Musik *music*
der Musiker(-)/die Musikerin(nen) *musician*
der Muskel(n) *muscle*
muslemisch *Muslim*
müssen *must,* or *to have to*
das Muster(-) *pattern*
die Mutter(") *mother*
die Mütze(n) *cap*

na *well ...;* **na und?** *so what?*
nach *after,* or *to;* **nach draußen** *outside*
der Nachbar(n)/die Nachbarin(nen) *neighbour*
nachher *afterwards*
die Nachlösegebühr(en) *excess fare*
der Nachmittag(e) *afternoon*
der Nachname(n) *surname*
die Nachricht(en) *message*
die Nachrichten [pl] *news*
die Nachspielzeit *injury time*
nächste(n) *nearest,* or *next*
die Nacht("e) *night*
der Nachteil(e) *disadvantage*
der Nachtisch(e) *dessert*
nackt *naked*
die Nadel(n) *needle*

der Nagel(") *nail*
die Nähe *proximity;* **in der Nähe (von)** *near,* or *close* (to)
naiv *naïve*
der Name(n) *name*
die Nase(n) *nose;* **die Nase in alles hinein'stecken*** *to be nosy;* **die Nase voll haben*** *to be fed up*
nass *wet*
national *national*
die Natur *nature*
natürlich *natural,* or *of course*
das Naturschutzgebiet(e) *nature reserve*
die Naturwissenschaften [pl] *natural science*
neben *next to*
necken *to tease*
nehmen *to take,* or *to get*
nein *no*
Nepp: so ein Nepp!* *it's a rip-off!*
der Nerv(en) *nerve*
der Nervenkitzel(-) *thrill*
nervös *nervous*
nervtötend *nerve-racking*
nett *kind,* or *nice*
neu *new*
neugierig *curious,* or *nosy*
Neujahr *New Year*
neulich *recently*
Neuseeland [n] *New Zealand*
nicht *not*
nichtalkoholisch *non-alcoholic*
Nichtraucher *non-smoking*
nichts *nothing*
nie *never*
niedergeschlagen *dejected;* **sich niedergeschlagen fühlen** *to be/feel down*
niedrig *low*
niemand *nobody*
niesen *to sneeze*

nirgendwo *nowhere*
noch *still* (even now); **noch mal*** *again;* **noch mehr** *more* (additional); **noch nicht** *not yet*
der Norden *north*
nördlich *north*
normal *normal*
der Notausgang("e) *emergency exit,* or *fire exit*
die Note(n) *mark* (at school)
der Notfall("e) *emergency*
nötig *necessary*
das Notizheft(e) *notebook*
die Notrufnummer(n) *emergency number*
November [m] *November*
die Nudeln [pl] *pasta*
Null *zero*
die Nummer(n) *number*
nur *only;* **nur so tun** *to pretend e.g.* **er tut nur so** *he's pretending*
die Nuss("e) *nut*
der Nussknacker(-) *nutcracker*
nützlich *useful*
nutzlos *useless*

obdachlos *homeless*
oben *above* (overhead), or *upstairs;* **oben ohne** *topless*
oberflächlich *superficial*
das Oberteil(e) *top*
das Objektiv(e) (camera) *lens*
obligatorisch *compulsory*
die Oboe(n) *oboe*
das Obst *fruit*
der Obstsalat(e) *fruit salad*
obszön *obscene*
oder *or*
offen *open*
offensichtlich *obvious*
öffentlich *public*
offiziell *official*
öffnen *to open*
oft *often*

ohne *without*
ohnmächtig *unconscious;*
ohnmächtig werden *to faint*
das Ohr(en) *ear*
Ohrenschmerzen [pl]
earache
der Ohrring(e) *earring*
okay* *OK*
die Ökologie *ecology*
Oktober [m] *October*
das Öl(e) *oil*
die Olive(n) *olive*
die Oma(s) *granny*
das Omelett(s) *omelette*
der Opa(s) *grandpa*
die Oper(n) *opera*
der Optiker(-)/die
Optikerin(nen) *optician*
optimistisch *optimistic*
orange *orange* (colour)
ordentlich *tidy,* or *proper*
Ordnung: in Ordnung *all*
right, or *OK;* **in Ordnung**
bringen *to fix* (mend)
organisieren *to organize*
der Ort(e) *place*
Orts~ *local* e.g. **Ortsgespräch**
local call
der Osten *east*
Ostern [n] *Easter*
Österreich [n] *Austria*
der Österreicher(-)/die
Österreicherin(nen)
Austrian
österreichisch *Austrian*
Osteuropa *eastern Europe*
out* *old-fashioned*

paar: ein paar *a few*
paddeln *to go canoeing*
der Palast(¨e) *palace*
die Pampelmuse(n)
grapefruit
die Panne(n) *breakdown,*
or *slip-up*
das Papier *paper*
die Papiere [pl] (identity)
papers

das Papiertaschentuch(¨er)
tissue
die Paprikaschote(n)
pepper
die Paranuss(¨e) *Brazil nut*
parken *to park*
das Parkhaus(¨er) (multi-
storey) *car park*
der Parkplatz(¨e) *car park*
die Partei(en) (political)
party
die Partie(n) *game*
der Pass(¨e) *passport*
der Passagier(e) *passenger*
passen *to fit,* or *to suit*
passieren *to happen*
die Pastete(n) *pie*
die Pauschalreise(n)
package tour
die Pause(n) *interval,* or
rest
Pech! *bad luck!,* or *too bad!*
das Pedal(e) *pedal*
peinlich *embarrassing*
perfekt *perfect*
die Periode(n) *period*
(menstruation)
die Persönlichkeit(en)
personality
die Pfanne(n) *pan*
der Pfeffer *pepper*
das Pferd(e) *horse*
der Pfirsich(e) *peach*
die Pflanze(n) *plant*
das Pflaster(-) *plaster*
die Pflaume(n) *plum*
Pflicht~ *compulsory*
pflücken *to pick* (gather)
das Pfund(-) *pound* (UK
money or German weight)
die Pfütze(n) *puddle*
die Phobie(n) *phobia*
der Pickel(-) *spot* (pimple)
das Picknick(s) *picnic*
das Pils(-) *lager*
der Pilz(e) *wild mushroom*
der Pinsel(-) *paintbrush*
die Pinzette(n) *tweezers*

die Pistazie(n) *pistachio
nut*
die Piste(n) (ski) *run*
das Plakat(e) *poster*
der Plan(¨e) *plan*
Plastik~ *plastic*
platt (slang) *stunned*
der Platten(-) *puncture*
der Platz(¨e) *place,* or
space, or (in town) *square,* or
seat, or (sports) *court*
platzen *to burst*
plaudern *to chat*
pleite *broke* (no money)
plötzlich *suddenly*
der Po(s)* *bum*
Polen [n] *Poland*
die Politik *politics*
die Polizei *police*
der Polizist(en)/die
Polizistin(nen) *police
officer*
Pommes* (or **Pommes
frites**) *chips*
das Portemonnaie(s)
purse
die Posaune(n) *trombone*
die Post *post,* or *post office*
das Postamt(¨er) *post
office*
die Postkarte(n) *postcard*
die Postleitzahl(en)
post/area code
praktisch *practical*
das Präservativ(e) *condom*
der Preis(e) *price,* or *prize*
prima *great,* or *fantastic*
privat *private*
die Probe(n) *test,* or
rehearsal
probieren *to try,* or *to taste*
prost! *cheers!*
protestantisch *Protestant*
die Prüfung(en) *exam*
das Publikum *audience*
der Pullover(-) (or **der
Pulli(s)***) *sweater*
pünktlich *on time*

die Qualität - der Roman(e)

die Qualität quality
die Qualle(n) jellyfish
die Quantität quantity
Quatsch* rubbish; **Quatsch reden*** to talk rubbish
die Quelle(n) spring (water)
die Querflöte(n) flute

der Rabatt(e) discount
die Rache revenge
das Rad(¨er) bike, or wheel
der Radfahrweg(e) cycle track
raffiniert cunning, or sneaky
der Rahmen(-) frame
ran'gehen* to answer (the phone)
(sich) rasieren to shave
der Rasierer(-) razor
die Rasierklinge(n) razor blade
der Rasierschaum shaving foam
rassistisch racist
das Rasthaus(¨er) service station
der Rat advice
raten to guess
das Rathaus(¨er) town hall
das Rätsel(-) puzzle
rauchen to smoke
Raucher smoking
das Rauschgift(e) drug
der Rechner(-) computer
die Rechnung(en) bill
das Recht law; **Recht haben** to be right
rechte(n) right (hand)
rechts on the right
die Regel(n) rule
regelmäßig regular
der Regen rain
der Regenbogen(¨) rainbow
der Regenmantel(¨) raincoat
der Regenschirm(e) umbrella

der Regentropfen(-) raindrop
die Regierung(en) government
die Region(en) region
der Regisseur(e)/die Regisseurin(nen) (film) director, or (theatre) producer
regnen to rain; **es regnet** it's raining
reiben to rub
reich rich
reicht: das reicht that's enough
reif ripe, or mature
der Reifen(-) tyre
der Reifendruck tyre pressure
die Reihenfolge order
rein pure, or (slang for **herein**) inside
der Reinfall(¨e) failure
die Reinigungslösung(en) cleansing solution
der Reis rice
die Reise(n) journey
das Reisebüro(s) travel agency
der Reisebus(se) coach
reisen to travel
der/die Reisende(n) traveller, or (train) passenger
der Reisepass(¨e) passport
der Reisescheck(s) traveller's cheque
reißen to rip
der Reißverschluss(¨e) zip
Reiten [n] riding
der Reiter(-)/die Reiterin(nen) rider
die Reithose(n) jodhpurs
die Reitjacke(n) riding jacket
die Reitkappe(n) riding hat
die Reitpeitsche(n) whip
der Reitstiefel(-) riding boot

die Reizung(en) irritation
reizvoll attractive
der Rekord(e) record
rennen to run
das Rennen(-) race
das Rennrad(¨er) racing bike
reparieren to repair
reserviert reserved
die Reservierung(en) reservation
der Rest(e) rest (remainder)
das Restaurant(s) restaurant
retten to rescue
die Rettung(en) rescue
der Rettungsschwimmer(-)/die Rettungsschwimmerin(nen) lifeguard
die Rettungsweste(n) life jacket
der/das Revers(-) lapel
das Rezept(e) recipe, or prescription
das R-Gespräch(e) reverse charge call
richtig correct, or right; **sich richtig aus'leben** to live it up
die Richtung(en) direction, or way
riechen to smell
der Riemen(-) oar
das Rindfleisch beef
der Ring(e) ring
das Risiko (pl: Risiken) risk, or chance
riskant risky, or dodgy
riskieren to risk
der Rock(¨e) skirt, or (music) rock
roh raw
Rollschuhlaufen [n] roller skating
der Rollstuhl(¨e) wheelchair
die Rolltreppe(n) escalator
der Roman(e) novel

romantisch *romantic*
rosa *pink*
der Rosé(s) *rosé wine*
rot *red*
der Rotwein(e) *red wine*
das Rouge *blusher*
die Route(n) *route*
der Rücken(-) *back*
Rückenschmerzen [pl] *backache*
Rückenschwimmen [n] *backstroke*
die Rückfahrt(en) *return journey*
rück mal! *move over!*
der Rucksack("e) *backpack*
rückwärts: rückwärts fahren *to reverse* (car)
das Ruder(-) *rudder*
das Ruderboot(e) *rowing boat*
rudern *to row*
die Ruderpinne(n) *tiller*
rufen *to call, or to shout*
die Ruhe *silence*
ruhig *calm, or quiet*
das Rührei(er) *scrambled egg*
der Rummel *funfair, or* (slang) *fuss*
rund *round*
die Runde(n) *round* (of drinks)
der Rundfunk *radio broadcasting*
Russland [n] *Russia*

die Sache(n) *thing, or matter*
der Safe(s) *safe* (for valuables)
der Saft("e) *juice*
sagen *to say, or to tell*
sagenhaft *terrific*
die Sahne *cream*
die Salami(s) *salami*
der Salat(e) *salad, or lettuce*

die Salbe(n) *ointment*
das Salz *salt*
salzig *salty*
sammeln *to collect*
Samstag [m] *Saturday*
der Sand *sand*
der Sänger(-)/die Sängerin(nen) *singer*
die Sanitäranlagen [pl] *washrooms* (and toilets)
sarkastisch *sarcastic*
satt *full*
der Sattel(") *saddle*
die Satteldecke(n) *saddle cloth*
sauber *clean*
sauer *sour, or* (slang) *cross*
Sauerkraut [n] *pickled cabbage*
die Sauerstoffflasche(n) *oxygen bottle*
saufen* *to drink, or to booze*
das Saxophon(e) *saxophone*
der Saxophonist(en)/die Saxophonistin(nen) *saxophonist*
Schach [n] *chess*
schade! *what a shame/pity!*
schaffen *to manage, or to succeed*
der Schal(s) *scarf*
die Schale(n) (apple) *skin, or* (egg) *shell*
sich schämen *to be ashamed*
scharf *hot* (spicy), *or sharp* (pointed)
der Schatten *shade*
schauen *to look*
das Schaufenster(-) *shop window*
der Schaumfestiger(-) *mousse*
das Schauspiel(e) *play*
der Schauspieler(-)/die Schauspielerin(nen) *actor/actress*

der Scheck(s) *cheque*
das Scheckbuch("er) *cheque book*
die Scheibe(n) *slice*
der Scheibenwischer(-) *windscreen wiper*
der Schein(e) *note* (money)
scheinen *to shine, or to seem*
schenken *to give*
die Schere(n) *scissors*
schick *smart* (elegant)
schicken *to send*
schieben *to push*
der Schiedsrichter(-)/die Schiedsrichterin(nen) *referee, or umpire*
schießen *to shoot, or to score* (a goal); **zum Schießen sein*** *to be a riot*
das Schiff(e) *ship*
das Schild(er) (road) *sign*
das Schimpfwort("er) *swearword*
der Schinken(-) *ham;* **gekochter Schinken** *boiled ham;* **roher Schinken** *smoked ham*
schlafen *to sleep*
der Schlafsack("e) *sleeping bag*
das Schlafzimmer(-) *bedroom*
schlagen *to hit, or* (sport) *to beat*
der Schläger(-) *thug, or* (sport) *bat, or racket*
die Schlägerei(en) *fight*
der Schlägertyp(en) *thug*
die Schlagsahne *whipped cream*
das Schlagzeug [n] *drums*
der Schlagzeuger(-)/die Schlagzeugerin(nen) *drummer*
der Schlamper(-)/die Schlamperin(nen)* *slob*
schlampig *scruffy, or sloppy*

121

die Schlange(n) *snake,* or *queue*

schlank *slim* (thin)

schlau *clever* (crafty)

schlecht *bad,* or *badly*

der Schlepplift(s) *drag lift*

schließen *to close,* or *to lock*

schlimm *bad,* or *badly*

die Schlinge(n) *sling*

der Schlitten(-) *toboggan*

der Schlittschuh(e) *skate*

das Schloss(¨er) *castle,* or *lock*

Schluckauf [m] *hiccups*

schlucken *to swallow*

der Schluss(¨e) *end*

der Schlüssel(-) *key*

schmecken *to taste*

schmeißen *to chuck* (throw)

Schmerzen [pl] *pain,* or *ache;* **Schmerzen haben** *to ache*

die Schmerztablette(n) *painkiller*

(sich) schminken *to put on make-up*

der Schmuck *jewellery*

schmutzig *dirty*

die Schnalle(n) *buckle*

der Schnee *snow*

schneiden *to cut*

schneit: es schneit *it's snowing*

schnell *fast,* or *quick*

der Schnorchel(-) *snorkel*

die Schnur(¨e) *string*

die Schokolade *chocolate;* **die heiße Schokolade** *hot chocolate*

schon *already*

schön *beautiful,* or *(weather) good;* **schön kalt** *nice and cold*

der Schotte(n)/die Schottin(nen) *Scottish*

schottisch *Scottish*

Schottland [n] *Scotland*

der Schrank(¨e) *cupboard*

die Schraube(n) *screw*

der Schraubenschlüssel(-) *spanner*

der Schraubenzieher(-) *screwdriver*

schrecklich *terrible*

schreiben *to write*

der Schreibtisch(e) *desk*

schreien *to shout*

der Schriftsteller(-)/die Schriftstellerin(nen) *writer*

schüchtern *shy*

schuften* *to work*

der Schuh(e) *shoe*

schuldig *guilty*

die Schule(n) *school*

die Schulter(n) *shoulder*

schulterlang *(hair) shoulder-length*

das Schulterpolster(-) *shoulder pad*

die Schüssel(n) *bowl,* or *dish*

Schütze [m] *(star sign) Sagittarius*

schwach *weak;* **mir wird schwach** *I feel faint*

schwafeln *to waffle*

schwanger *pregnant*

der Schwanz(¨e) *tail*

schwänzen *to bunk off*

schwärmen (für) *to enthuse (about);* **ich schwärme für ihn/sie** *I've got a crush on him/her*

schwarz *black*

schwätzen *to natter*

schweigen *to be silent*

das Schwein(e) *pig*

das Schweinefleisch *pork*

die Schweinerei* *mess,* or *dirty trick;* **Schweinerei!** *disgusting!*

der Schweiß *sweat*

die Schweiz *Switzerland*

schwer *heavy,* or *hard (difficult),* or *serious*

die Schwester(n) *sister*

schwierig *difficult*

das Schwimmbad(¨er) *swimming pool*

schwimmen *to swim*

der Schwimmflügel(-) *(swimming) armband*

der Schwimmreifen(-) *(swimming) rubber ring*

die Schwimmweste(n) *lifejacket*

die Schwindelei(en) *fib*

schwindlig *dizzy*

schwitzen *to sweat*

schwören *to swear*

schwul *gay*

der See(n) *lake*

die See *sea*

seekrank *seasick*

das Segelboot(e) *sailing boat*

segeln *to go sailing*

sehen *to see*

sehr *very,* or *a lot*

die Seife(n) *soap*

das Seil(e) *rope*

sein *to be,* or *(or* **seine***) his*

seit *for,* or *since*

die Seite(n) *page,* or *side*

die Sekunde(n) *second*

die Selbstbedienung *self-service*

selten *rare* (uncommon)

seltsam *strange,* or *weird*

das Semester(-) *six-month university term*

der Sender(-) *radio station*

die Sendung(en) *TV/radio programme*

der Senf(e) *mustard*

September [m] *September*

die Serie(n) *series*

die Serviette(n) *napkin*

der Sessellift(s) *chairlift*

der Sex *sex* (intercourse)

sexistisch *sexist*

sicher *sure,* or *safe*

die Sicherheit *safety*

der Sicherheitsgurt(e) *safety belt*

die Sicherheitsnadel(n)
safety pin
sie *her,* or *she,* or *them,* or
they, or *it*
Sie *you* (polite)
der/die Sikh(s) *Sikh*
das Silber *silver*
Silvester [n] *New Year's Eve*
singen *to sing*
der Sinn(e) *sense*
sitzen *to sit* (to be sitting
down)
der Sitzgurt(e) *harness,* or
safety belt
der Ski(s) *ski*
der Skianzug(¨e) *ski suit*
die Skihose(n) *ski pants*
Skilaufen [n] *skiing*
Ski laufen *to ski*
der Skiort(e) *ski resort*
der Skipass(¨e) *ski pass*
der Skistiefel(-) *ski boot*
Skorpion [m] (star sign)
Scorpio
der Slip(s) *knickers*
so *so,* or *like this/that;*
(genau) so ... wie (just) *as ... as*
die Socke(n) *sock*
sofort *immediately,* or
straight away
**der Soldat(en)/die
Soldatin(nen)** *soldier*
sollen *to be supposed to*
der Sommer(-) *summer*
Sonnabend [m] *Saturday*
die Sonne *sun*
sich sonnen *to sunbathe*
die Sonnenblende(n) *lens
hood*
die Sonnenbrille(n)
sunglasses
die Sonnencreme(s) *sun
cream*
der Sonnenhut(¨e) *sun hat*
die Sonnenliege(n) *sun
lounger*
der Sonnenschirm(e)
parasol

das Sonnenschutzmittel(-)
sun cream/lotion
der Sonnenstich(e)
sunstroke
der Sonnenuntergang(¨e)
sunset
sonnenverbrannt
sunburned
sonnig *sunny*
Sonntag [m] *Sunday*
sonst *else,* or *otherwise;*
sonst noch etwas? *anything
else?*
die Sorge(n) *worry;* **keine
Sorge!** *not to worry!*
die Sorte(n) *sort,* or *flavour*
soso *so-so* (not great)
die Soße(n) *sauce*
Spanien [n] *Spain*
die Spannung *suspense*
sparen *to save* (money, energy)
der Spaß *fun;* **zum Spaß** *for
a joke;* **Spaß machen** *to be
fun,* or *to be joking*
spät *late* (not early)
spazieren gehen *to go for
a walk*
der Spaziergang(¨e) *walk*
die Speisekarte(n) *menu*
der Speisewagen(-)
restaurant car
die Spezialität(en) *speciality*
der Spiegel(-) *mirror*
das Spiegelei(er) *fried egg*
das Spiel(e) *game* or *match*
spielen *to play,* or *to act*
**der Spieler(-)/die
Spielerin(nen)** *player*
die Spielhalle(n)
(amusement) *arcade*
der Spielstand *score*
der Spinat *spinach*
die Spinne(n) *spider*
spinnen* *to be nuts* (crazy)
**der Spion(e)/die
Spionin(nen)** *spy*
die Spitze(n) *end,* or *tip*
der Spitzname(n) *nickname*

spontan *spontaneous*
sportlich *sporty,* or *athletic*
die Sportschuhe *trainers*
die Sprache(n) *language*
die Sprechanlage(n)
intercom
sprechen *to speak,* or *to talk*
springen *to jump,* or *to dive*
die Spritze(n) *injection*
der Sprudel *fizzy mineral
water;* **süßer Sprudel**
lemonade
das Sprungbrett(er)
diving-board
spucken *to spit*
das Spülmittel(-) *washing-
up liquid*
**die Staatsangehörig-
keit(en)** *nationality*
die Stadt(¨e) *town*
die Stadtmitte *town centre*
der Stadtplan(¨e) *map* (of
town)
der Stadtrand *suburbs*
stark *strong*
die Station(en)
(underground) *station,* or
(hospital) *ward*
statt dessen *instead*
der Stau(s) *tailback,* or
traffic jam
stechen (insect) *to bite,* or *to
sting*
stecken *to put* (in pocket/bag)
der Stecker(-) (electric) *plug*
stehen *to stand,* or *to suit*
e.g. **es steht dir/Ihnen gut** *it
suits you*
stehlen *to steal*
steif *stiff*
der Steigbügel(-) *stirrup*
steil *steep*
der Stein(e) *stone*
Steinbock [m] (star sign)
Capricorn
steinreich* *loaded* (rich)
die Stelle(n) *job,* or *place;*
eine freie Stelle *a vacancy*

stellen to put; **eine Frage
stellen** to ask a question;
lauter/leiser stellen to turn
up/down (volume)
stempeln: stempeln gehen
to be on the dole
sterben to die
die Stereoanlage(n)
stereo
der Stern(e) star (in sky)
der Stich(e) insect bite
stickig stuffy
der Stiefel(-) boot
der Stiel(e) stalk
Stier [m] (star sign) Taurus
der Stift(e) pen
still silent
die Stimme(n) voice, or
vote
stimmt: das stimmt that's
right
stinken to stink
**das Stipendium
(pl: Stipendien)** grant
das Stirnband(¨er)
headband
der Stock(-) floor (level)
der Stoff(e) material (cloth)
der Stollen(-) stud (on
boot)
stolz proud
der Stöpsel(-) plug (for
water)
stören to disturb
stoßen to push; **stoßen
gegen** to bump into
die Stoßzeit(en) rush hour
der Strand(¨e) beach
die Straße(n) road, or street
die Straßenbahn(en) tram
die Straßenkarte(n) road
map
das Streichholz(¨er) match
der Streit(e) quarrel
sich streiten to have an
argument, or to quarrel
streng strict
der Strom electricity

der Strom(¨e) (large) river
die Strumpfhose(n) tights
das Stück(e) piece, or bit,
or (theatre) play
studieren to study
die Stufe(n) step, or level
der Stuhl(¨e) chair
die Stunde(n) hour, or
lesson
der Stundenplan(¨e)
timetable (school)
stur stubborn
der Sturm(¨e) storm
suchen to look for
der Süden south
südlich south
der Sunblocker sunblock
die Suppe(n) soup
das Surfbrett(er) surf
board, or windsurfer (board)
surfen to surf
**der Surfer(-)/die
Surferin(nen)** surfer, or
windsurfer (person)
süß sweet
die Süßigkeit(en) sweet
sympathisch likeable
synchronisiert dubbed

der Tabakladen(¨)
tobacconist's
die Tablette(n) pill
der Tag(e) day; **am vorigen
Tag** the day before
die Tage [pl] period
(menstruation)
das Tagebuch(¨er) diary
die Tageskarte(n) daily
travel pass
die Taille(n) waist
der Tampon(s) tampon
die Tankstelle(n) petrol
station
tanzen to dance
**der Tänzer(-)/die
Tänzerin(nen)** dancer
tapfer brave
die Tasche(n) bag, or pocket

das Taschenbuch(¨er)
paperback (book)
die Taschenlampe(n) torch
das Taschenmesser(-)
penknife
die Tasse(n) cup
taub deaf
Tauchen [n] diving
**der Taucher(-)/die
Taucherin(nen)** diver
der Taucheranzug(¨e)
wetsuit
die Tauchermaske(n)
(diving) mask
tauschen to swap
sich täuschen to be mistaken
der Tee tea
der Teil(e) part
das Teil(e) spare part
teilen to share
das Telefon(e) phone
das Telefongespräch(e)
telephone call
telefonieren to phone
die Telefonkarte(n) phone
card
die Telefonzelle(n) phone
booth
der Teller(-) plate
das Tempo speed
der Termin(e) appointment
(with doctor/lawyer), or
deadline
der Terminkalender(-)
diary
teuer expensive
die Textverarbeitung
word processing
das Theater(-) theatre;
Theater machen* to make a
fuss
das Theaterstück(e)
(theatre) play
die Theke(n) bar, or counter
das Thema (pl: Themen)
subject
das Thermometer(-)
thermometer

die Thermosflasche(n)
Thermos® flask
der Thunfisch(e) *tuna*
tief *deep*
das Tier(e) *animal*
der Tisch(e) *table*
Tischfußball [m] *table
football*
Tischtennis [n] *table tennis*
todunglücklich *heart-broken*
die Toilette(n) *toilet*
toll* *stunning, or amazing,
or brilliant*
die Tomate(n) *tomato*
der Ton(¨e) *sound*
der Topf(¨e) *saucepan*
das Tor(e) *gate, or goal*
der Tormann(¨er)
goalkeeper
das Törtchen(-) *small tart*
die Torte(n) *tart, or gâteau*
tot *dead*
töten *to kill*
die Tournee(n) *(music) tour*
tragen *to carry, or to wear*
der Trainingsanzug(¨e)
tracksuit
trampen *to hitch (a ride)*
**der Tramper(-)/die
Tramperin(nen)** *hitch-hiker*
die Träne(n) *tear (in eye)*
die Traube(n) *grape*
der Traum(¨e) *dream*
traurig *sad*
treffen *to meet, or to hit*
trennen *to separate*
die Treppe(n) *stairs*
treu *faithful*
der Trickfilm(e) *cartoon
(film)*
das Trikot(s) *team shirt*
trinken *to drink*
die Trinkflasche(n) *water
bottle*
das Trinkgeld(er) *tip (money)*
der Tritt(e) *kick*
trocken *dry*
trocknen *to dry*

der Trödel *junk*
die Trompete(n) *trumpet*
tschau* *bye*
**die Tschechische
Republik** *Czech Republic*
tschüs* *bye*
tun *to do, or (slang) to put*
die Tür(en) *door*
**der Türke(n)/die
Türkin(nen)** *Turkish*
die Türkei *Turkey*
turnen *to do gym*
die Turnhalle(n) *gymnasium*
die Tüte(n) *bag*
der Typ(en)* *bloke, or guy*
typisch *typical*

die U-Bahn *underground
(trains)*
üben *to practise*
über *over, or above*
überall *everywhere*
die Überfahrt(en) *(sea/
river) crossing*
überfallen *to attack*
das Übergewicht *excess
weight*
überholen *to overtake*
übernachten *to stay
(overnight)*
überprüfen *to check*
überqueren *to cross*
die Überraschung(en)
surprise
überschätzt *overrated*
übersetzen *to translate*
übertreiben *to exaggerate*
übertrieben *over the top,
or (price) excessive*
üblich *usual*
übrig *spare*
übrigens *by the way*
die Übung(en) *exercise, or
practice*
die Uhr(en) *watch, or clock;*
drei Uhr *three o'clock;* **elf
Uhr zwanzig** *twenty past
eleven*

um *at, or around*
umarmen *to hug*
sich um'drehen *to turn
around/back*
der Umkleideraum(¨e)
changing room
die Umleitung(en) *detour*
um'rühren *to stir (cooking)*
der Umschlag(¨e) *envelope*
sich um'sehen *to look
around (in shop etc.)*
der Umweg(e) *detour*
die Umwelt *environment*
umweltfreundlich
environmentally friendly
der Umweltschaden(¨)
damage to the environment
der Umweltschutz
conservation
**die Umwelt-
verschmutzung** *pollution*
um'ziehen *to move house;*
sich um'ziehen *to get
changed*
unabhängig *independent*
unangenehm *unpleasant*
und *and*
unentschieden *drawn
(match)*
unerhört *outrageous*
der Unfall(¨e) *accident*
Ungarn [n] *Hungary*
ungefähr *approximately*
ungerecht *unfair*
ungewöhnlich *unusual*
das Ungeziefer *creepy
crawlies*
ungezwungen *easy-going*
unglaublich *unbelievable*
das Unglück(e) *accident*
unheimlich *creepy, or
weird, or (slang) really, or very*
unhöflich *rude*
die Universität(en) *(or die
Uni(s)*) university*
die Unordnung *mess*
Unrecht: Unrecht haben *to
be wrong (not right)*

unschuldig *innocent*
unser (or **unsere**) *our*
unter *under*
das Unterbewusstsein
subconscious
die Unterführung(en)
subway
sich unterhalten *to chat*
die Unterhose(n)
underpants
die Unterkunft
accommodation
unterrichten *to teach*
die Unterschrift(en)
signature
der Untertitel(-) *subtitle*
die Unterwäsche
underwear
der Urlaub(e) *holiday*
ursprünglich *original*

der Vater(") *father*
die Verabredung(en)
appointment, or *date* (with
boy/girlfriend)
verabscheuen *to loathe*
verantwortlich *responsible*
verärgert *angry*
der Verband("e) *bandage*
verblüffend *stunning*
verboten *forbidden*
verbrennen *to burn,* or *to
sting*
verbringen *to spend* (time)
**verdammt: verdammt
noch mal!*** *damn!*
verderben *to spoil* (ruin)
verdorben *rotten* (off)
**der Verehrer(-)/die
Verehrerin(nen)** *admirer*
der Verein(e) *club*
**die Vereinigten Staaten
[pl]** *United States*
sich verfahren *to get lost*
(in car)
vergessen *to forget*
die Vergewaltigung(en)
rape

verhindern *to prevent*
der Verkauf("e) *sale*
verkaufen *to sell*
der Verkehr *traffic*
das Verkehrszeichen(-)
traffic sign
verkehrt *wrong*
verknallen: sich in ...
verknallen* *to fall for* (a
person), or *to have a crush on*
verlassen *to leave*
sich verlaufen *to get lost*
(on foot)
verlegen *embarrassed*
verleihen *to lend*
die Verletzung(en) *injury*
verliebt *in love*
verlieren *to lose*
vermieten *to rent*
vermischen *to mix*
vermissen *to miss*
vernünftig *sensible*
verpassen *to miss*
verrückt *crazy,* or *mad*
verschieben *to postpone*
verschieden *different*
die Verschlussklappe(n)
lens cap
die Verschmutzung
pollution
verschwenden *to waste*
die Versicherung(en)
insurance
verspätet *delayed*
die Verspätung(en) *delay*
das Versprechen(-)
promise
der Verstand *common
sense*
die Verstauchung(en)
sprain
verstecken *to hide*
verstehen *to understand*
verstopft *blocked,* or
constipated
versuchen *to try*
verteidigen *to stand up for*
vertrauen *to trust*

verwirren *to confuse*
verwöhnt *spoiled* (child)
verzeihen *to forgive*
Verzeihung *sorry*
das Video(s) *video*
viel *much,* or *a lot of*
viele *many*
vielleicht *perhaps*
das Viertel(-) *area* (in
town), or *quarter;* **Viertel
nach neun** *a quarter past
nine;* **Viertel vor eins** *a
quarter to one*
der Vogel(") *bird*
das Volksfest(e) *funfair*
voll *full*
völlig *completely*
das Vollkornbrot(e)
wholemeal bread/loaf
die Vollwertkost
wholefood
von *of,* or *by,* or *from;* **von
wegen!*** *no way!*
vor *in front of,* or *before,* or
ago, or (with time) *to,* e.g.
zehn vor acht *ten to eight*
vorbei *over* (finished)
vorbei'gehen an *to pass*
vorbei'kommen *to drop in*
vor'bereiten *to prepare*
Vorfahrt [f] *right-of-way*
das Vorhängeschloss("er)
padlock
vorher *beforehand*
der Vormittag(e) *morning*
vorn (or **vorne**) *at/in the
front;* **von vorn** *from the
beginning*
der Vorname(n) *first name*
vor'lesen *to read* (aloud)
der Vorort(e) *suburbs*
vor'schlagen *to suggest*
vorsichtig *careful*
die Vorspeise(n) *first
course*
vor'stellen *to introduce*
(people); **sich vor'stellen** *to
imagine* (to picture a situation)

die Vorstellung(en) *performance*, or *idea*
der Vorteil(e) *advantage*
vorübergehend *temporary*
die Vorwahl(en) *(phone) code*
vor'ziehen *to prefer*
Waage [f] *(star sign)* Libra
wachsen *to grow*
wagen *to dare*
der Wagen(-) *car*, or *(train) carriage*
die Wahl *choice*, or *election*
wählen *to choose*, or *to vote*
wahnsinnig *mad*
wahr *true*
während *while*
die Wahrheit *truth*
wahrscheinlich *likely*, or *probably*
der Wald("er) *forest*
der Waliser(-)/die Waliserin(nen) *Welsh*
walisisch *Welsh*
die Walnuss("e) *walnut*
wandern *to hike*
die Wanderung(en) *walk*
wann *when*
warm *warm;* **es ist sehr warm** *it is hot*
die Warnung(en) *warning*
warten *to wait*
der Wartesaal (pl: Wartesäle) *(station) waiting room*
das Wartezimmer(-) *(doctor's etc.) waiting room*
warum *why*
was *what*, or *(slang) something;* **was läuft?** *what's on?*
waschen *to wash*
die Waschmaschine(n) *washing machine*
das Waschpulver(-) *washing powder*
der Waschsalon(s) *launderette*

das Wasser *water*
wasserdicht *waterproof*
der Wasserfall("e) *waterfall*
der Wasserhahn("e) *tap*
der Wasserkanister(-) *water bottle*
Wassermann [m] *(star sign)* Aquarius
die Wassermelone(n) *watermelon*
Wasserskilaufen [n] *water-skiing*
Wasserski laufen *to waterski*
die Watte *cotton wool*
der Wechselkurs(e) *exchange rate*
wechseln *to change*
die Wechselstube(n) *foreign exchange office*
der Wecker(-) *alarm clock*
weg *away*
der Weg(e) *path*, or *way*
wegen *because of*
weg'gehen *to go away*
weg'laufen *to run away*
weg'räumen *to put away*
der Wegweiser(-) *signpost*
weg'werfen *to throw away*
weh tun *to hurt*
weich *soft*
Weihnachten [n] *Christmas*
weil *because*
der Wein(e) *wine*
der Weinberg(e) *vineyard*
weinen *to cry (weep)*
die Weinprobe(n) *wine-tasting*
die Weinrebe(n) *vine*
die Weinstube(n) *wine bar*
weiß *white*
der Weißwein(e) *white wine*
weit *far*
weiter'machen *to continue,* or *to keep on* (doing something)
welche (or **welcher** or **welches**) *which*

die Welle(n) *wave*
die Welt(en) *world*
der Weltraum *(outer) space*
wenig *little*
wenige *few* (not many)
wenn *if*, or *when*
wer *who*
die Werbung(en) *(cinema, TV) advertisement*
werden *to become*
werfen *to throw*
die Werkstatt("en) *garage,* or *workshop*
das Werkzeug(e) *tool*
der Werkzeugkasten(") *tool box*
die Wertsachen [pl] *valuables*
die Wespe(n) *wasp*
die Weste(n) *waistcoat*
der Westen *west*
der Wettbewerb(e) *competition*
das Wetter *weather;* **wie ist das Wetter?** *what's the weather like?*
die Wettervorhersage(n) *weather forecast*
wichtig *important*
Widder [m] *(star sign)* Aries
widerlich *obnoxious*
wie *how*, or *as* (like); **wie bitte?** *pardon? (what?);* **wie geht's?** *how are you?;* **wie ist er?** *what's he like?;* **wie oft?** *how often?;* **wie üblich** *as usual*
wieder *again*
wiederholen *to repeat*
Wiederhören *(on the phone) goodbye*
wieder sehen *to see again;* **auf Wiedersehen** *goodbye*
das Wiener Schnitzel(-) *veal or pork escalope in breadcrumbs*
wie viel? *how much?,* or *how many?;* **wieviel Uhr ist es?** *what time is it?*

willkommen welcome
die Wimperntusche(n) mascara
windig windy
der Windschutz windbreak
die Windschutzscheibe(n) windscreen
der Winter winter
wir us, or we
wirklich really, or truly
die Wirkung(en) effect
die Wirtschaft(en) pub which serves food
wissen to know
die Wissenschaft(en) science
der Witz(e) joke
wo where
die Woche(n) week
das Wochenende(n) weekend
woher? where from?
wohin? where to?
wohl: sich wohl fühlen to feel well, or to feel comfortable
wohnen to live, or to stay
das Wohnmobil(e) camper van
die Wohnung(en) flat
der Wohnwagen(-) caravan
das Wohnzimmer(-) living room
die Wolke(n) cloud
die Wolle wool
wollen to want
das Wort(¨er) word
das Wörterbuch(¨er) dictionary
worüber? what about?
worum: worum geht es? what's it about?
wozu? what for?
wunderbar wonderful
die Wundsalbe(n) antiseptic cream
der Wunsch(¨e) wish

wünschen to wish (hope for)
der Würfel(-) dice
wurscht: das ist mir wurscht!* I don't care!
die Wurst(¨e) sausage, or cold meats such as ham, salami, pâté, etc.
das Würstchen(-) sausage
würzig spicy
der Wutanfall(¨e) fit, or tantrum
wütend furious

zahlen to pay
zählen to count
der Zahn(¨e) tooth
der Zahnarzt(¨e)/die Zahnärztin(nen) dentist
die Zahnbürste(n) toothbrush
die Zahnpasta toothpaste
Zahnschmerzen [pl] toothache
die Zange(n) pliers
der Zaum(¨e) bridle
das Zeichen(-) sign
zeichnen to draw
zeigen to show, or to point at
die Zeit(en) time; zur Zeit at the moment
zeitgenössisch contemporary
die Zeitschrift(en) magazine
die Zeitung(en) newspaper
der Zeitungshändler(-) newsagent's
das Zelt(e) tent
zelten to camp
das Zentrum (pl: Zentren) centre
zerreißen to rip (to shreds)
sich zerstreiten to fall out with (a person)
das Zeug stuff
ziehen to pull

ziemlich quite
die Zigarette(n) cigarette
das Zimmer(-) room
der Zirkus(se) circus
die Zitrone(n) lemon
der Zoll customs, or toll
zollfrei duty-free
das Zoom(s) zoom lens
zu to (towards), or closed, or shut, or too (too much)
der Zucker sugar
zuckerkrank diabetic
zuerst first, or at first
der Zufall(¨e) chance, or coincidence
zufällig by chance
der Zug(¨e) train
die Zügel [pl] reins
zu'hören to listen
zu'machen to close, or to do up (fasten)
zu'nehmen to put on weight, or to increase (grow)
die Zunge(n) tongue
zurecht'kommen to cope, or to manage
zurück back
zurück'kommen to come back
zurück'rufen to phone back
zurück'zahlen to pay back
zusammen together
zusätzlich extra (additional)
zu'schauen to watch (look at)
der Zuschlag(¨e) supplement
das Zweibettzimmer(-) twin room
zweifelhaft dodgy
die Zwiebel(n) onion
der Zwilling(e) twin (brother/sister)
Zwillinge [pl] (star sign) Gemini
zwischen between
die Zwischenstation(en) stopover

Index

If you can't find the phrasebook section you want from the Contents page, try looking here. If you still can't find it, you can use the dictionary to look up individual words.

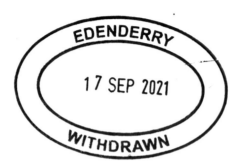